COVENANT HOUSE

COVENANT HOUSE

Lifeline to the Street

Bruce Ritter

Doubleday
NEW YORK
1987

This book, like Covenant House itself, exists because of the dedication and effort of countless people.

My special thanks to John F. Kells, whose vision and energy led us to take the first steps toward publication; to Dorianne Perrucci, whose patience, perseverance, and persuasion shaped and refined fifteen years of newsletters into a book; and to Duran Ben-Ami, whose illustrations capture moments from the daily life of our kids at Covenant House.

Grateful acknowledgment to the following for permission to quote from song lyrics in this book:

"Do You Know the Way to San Jose?" by Burt Bacharach and Hal David. Copyright © 1968 Blue Seas Music, Inc. and Jac Music Co., Inc. Used by permission. All rights reserved.

"So Far Away" by Carole King. Copyright © 1971 by Colgems-EMI Music Inc. Used by permission. All rights reserved.

"I Want to Know What Love Is." Written by Mick Jones and performed by Foreigner. Copyright © 1984 Somerset Songs Publishing, Inc. Used by permission.

Library of Congress Cataloging-in-Publication Data

Ritter, Bruce, 1927–
Covenant House.

Bibliography: p.
1. Covenant House (New York, N.Y.)—History.
2. Abandoned children—New York (N.Y.)—History.
3. Runaway children—New York (N.Y.)—History.
4. Ritter, Bruce, 1927–   . I. Title.
HV885.N49R63   1987   362.7'6   87-6829
ISBN 9780385260046

146721804

DEDICATED

to the thousands of
good & brave & beautiful bought & sold kids
who never make it back because no one
reached out to them in time . . .

Contents

Introduction
Even Now It Hurts
to Write About It

In the almost twenty years of our existence we have tried our best to help the more than one hundred thousand kids we have taken off the streets into residence in our programs. We believe that we have been able to help about one third make it back.

The rest? I think most of them don't make it. They die young. Or they go to jail, or join the tragic throngs of emotionally racked, alcoholic, and drugged inhabitants of what is becoming a vast and barely human national shelter system.

Kids don't survive very long on the street—at least in any recognizably human way. The distortion of the personality, the erosion of character are swift and massive and almost always irreversible.

If this be true—and I am quite certain it is—then the ethical and moral imperative to help as many of these kids as possible, before it is too late, becomes a matter of conscience for me and my staff, for other helping agencies and service providers, and for our public servants who are also obliged by office to hear the cry of the poor.

More than thirty years ago, in 1956, in Rome, I was ordained a priest of the Roman Catholic Church as a member of the Franciscan Order. I have never wanted to be anything else. I certainly didn't know at the time that I would wind up in Times Square taking care of thousands of kids who had been bought and sold like so many potatoes.

The kids came into my life by accident. Or so I thought at the time. Ten kids who had no place to live, who had been pimped by a bunch of junkies, and who had been forced to make a porn film because they were hungry, just couldn't take it anymore and fled to my apartment in the slums of the Lower East Side of New York City. I didn't have the guts to kick them out and I couldn't find anybody else who wanted them, so I kept them. Or, as one of the kids gleefully chortled, "Bruce, we're going to give you a chance to own us, to be our father." Since, as you probably know, being a priest can get pretty lonely at times, I didn't mind it a bit. "It's like having your cake and eating it, too, Bruce," one kid said. "What gives you the right to know me so well so soon?" I said.

I never forgot what happened to those first kids. Nor can I forget or overlook or keep quiet about what's happened to thousands of others of my kids who, because they needed food and shelter, or maybe some money, and always some love—or all of these things— took their clothes off in front of a camera and let somebody make a permanent record of their need and their shame. And forced them to smile and not to cry.

The way I see it, those who would exploit and destroy children this way for the sake of making money are the kind of sinners Jesus spoke about when He said it would be better if they had millstones tied around their necks and that they be drowned in the sea.

When it comes to loving sinners, I've got a rather spotty record. I guess I can love some easier than others. It helps if they haven't sinned against me!

I mean, I find it very easy to love a kid who's into "the life" because he or she doesn't really have many choices and is looking for love in all the wrong places.

What would I do in their place, I ask? The answer is, very often, I don't know what I would have done—or, God help me—maybe the same thing.

But the fact is, what most of these kids have to do with their bodies in order to stay alive doesn't hide how good they are. Or change it. At least not for a while. It's easy for me to love them.

I find it harder to forgive or to care about the johns, the customers who buy these kids, but I can usually manage that pretty well. Most johns are sad and lonely guys trying to buy some friendly company for a few minutes at a time. I mean, sometimes the commodity being exchanged is not only just sex, whether it's the kid selling or the john buying. Sometimes it's a lonely, desolate kind of love, two needs meeting in a quick, anonymous encounter. (Nobody ever uses his real name.)

When some john abuses a kid or hurts him, my ability to love and forgive diminishes rapidly. Nothing, ever, excuses cruelty. Whatever loneliness and need mean in an erotic commercial relationship, deliberately causing someone pain is simply inexcusable. Jesus said it is still forgivable. I'll take His word for it.

Pimps are another story altogether. Where pimps are concerned, my ability to forgive flies out the window. I loathe and despise them. I hate what they do to kids. I hate their cruelty and viciousness. I wish I could say that I loved the sinner but hated the sin. I can't and don't where pimps are concerned. If I could put every pimp in jail for thirty years, I'd do it. Longer . . .

If I hate and despise pimps who sell real bodies of real people, I hate and despise even more the greedy-hearted businessmen who publish and distribute the vicious and violent and degrading pornography that floods this country and corrupts our kids, and adults, too.

They are nothing more than white-collar pimps who hypocritically shroud themselves in the First Amendment and shriek censorship at anyone who objects to their vile business. They should be called by their right name: They are pimps and procurers to a nation.

The organized-crime animals who sell sex for profit and casually kill anybody who interferes with their filthy business make me gag. I'd have a tough time burying any of these wretched men from a church. I'd have a tough time believing in their deathbed repentance.

Covenant House receives a lot of contributions from people who care about my kids. It's how we survive. In eighteen years I can only recall refusing three gifts.

The first was from a pimp who ran a really rotten low-life brothel across the street from our center on Eighth Avenue. He collected $84.20 from his girls and their johns—nickels, dimes, and quarters—and brought a milk carton full of coins over to me because he liked what we did for kids.

I couldn't take the money. I just couldn't. He was hurt. He couldn't understand. He thought I refused a gift to God. He drove off in his gold Eldorado to give the money to another church down in Greenwich Village.

The second gift I refused was from a politician who offered me a lot of money—I mean a lot of money—from his private foundation. The only catch was that I had to ask for it and that he had a long and public history of buying and exploiting kids. Since I was then denouncing him by name from every pulpit I could find, I presume he wanted me to stop talking about his vices in public. I didn't take his money, and I didn't stop talking.

The third contribution came in a plain envelope that contained a check for twenty dollars and a note. The note said simply, "The men here on death row collected this money for your kids." It was signed John Gacey. John Wayne Gacey murdered at least twenty-six boys, most of them runaways and homeless kids, after he sexually abused them.

When I saw his signature I dropped the letter on my desk, afraid to touch it. I sat there for a while, just staring at the letter, oppressed and afraid of the images that crowded into my mind. In all my life I have never felt so close to pure evil.

After a few minutes, without thinking about it, without thinking it through, without trying to understand my motives, I picked up the letter and check, tore them in little pieces, and threw them into the wastebasket. I went into the bathroom and washed my hands for a long time. I can still remember the look of horror on my face as I stared in the bathroom mirror. Even now it hurts to write about it.

God forgive me for not being able to forgive him. Maybe when I can forget those twenty-six anonymous kids. Maybe when I can forget the thousands of others who have come to Covenant House in the last eighteen years who suffered the same kind of sexual exploitation. Maybe if I go downstairs today and don't see another thirty kids who came in last night I can forgive him.

Underlying every great and noble work is a very simple vision of what that work is. The vision of Covenant House is quite simply this: Kids should not be bought and sold. They should not be exploited. It should not be infinitely dangerous to be alone and homeless on the streets of our cities. There must be a place where they can all get help. And when they need it: before it is too late. And from people who love and respect them. With no strings. No questions asked.

And in a place where nobody gets excluded. That's what "catholic" is supposed to mean.

"Catholic" is supposed to mean universal. "Catholic" is supposed to mean that nobody is excluded.

Jesus had a hard time making that point. He still does.

Just about all His friends—and certainly most of His enemies—wanted to make Jesus sectarian.

His friends and His enemies alike didn't want Him to associate with lepers or Samaritans, or publicans or sinners—or even women. The disciples of John and Jesus had their own turf battles over who were greater. And everybody thought it was okay to hate the Romans.

If you want to hate somebody, or to exclude them from your company, or make yourself better than they are, you can always find some religious, economic, social, cultural, ethnic, or historical reason to do so.

When Jesus finally—with some impatience, I think—taught us who was going to make it into His kingdom, He did so without reference to doctrinal or sectarian conditions.

He said very clearly that it was mercy, not doctrine; pity, not dogma; love, not credal statements that got you into His company. He said we are welcome into His kingdom if we feed the hungry, clothe the naked, shelter the homeless, comfort the afflicted. And if we don't do these things we're not welcome.

Far too often well-meaning men and women have tried to exclude others from their love on the basis of doctrine or race or money or sexual orientation—or for dozens of other reasons.

We make ourselves uncatholic that way.

Love doesn't exclude anybody.

God is nonsectarian.

So is Covenant House. We are proud to be an agency that strives very hard never to become uncatholic.

Nobody gets turned away.

It is a matter of promises to keep. To you, to my kids. To God.

When all is said and done, there aren't many good reasons for doing good.

For some of us the good itself is sufficient reason. For others, it is the simple need of good and brave and beautiful kids who sometimes have lost even the ability to inspire our pity.

Others perhaps look beyond the goodness of the simple deed, and beyond the goodness of the kids themselves, to a perfect and compelling goodness they find in God alone.

I really don't think it matters very much to God, who is quite above our need to praise Him for the good we should do.

However, and whyever, we are led or drawn or choose to do good for the kids who need us, it is enough that we do it.

It means a lot if we do it for love.

St. Francis, at the end of his life, left one simple injunction for his friends: *Dum tempus habemus, operemur bonum!* Brothers and Sisters, while we have time, let us do good.

DYING
FOR LOVE
1972–76

"Bruce, this is Ernie.
We found him sleeping in a garbage can."

"How long will it be before you guys sell out? To money, power, ambition . . . ? Will you sell out by the time you're twenty-five?"
I finished my sermon on that note and turned back to the altar to continue the celebration of Mass. I was proud that almost four hundred students had come to church that brilliant Saturday afternoon in October 1966.
It was a good sermon. I liked that sermon. I had worked hard on it. It was all about zeal and commitment and how the students at Manhattan College in New York City should be more involved in the life and work of the Church.
One of the students, Hughie O'Neill, stood up in church and said, "Wait a minute, Bruce." He happened to be the president of the student body and captain of the track team.
"Bruce," he said, "you're making two mistakes. The first mistake you're making is that we are not going to sell out by the time we're twenty-five; we'll undoubtedly do so by the time we're twenty-one. Your second mistake, and your bigger one, is that you're standing up there telling us this and not leading us by your example and life-style not to.
"We all think you're a pretty good teacher, Bruce, but we don't like your sermons. We think you should practice what you preach."
That's a pretty heavy shot to take from your students on a Saturday

afternoon. *(There was a general murmur of agreement from the other kids in church.)*

I thought about it a lot over the next few days and realized, of course, that Hughie O'Neill was correct. The next Sunday, at all the Masses on campus, I apologized to the student body—for not edifying them—and asked my superiors and the archbishop for a new assignment: to live and work among the poor on the Lower East Side of Manhattan.

Quite frankly, neither my superiors nor the archbishop liked the idea very much. You see, when I made that request it was a time in the Roman Catholic Church when thousands of priests, brothers, and nuns were leaving their communities, their dioceses, their orders and returning to secular life, often using as their avenue out of the Church these new and exotic ministries. Consequently, bishops had become very reluctant to approve any more of them.

(I'm quite convinced that it was only because I made my request in impeccable Latin that they thought me conservative enough to undertake this new ministry.)

The archbishop and my superior agreed, reluctantly, to let me do this, on the conditions that I not represent anything I did as sponsored by the Church or my Order and that I not ask for financial assistance from either. As my superior put it to me bluntly, "Bruce, you're on your own. If you fail, it's your neck; if you succeed, it's to God's glory."

On those conditions, in May of 1968, on Holy Thursday, I moved off campus and found an apartment in the East Village, on East Seventh Street near Avenue D. A couple of junkies had just been busted so I was able to take over their tiny three-room apartment. Me and 10 million cockroaches. The bathtub was in the kitchen, which made it handy for washing dishes. The toilet was in the hallway.

Most of my neighbors were junkies, dealers, and speed freaks. In fact, of the seventy-two apartments in my tenement at least half were occupied by junkies. For the first couple of months my neighbors left me completely alone—they thought I was a "narc" (an undercover narcotics agent) trying to get evidence on the drug scene.

When they found out that I really was a dumb priest, and had made the mistake of bringing some possessions into the East Village, like a stereo and a TV, they decided to redress the economic imbal-

ance. They robbed me at least once a day—no exaggeration—for over a month. When I had nothing left to steal, they stopped.

Since I had no specific ministry—my assignment was simply to be useful to the poor—I became involved in all the problems you'd expect to find if you lived and worked in a slum: the poverty, the violence, the drug scene, the unemployment, the police corruption that was rampant in New York City in the sixties.

I had no intention of becoming involved with the kids of the neighborhood.

For almost a year I worked at anything and everything I could find. My expenses were low. My rent was sixty dollars a month! My ministry to the poor didn't seem to be getting anywhere, but I was pretty content. I figured that God would mess around in my life again. And I really liked the people! Maybe they didn't know what fork to use and maybe they were pretty casual about a lot of the things I had simply taken for granted—like paying bills and whom they were sleeping with at the moment—but I found them to be generous, kind, and forgiving, compassionate and helpful to a friend in trouble. They were also enormously protective about an un-street-wise Franciscan who had moved onto their turf.

I became involved with the kids of the neighborhood quite by accident—and, quite frankly, against my will.

One night, at two in the morning of a bitter day in February 1969, six kids knocked on my door. It was very cold and snowing very hard, and the four boys and two girls looked half frozen. They were quite young—all sixteen and under—and asked if they could sleep on the floor of my apartment.

What could I do? It was snowing outside and cold. What would you have done? I invited them inside, gave them some food and blankets, and the kids bedded down on my living-room floor. One of the boys looked at me. "We know you're a priest," he said, "and you don't have to worry. We'll be good and stay away from the girls." I thanked him for that courtesy!

The next morning it was still very cold and still snowing very hard. The kids obviously did not want to leave. They had no place to go. The girls got up and cooked my breakfast and burned it; the boys cleaned my apartment and cased it.

One boy went outside for just a few minutes and brought back four more kids. "This is the rest of us," he said, "the rest of our family."

*They were afraid to come last night. They wanted us to check you out
first. I told them that you didn't come on to us last night so that it was
probably okay."*
    *These ten kids had been living down the block in one of the aban-
doned buildings with a bunch of junkies who were pimping them. The
junkies had just forced the kids to make a porn film before they would
give them some food. The kids hated that. They really hated that. In
disgust and a kind of horror at the direction their lives were taking,
they fled the junkies and came down the street to my place.*
    *I tried very hard to find some child-care agency that would take
these kids in. I called over twenty-four different agencies. Far be it
from me to be sectarian about it! I called Catholic, Protestant, and
Jewish agencies. When I called a Catholic agency I was "Father Ritter," and when I called a Jewish agency I was "Dr. Ritter," but it
didn't do any good. No matter who I was, nobody wanted these kids.*
    *They were either too old or too young, too sick or not sick enough.
They were from out of state, they were not "certified for care" (meaning that they were not "reimbursable"—meaning nobody would pay
for them). Whatever the reason, nobody would touch these kids.*
    *Finally, in desperation, I called a very high official in the child-
welfare system and told him about the ten kids sleeping on my floor.
He told me about all the laws I was breaking. I was guilty of harbor-
ing and contributing to the delinquency of a minor, probably of interstate commerce in minors, and of a crime I had never even heard of
before: the alienation of affection of children—which means that if the
kids began to like me enough, they wouldn't want to go home again—
and that's a crime in New York!*
    *"Look," he said, "you've destroyed your reputation. There's only
one reason people will think you've taken kids off the street. You've got
to have them arrested. That's the only way to get them into care."*
    *I couldn't do that. That wasn't the agreement I had made with the
kids. So I kept them.*
    *I wish I could tell you that my motives were honorable. I wish I
could say that I acted out of zeal, compassion, kindness. My motives
were not that noble—they were much closer to anger, stubbornness,
pride, vanity. I am a very competitive person. I hate to lose. I had just
been driven off campus by my students; my assignment was to be
useful to the poor, and I didn't want to lose another encounter with a
bunch of kids.*

So I kept them. I got some old bunk beds, and the kids moved off the floor into beds.

I really liked these kids. They were great kids!

The problem was, the next day two more kids came in, and then the day after that two more. The word got around fast. You see, my kids were telling other kids that I was a pretty good cook, there were no rats in the apartment, and that if they knocked on my door, I wouldn't have the guts to kick them out. They did, and I didn't.

One day my kids (right from the start I began to think of them as "my kids") brought me another kid and they said to me, "Bruce, this is Billy. He's sixteen. He's been living in a car for a year."

Every day, to keep warm, Billy would break into a car, jump-start the motor so he could run the heater, and play the radio. If the cops chased him, or the owner did, Billy would walk around the block, break into another car, jump-start the motor, play the radio. . . . He survived that way for more than a year, panhandling, hustling.

I remember another scruffy kid they brought me. "Bruce, this is Ernie. He's twelve. We found him sleeping in a big plastic garbage can." And they would look at me.

What could I do? What could anybody do? What would you have done? You would have taken them in, of course. I didn't do anything special.

So many kids began to come that I needed more space and more help.

To get the help, I went back to Manhattan College. I decided on revenge. I told those kids who drove me off campus to come down to the East Village and help me practice what they preached. And they did. Half a dozen guys moved off campus, including Hughie O'Neill, to help me care for all the kids who were knocking on my door.

A couple of girls from Mount St. Vincent's nearby, and a couple more from Marymount, four girls from St. Joe's College in Brooklyn, a couple of kids from Fordham, three from St. John's, a kid from Iona —they all moved off campus to help me with my kids.

I couldn't pay them. I didn't have any money. For room and board alone they worked sixty to eighty hours a week, because they cared about these kids. After a semester or two they would get pretty burned out and return to school to finish their education.

Most of these college kids would have been considered to be alienated from the so-called institutional Church. I guess that was true.

They certainly were not alienated from God. They knew exactly why they did what they did.

A thousand times, when I wanted to quit, to pack it in and return to teaching—like every day—I just couldn't do it. I could never figure out what to do with all the kids who were living with me, and I couldn't bear to let down the college kids who had such unreasonably high expectations of me. Actually, I looked up to them. It does not do great things for your ego when you realize that you have heroes and role models a generation younger than yourself.

To get the space I needed was simple. I just kept taking over more and more of the apartments in my tenement. Most of them, as I mentioned, were occupied by junkies, dealers, and speed freaks. That's a very transient population. They move around a lot; they die; they get busted; they just disappear.

As they did all these things, I would take over their apartments, paint them, and move some kids in. I wound up with twenty-six apartments that way.

And sometimes, if the junkies were bothering my kids, and they wouldn't stop—and by bothering I mean trying to exploit them sexually, trying to pimp them—I would hire some friends for fifty dollars to break into their apartments, steal their clothes, steal the furniture, and remove the plumbing. The junkies would come back to their apartment from trying to cop some heroin, realize they were unwanted, and move away. I took over half a dozen apartments that way and made the building a lot safer for the rest of us.

It was a kind of, if you will, muscular Christianity. The Holy Spirit made me do it.

Seriously, I don't know what you really think of the ethical or moral quality of what I did. Many of you undoubtedly come from backgrounds where you were taught that property is more important than people.

But my time and space were different. You could not count on any help from the police. In the late sixties and early seventies nobody in the East Village expected anything but hassles from the police. It was a time in the NYPD when the Knapp Commission had just declared that "corruption was pervasive throughout the entire NYPD," and that "a substantial majority of the NYPD were corrupt."

The Sixth Precinct, where I lived, was the "punishment precinct" for the NYPD. The alcoholic cops, the maligners, the psychotic cops, the cops under discipline were assigned there. In fact, one of the most lethal things you could do in the East Village, as I discovered to my sorrow, was to uncover police corruption.

(Note: Having said that, in justice to the NYPD I must say that under a series of reform-minded police commissioners and mayors, there has been a substantial cleansing of the NYPD. It is now considered to be not only one of the most professional but one of the cleanest of the big-city police departments. It was not so when I lived in the East Village. If you wanted to be protected, you protected yourself.)

By now, hundreds of kids—urban nomads, as I had begun to call them—were coming to what my friends and I now termed Covenant House. We were illegal, unofficial, unchartered, and unfunded. To get the money I needed, I begged, I preached in a local church for forty dollars a weekend. I did whatever I had to do.

We never had enough for food or rent. I would pay my bills with my MasterCharge card, which I had obtained while teaching at Manhattan College, and hope that I would get enough money to pay it off when the bill came in.

My kids would play a game with any unwary visitors who happened to drop in somewhere near mealtime. "What's for dinner tonight, Bruce?" one kid would yell from the kitchen. "I don't know," I'd yell back. "What's in the refrigerator?" "There ain't nothing, Bruce," the kid would yell back. Generally my visitor would get the hint and take a couple of my kids out to the local supermarket to spend the contents of his wallet on whatever my kids could persuade him to buy.

Those first four years—from 1968 to 1972—were pretty bloody. I won't hide that from you. A thousand times I wanted to quit and go back to teaching. So many kids, so many lost, dying kids came to Covenant House in those early years. We did what we could—which was to provide a clean bed, some food, somebody safe to be with. Mostly we loved them and the kids knew that.

I don't like to think about those early years. There was a lot of love there in the East Village. I loved the kids. But there was also a lot of pain.

Every few months my superior, who was a very dear friend, would call me up and say, "Bruce, how're you doing? Don't tell me or I'll have to tell you to stop." So I never did.

In 1972 I made the decision that was to change my life definitively. There were so many kids, and we just could not do enough for them;

we couldn't meet their urgent needs because of our highly unofficial, illegal, and unrecognized status. So I decided to become legal, to get a charter, to incorporate Covenant House as a licensed, nonprofit, child-care agency specializing in the care of runaways, urban nomads, and street kids. We obtained our charter in October of 1972.

In a sense, that's where this book begins. In a desperate effort to raise the funds we needed to feed our kids, I began writing a brief newsletter to a few hundred people whom I had dragooned, coaxed, and seduced into caring about my kids. I wrote the first letter in May of 1972.

I've been writing them once a month for the last sixteen years. Nobody else writes them. People say that I'm very hard to know. My students would never say that. Neither would my kids. If you think it at all important for you to know who I am, read these newsletters. Who and what I am, for better or worse, is smeared all over these pages.

Father Bruce Ritter

FEBRUARY 1987

Grab Him Back with Love and He Will Let You Go

You always own somebody you know that well, love that much.

May 1972

I don't know exactly what to call this letter. It's a first for us here. For far too long an urgent need to communicate with the friends who are responsible for Covenant House has been blistering my conscience. There is no possibly adequate way I and my friends and our kids can express our gratitude for your help.

We like to think we "own" kids—certainly in all the basic human ways they are our own and we don't shrink from that commitment. That they are also your own kids is part of what binds us together.

When our staff gathered last New Year's Eve to celebrate, we made a common resolution: to just once in a while to be quiet together, to enjoy a state of happy calm, free from the sense of crisis and concern that is so much part of the lives of our children and therefore our own lives.

Our younger children are hungry, jealous goslings, jostling each other away from the mother/father source of warmth and food. Our older kids, hurt more, more suspicious, hawkish, and wary, circle in erratic near, then far, orbits. Owning them is risky, and we fail with more than we can easily bear.

Tyrone David Jackson Ritter (he insisted on adopting me), fifteen, impatient, and importunate, is throwing a nicotine fit on my floor.

After suitably paternal admonitions about the evils of smoking I shall preserve his sanity and mine by staking him to a pack of Kools. Thanks for staking us to our kids.

June 1972

Tim graduates from high school next week with high marks and has been accepted into City College; Eddie has passed with honors into his sophomore year; Billy, age sixteen, hasn't had a drink in four months and has "graduated" from Covenant House; John has pretty well given up drifting and wants to begin college in September.

Milton's attitude is actually changing, and he goes to school every day—for him a great accomplishment. Mike has a steady job and has kept it for three months.

Another John, much loved and sadly missed, is back in jail for drug possession. Two kids named Angel are beautiful, straight out of a Botticelli painting, both fourteen, both sick maybe, maybe just bad, out of control and corrupted. Paul and Stephen are lurching in and out of their sad/funny/bizarre fantasies.

Our kids here are a heartrending, mind-bending mixture of naïveté, callowness, and adult scarifying experience. Some, brutalized and victimized by the street scene, have only a minimal ability to be "good," and that for just a few minutes at a time. In some, even the perception of the possibility of their being "good" is overwhelmed by the hopeless conviction that they are bad.

They look with longing suspicion and disbelief on our efforts to convince them they are, can be, should, might be good. Some learn this: the Mikes, Tims, and Eddies. Many more don't. We didn't succeed in teaching them that we loved them—or they didn't believe it.

Most of the staff are very tired and looking forward to some time away from Seventh Street. Renovations are under way in our fourth-floor apartments. If the landlord can provide some water pressure we might even put in a shower. Eighty-year-old plumbing, clogged and leaky pipes, bathtubs in the kitchen do not encourage daily bathing.

I made friends with King, a 140-pound white German shepherd. King, at first suspicious and snarly, chomped on my left hand. As Paul has endlessly chortled to anyone who would listen, "It was love at first bite." I tell everyone King was sorry.

We're a little late writing to you this month, although our bills,

like yours, always keep coming in on time. Sometimes I wish the
Lord wouldn't always bring it right down to the wire: not having
rent money for June last Saturday, preaching in Our Lady of Angels
Church in Albany on Sunday and having it. They were very generous. He always is.

July 1972

At our regular weekly house meeting last Monday I talked to our
kids about what it means to be part of a "covenant." The word has
an ancient and sacred history—it goes back thousands of years and
refers to a really solemn pact or agreement between persons to commit themselves to each other, to honor, respect, support, and love
each other.

The covenant we have with each other, I explained endlessly—
having a congenital tendency to run off at the mouth—means we are
sworn to love and care for them and, if they want us to, to own them.
We want and expect the same back from them.

I saw four pairs of eyes dart around the room suspiciously. The
other kids played it cool. I hastened on: Your primary obligation
with us is to try to be happy and human. One kid snorted unbelievingly (but not cynically; I think he really wanted to hope it was true).
I haven't been happy since the day I was born, Bruce.

Looking a gaggle of blighted, tough-as-nails street kids smack in
the eye and telling them they have an obligation to love you back
takes a certain amount of guts. Maybe just not to street kids either;
maybe to say it to anyone. Anyway, they didn't laugh, probably
because I scowled menacingly as I said it.

Some really great news: We are praying that a number of Franciscan sisters will be sent by their community to open a Covenant
House for girls here in the East Village. The situation of runaway or
homeless teenage girls here in New York City is even more serious
and hopeless than that of the boys.

Thanks for joining and sharing our covenant with our children.
When all is said and done, I guess the most healing thing we can do
to each other is to make a covenant to love each other and be good to
each other.

August 1972

Autumn premonitions: in New York: Our kids were scrabbling for blankets last week after a steamy hot spell that had us all longing for snowballs and icicles.

Progress toward opening a Covenant House for girls is rapid and encouraging. We must still find a place for the residence, raise some money (as always) for its support. I am really happy and confident that the Lord wants this. Their need is so overwhelming.

One of our graduates returned a few days ago for a visit while on leave from the Air Force. After some excited greetings he handed me a very official-looking document that legally changed his name from the Bernard Baez he was born with to Eric Life.

His reason for the change was compelling: His first seventeen years were so awful that the young Bernard, out of a desperate need for survival, could only shrug and say "that's life." For him now, at eighteen, to choose to identify his suffering, mistake-filled, messed-up childhood with life—to choose to be called by his true name—lays waste our understanding and besieges our hearts.

FOR RENT: the services of one itinerant, mendicant preacher (me). Anxious to talk to large and small gatherings, convocations, assemblies, at breakfasts (Communion), luncheons (business), or dinners (any kind). Subject: Covenant kids. Aim: As St. Francis put it when asked why he thought God willed the existence of his Order: to give good people who love the Lord a chance to show their love for the poor.

September 1972

He was a street kid, sixteen, long and skinny, eaten by hunger and lice, bones and lungs rattling, scowling-weak and desperate from too many months on pizza and Coke and acid and loneliness. Dark, opaque eyes looked at nothing and missed nothing.

Infinitely armored (a knife, a club, and a piece of taped pipe carefully stashed under pillow and mattress), he mistrusted clean sheets and underwear, showers, doors, windows, people, food, words, eyes. Infinitely vulnerable, he could only eat and sleep and eat, crouch, huddle, and posture before the TV, letting himself be absorbed into the benign world of the children's cartoons. I heard him break si-

lence after three weeks—a harsh, humorless, barking guffaw, deliber-
ate and calculated. I think he wanted to assure me he liked it here.
Afraid, like most street kids, of place and space, he didn't really
settle in so much as gingerly occupy the premises, always tentative in
his acceptance of the fact that it was his bed, his room. It never
crossed his mind that we were. After the first month he gave me his
club, and then a few weeks later his iron pipe. I had to wait six
months for his knife.

The breakthrough, when it came, was massive. One of us—afraid,
too busy, too tired, impatient—rejected him. Snarling and ugly, he
went to his room and sat on his chair, folding his hands tightly in his
lap. He began to cry, harder and harder. After a while he could not
sit on the chair anymore and fell on the floor, curled fetus-like for
two hours, straining out a grief he couldn't name.

The visible change that began then was wrenching for us all. He
began to grow up all over again, and like a small child needed to
touch and feel things and persons: us, our alarmed visitors, our kids.
Always with a scowl, a threat of violence, the bleak opaque stare,
always at the door to block your path, pin your arms, take your keys,
your books, your cigarettes, records. I said that if he grabs you, why,
grab him back with love and he will let you go and run away. He did.

Testing us incessantly, he pushed out our limits. We had always to
find new resources and new understanding. He tried one, then two
jobs and failed, and acted out his discouragement with violence, re-
jecting us and our covenant for the cruelty and exploitation of the
street scene. Shattering confrontations with me and Dave and Dan
drove him back to the street. He returned a month later, sick, sadder,
more understanding.

We found him another job, in a day-care center—five hours a day
letting two- and three-year-old children climb on him, wet him,
punch and grab him, love him and need him. He stopped grabbing us
and punching us; he stopped, mostly, the blank, hard stares and
became capable, more and more, of human speech, conversation.

We own him. I think for good, in the sense that you always own
somebody you know that well, love that much. Covenant becomes a
need after a while, and it is no longer possible to say if it is his need
or your need. It goes beyond the certain conviction he still has a long
way to go, and that still, maybe, he won't make it. He now has a

need for his own space and place to grow. To grow away from us, to become independent of us and free of us.

P.S. Our bed linen supply is just about nonexistent. Anyone with some extra sheets and pillowcases or blankets can win some points with the Lord.

I thought, too, that perhaps some of you might have used winter outerwear: warm coats or jackets, hats, socks, even rubbers and galoshes—things your own teenagers have outgrown. Sweaters, too, and gloves???

Underwear! Grab a pair of shorts and T-shirt from your son (or skinny husband). He'll never miss them.

A couple of bars of soap and a toothbrush. I don't think our kids will ever think that cleanliness is next to godliness but it sure beats buying Right Guard.

And towels and toothpaste?

My Kids Have Dirty Hearts

He was saying goodbye
all the way to the ground.

October 1972

I don't know who said God can appear to a hungry man only in the form of bread. We all know who said, "Blessed are the merciful. When I was hungry, you fed me, when I was thirsty, you gave me to drink, when I was homeless, you took me in."

But when you put names and faces and smells to it . . . Many of our kids can be good only a few minutes at a time. (Ralphie lived here, betrayed and robbed us, is dying of glue and aloneness, has no morals, is beautiful, evil, needful and hungry and homeless.) When I was hungry . . . does it mean Ralphie? Most of you can be saints for a few minutes at a time. It is easy to see the Lord in you and to love you—you would, after all, be unfailingly grateful. (Hector was sixteen, gone on bad trips, a jumper-out-of-windows, illiterate, and a moron, maybe. He will never learn to read and write, hold a job, how to get married, how to be happy, how to be good.) When I was homeless, you took me in . . . does it mean Hector? How far must we go?

November 1972

The horror of it is still there deep in our guts and behind our eyes. Jack found Dave wandering aimlessly, dazed, in a drenching rain and brought him home to us. He was eighteen, very sick, and very, very sad. Dave stayed with us for a few days, silent, totally alone, and then left suddenly, in the rain, to find his parents again. It was raining when he returned for something to eat and a night's sleep two days later. For another week Dave drifted in and out of our house and our lives, grabbing a sandwich and us, sadder and unhappier than before. We suggested and hoped that he would stay.

Last Sunday he went up to his room on the fifth floor, said good-bye to one of our kids, and jumped out the window. He was saying good-bye all the way to the ground. He landed feet first on the hood of a car—it broke his fall somewhat—and fell to the street among the garbage cans.

I had been upstairs trying to write this newsletter when I heard his crash into the car and got to him almost immediately. He never lost consciousness, said he loved us and was sorry to cause us all this trouble. It took the ambulance twenty-five minutes to get here. The doctors in the emergency room at Bellevue were quick, kind, and thorough. Outside of a smashed ankle and some bad bruises he is okay—no other injuries.

He should have died, but he didn't. We don't know yet if Dave will return to us after his release from the hospital. I rather suppose he will. We hope he does.

I have the absolute conviction that God cares for and watches over our kids. It would be hard to convince me, or anyone else here, that the Lord did not guard this boy from his own sadness.

Occasionally someone will remark to me (when I tell them that Covenant House is supported solely by small donations from six or seven hundred people) that—whatever God's motives may be—most of those who help us are working off a middle-class sense of guilt for having so much of this earth's abundance, that a sense of grim duty or a social conscience rather than love underpins their generosity.

I get pretty mad when I hear that. I believe that our friends who have chosen to share with us the responsibility for our kids do so out of love, not guilt.

A sound theology supports this view. Any choice that does not spring from love is rather useless to the Lord and to ourselves. It does not make us any better; it does not please Him, it does not really help. It only pays the bills. Down with guilty givers. Our kids are painting their rooms (this old place is much like a ship; it needs continual painting to remain at all presentable). The kids aren't too happy about it; their eagerness to redecorate evaporated quickly when I vetoed their choice of Day-glo orange and purple, red and black stripes with polka dots. . . . I can only bear the sight of ten kids wielding paintbrushes for about five minutes before I long to flee to the relative peace and safety of a street riot.

Christmas 1972

Christmas is a kind of quirky, messed-up time for all of us here. It is not the time of tinselly trees and presents, with turkey and innocence and sharing and love and giving that made our own childhood's Christmases a wonder and delight. The urgent fantasies that protect our kids and that they live by carefully insulate them from that kind of Christmas. Our kids are afflicted with that special kind of poverty and abandonment that Jesus suffered all his life.

Our children are afflicted, but they are happy, they are loved. First and most of all by the Lord. And then by us. You are, too. More than you know and need, extravagantly, unilaterally, no strings, not because you (we) are good, or deserve it, or merit it, but because He simply loves us and said so, for all time, beyond any possible doubting, visibly, humanly, humbly, 1,972 years ago, in a stable.

It's just not my kids who find it hard to believe they are loved this much, so absolutely and totally, so unreservedly—it's all of us. We are all poor and afflicted together until we believe in and experience that love.

March 1973

The street gangs are back in New York City. Twenty years ago there were dozens of them, some with memberships of thousands, giving absolute obedience to their presidents and war counsellors. Drug addiction (a junkie is incapable of loyalty and discipline) and some fine work by New York City street workers destroyed the gangs.

They are back again. With a vengeance. More volatile, more vio-

lent, better armed. There are fewer social controls now, and a bitter
erupting racism fuels them. Doc's story is true, even truer than he
writes it. The events happened a short time before he came to Covenant House. Doc has settled in here, we hope for good, and he goes
to school (a different one) every day.

Doc and The Black Spades

Once I was coming from school. I was walking down the hall.
This is the whole truth.
I met a bunch of boys. They stopped me. One of them knew
me. He called my name.
"I want to speak to you, Doc."
I was a little shaky. He said, "Seven of your friends jumped
me."
"No, not any of my friends. Let's go and see if it was any of
my friends."
The guy told me as we were walking that he was making a
gang. He says, "Maybe the guys who jumped me weren't
your friends. Doc, I want you to join with us."
I said, "Join what?"
He said, "We are making up this gang, The Black Spades.
Are you with us or not, Doc?"
"Okay. I'm with you. But before I will be with you, you have to
make me something high and powerful. Something like Con-
troller of the Gang Fighters."
"I can't make you President or Vice-President, but I'll make
you War Counsellor because have nerve."
I was in the gang about a month, jumping and mugging peo-
ple. One boy in The Black Spades got jumped by The Seven
Immortals.
Everybody said, "Yeah, that's all we need! Our first gang
fight."
We went to the school, P.S. 185, and met The Seven Immortals in the schoolyard. When we were getting ready to
fight, a boy named Black Benjy jumped in the middle.

The Seven Immortals said, "What you doing, jumping in the middle and stopping our fight?"
Black Benjy said, "I'm just trying to make peace."
The Seven Immortals said, "I bet you he's one of The Black Spades. Let's go get that nigger." Benjy said, "Hold it. I'm in no gang."
The Seven Immortals all ran up on him. The Black Spades just stood there and looked. Then The Black Spades ran in to help the dude. One of The Seven Immortals said, "We're going to kill that nigger," and one of them went into his pocket and pulled out a brass knuckles. He started beating Benjy in the head and face, and I heard Benjy scream.
While we were fighting really hard we started getting stabbed and stabbed back. I dove over the crowd to try to get to Benjy and help him. They were stomping on me and him. There were three gunshots. I pulled the chain off me and hit The Seven Immortals with it. Then I heard the sirens as the cops started to come. I turned my head and the one with the brass knuckles hit me.
When I woke up, I was in the paddy wagon. I saw Benjy was dead. He was dead. The cops said, "Get in that room." My eye was puffed up. Then they put me in Juvenile Center. I had to go to court. I was in for fifteen days. I went to court and the judge gave me a hassle: He told me I could go, but if I was in another gang fight, I would be put away for a year.
    Sometimes I think about Benjy. What a man he was. He reminds me of Martin Luther King.

Doc is still very much attracted by the strength and power and violence and excitement of his gang. It brought a lot of romance and brotherhood into his pretty bleak fifteen-year-old life. Doc knows that if he goes back to the gang he can't stay with us, and he wants to do both very much. Doc said it's "taking a big risk and too scary" to let people love you. But he wants to. We hope he lets us.
    And lets you, too. Doc doesn't understand anything about long-distance love. Who does? And people whose names are on a mailing

list but who are not just names on a mailing list. When he gets his full growth maybe he will. And maybe, if we have loved him enough, he will be able to understand and accept our gratitude.

THEY ARE HERE! Sister Gretchen and Sister Mathias with Sister Frances Marie on her way! The girls' residence has just opened, and is full.

June 1973

Kids come to Covenant House because they have no place to go. Most are in flight from deplorable living situations, hungry, and very scared. Some are in flight from themselves. The problem is, for all of them, very simple: Where am I going to sleep tonight? Or eat tonight? Who will take care of me tonight?

In a much deeper and totally unromantic sense the question is even more searing: Who will love me and care about me? Why doesn't someone? Sometimes the answer is devastatingly frank and brutal: Because we can't. Because you won't let us. Because you do bad things to people.

Like Paul. Paul was sixteen and a thief with a real natural-born talent for thievery that he cultivated assiduously. He stole everything and anything—a turnip the cook was going to serve for dinner, wallets and radios and money, your socks and keys (Paul had a special fondness for keys). He stole every day, and the more he liked you the more he had to steal from you. We all liked him, too.

Having Paul for your friend was a real drag. Periodically he would beam at us all and proudly announce to his unwilling victims at Covenant House that he had managed to cut down on his stealing.

It got so bad one week that the other kids, in desperation, came to me and demanded that something be done before Paul got himself killed by an angry posse being formed in our living room. They wanted his blood bad, and intended to stretch his neck from the nearest fire escape. It was a real crisis. I wondered out loud whether I should throw Paul out, and my kids, in real disgust (remembering, maybe, their own past derelictions), said no, of course not, but that I had to do something, anything. We talked it over for a long time and I announced my decision.

Paul would be called before the entire staff, warned for the last time, and asked to undergo a retraining and purifying process: Everything would be removed from his room except his bed. He would be given a large blanket, and, in exchange, he would give us all his clothes, particularly the ones he was wearing. For two weeks Paul had to live in his blanket—and having nowhere to go, and especially no pockets, would be unable to steal anything. The only promise I could make to Paul was that sure death awaited any kid who stole his blanket. If Paul couldn't agree to this procedure, he had to leave. I gave him five minutes to make up his mind and watched incredibly large tears roll down his cheeks. He went to his room and we all waited, afraid. Ten minutes later, Paul returned, swathed in a blanket, cheating only a little—he had kept his underwear. We demanded that, too.

For two weeks Paul lived in his blanket. Not once did any other kid bother him. Not once did he steal. After two weeks we ceremoniously gave him back his underwear and, a week later, his shirt. Still no stealing. Another week and we gave him back his pants—and waited anxiously. Nothing happened, so we returned his shoes and socks and restored him to full membership in our covenant. He didn't steal for almost three months. And then it happened. Paul fell off the wagon, hard. He went on a perfect binge—an orgy of stealing —anything, everything, from anybody, all the time, and we had to ask him to leave.

Paul has been away nine months, sadly, but relievedly, missed by all. He appeared out of nowhere the other day. He wants to come back and has no other place to go. Who would want a sticky-fingered, larcenous, and large-pocketed walking vacuum cleaner around to suck up your possessions? The staff happily assumes that I am going to say yes. Things have been getting pretty quiet around here, I guess. Do you think I should greet Paul with a hug first and then his blanket, or vice versa? I mean, it's really dangerous to get close to that kid if he has pockets.

July 1973

Curb-to-curb people is what we have on Seventh Street, when the weather turns reeking hot and the thermometer climbs into the nineties. The fire escapes become your terrace then, the stoops and the garbage cans your lawn chairs and front yard. The kids and adults exercise their inalienable right to sit on any parked car and open a fire hydrant.

There's a game the kids play. It doesn't have any name yet, but it's great fun. What you do is grab a beer can from the gutter—a good strong tin one, not the easily collapsible aluminum cans—and cut off both ends. You then approach with caution, and from the rear, a runaway fire hydrant (a wide-open one spews out a thousand gallons a minute). The game calls for a kid to sit down behind the hydrant and wrap his legs around the bottom while he reaches around with both arms and inserts his beer can into the heart of the gushing torrent. It makes a dandy nozzle.

The object of the game is of course to fill up your front seat with water as you drive by. An experienced nozzler can get you at a range of fifty feet.

It doesn't pay to get mad. In fact it's downright unhealthy. When a stranger enters hostile territory he is expected to pay tribute, or at the very least to provide some fun for the local Indians. Running the gauntlet Lower East Side–style is a lot of fun for everybody. It creates a lot of camaraderie among our neighbors.

Except the fire department, which doesn't like it very much because they have a lot of trouble putting out fires when a thousand open hydrants lower the water pressure. Except anybody above the third floor who wants to take a bath and can't because there's no water. But everybody's a good sport about it.

A million kids get hosed down every day, a lot of garbage is washed down the sewers, and there's a lot of laughs at the expense of the unwary convertible owner who suddenly finds himself sitting in two hundred gallons of water—or in watching a dozen bus passengers hastily ducking for cover.

The kids respectfully—or at least prudently—let the squad cars go by unscathed and unsquirted. Everybody else is fair game.

I wish it would snow. Or rain every day. Anything that would keep the kids off the streets and out of trouble. I hate the summertime and the long hot days when the neighborhood kids have nothing much to do but hang out in the gathering menace of a deadly and foreboding boredom.

Today's Gospel was about unclean spirits. Jesus said that those who preach the Gospel would have authority over them. He also said, in the same breath, that to preach the Gospel we should go two by two with no staff, no food or money, and only the clothes on our backs. Maybe our authority over unclean spirits depends on how we preach the Gospel. Maybe if we want to cast out unclean spirits we must be as poor as Jesus, or Francis.

My kids are afflicted by unclean spirits, my kids have dirty hearts. Many are cruel and vengeful, selfish and carnal. Some of my kids lie and cheat and steal at times, and there is little truth in them at times. They exploit and are cynical, lazy, and dishonorable at times. They don't bathe often enough either, and their feet stink. . . .

They want their evil, vengeful, exploiting, cynical, cruel, and selfish spirits cast out. They want it very much. When we can't—maybe because we, and you, haven't prayed and fasted enough—they are disillusioned and hurt, and sometimes very frightened.

August 1973

Covenant House has expanded, even in the past nine months, from one to six houses, all in New York City. It has been a hectic, even frantic time for us. Most of my friends didn't understand the urgency: Why, if we were so broke all the time, open yet another residence and spend money we didn't have? Where would we find the staff? My answer was then and is now, That's God's problem. Because the kids have a problem.

It is impossible to refer dispassionately and unemotionally to the sad, sick, and murderous events that over a period of three years took the lives of at least twenty-eight young boys, many of them runaways, in Houston, Texas. The homicidal insanity, the grossness that occurred there has aroused great revulsion and great anxiety in us all.

Nobody, nobody can afford to shrug or throw up his hands and say the kids shouldn't have run away in the first place. Kids have always run away and probably always will. They are, after all, just that, kids, and don't understand what they're getting into.

Besides, the overwhelming majority of runaways are scared, sick, rejects, in flight not to any particular person or place, but very definitely running from a human situation with which they are unable to cope. Our experience at Covenant House has amply demonstrated that the runaway problem is an adult one and must be solved by adults.

There's an even bigger problem in our country involving more kids and just as great suffering. It is still largely unrecognized by sociologists and child-care agencies: the problem of the fourteen-, fifteen-, and sixteen-year-old urban nomads, homeless, rootless, exploiting, and exploited. Some were originally runaways, but most are the walkaway, throwaway kids, kids who are left stranded, high and dry, on the concrete reefs of the city when their shipwrecked families founder and go under.

If they get into trouble and get caught, concerned judges in Family Court don't really have many good places to send them. And no cop wants to bust a kid and then spend an entire day in court, only to have the kid released to the custody of some unconcerned, uncaring, and incompetent parent or relative. Most cops just don't want to pick up runaways or urban nomads or throwaway kids.

Rotten things happen to them. The rottenest is not the individual act of abuse or exploitation, however criminal and ugly—most kids can and do survive that. It's the acceleration of the dying process, the quickness with which the poison works, the speed with which irreversibility sets in: to see a boy or girl of sixteen or seventeen or eighteen who is really a twenty-five-year-old derelict. And public concern seems to fade to that exact degree that a child ceases to look like a child and act like a child and loses the beauty of a child. Time telescopes on and collapses upon children of the streets, their dying prolonged beyond those of Houston.

The Houston police tell us that at least five thousand teenagers in that city ran away last year. Nationwide, the estimates run about a million. While we are proud of our runaway houses and our own efforts, the staggering dimensions of the problem demand a concerted community/government approach on a nationwide scale. Houston is the mere tip of the iceberg. The harsh realities for these million temporarily or permanently homeless kids are not pleasant. Most are not in some good place with good people.

Smelling How Bad You Smell Can Take Your Voice Away

Madness would leap out of his darkness and clutch him by the mind again.

January 1974

L ast week, at two in the morning, somebody called us. They had found this kid who wouldn't talk wandering around. Tall, seventeen maybe, blond. Really dirty. A coat at least six sizes too big drooped over a pair of pants so ragged and torn that he was two threads and a rip away from being naked. He smelled pretty bad.

He couldn't tell us anything except that he was from Washington. He was scared and his face had gone slack (hunger maybe). He couldn't walk straight, either—just graceful wooden Pinocchio-like lurches. All the kids stayed away from him. That's a really bad sign. Kids read kids pretty well.

Preliminary diagnosis: mild schizophrenia, mildly retarded. Gut reaction: hungry, lost, exhausted, panicked, hopeless, a nobody in a nowhere, no place to start from to pass Go . . . We cleaned him up, gave him some underwear, a pair of pants, food. He didn't talk. Just sat on the couch without moving anything except his eyes. I stopped over at our crash pad the next morning to see how he was doing. He was still sitting on the couch, with a couple of other kids.

"Hey, you came in yesterday!" I didn't give him a chance to answer, but began talking to the kid sitting next to him. A couple of minutes later I walked past him again. "You're from Washington," I

said, and walked away before he could answer, circled back, said I
was glad he had some clean clothes, and walked away again to joke
with another hairy-monster kid that wanted to be joked with. Then I
came back, stepped on his foot just a little, said I was really glad he
was here, and walked over to the stove to stir the mashed potatoes.

The boy got up, walked over to the stove, and bumped into me,
except that he didn't move away. We stood there, his right side to my
left side, foot, calf, thigh, hip, shoulder pressed together. I stirred the
carrots and peas, said I hoped he was hungry, and moved over to the
broiler to check out the hamburgers.

The boy walked around the table and into me, bumping me, and
did not move away, his left side to my right side, foot, calf, thigh,
hip, shoulder pressed together. I stuck a fork in the hamburgers,
pronounced them ready, said it was great having him around,
punched him on the arm, and went back to my office.

The boy never said a word. I never heard his voice. But he com-
municated superbly well. I went back yesterday. He was sitting on
the couch, moving only his eyes. When he saw me he got up, walked
over to the table, and set up a chessboard, arranging all the pieces.
He didn't say a word. I have still never heard him speak. Maybe
tomorrow.

A true story, word for word. You interpret it. Fear, exhaustion,
loneliness (especially that), hunger, smelling how bad you smell, can
take your voice away and unhinge your face, keeping only your eyes
alive.

We have a lot of kids and a lot more who want to come live with
us. Help us, please. Thank you for sharing our conviction that children should not have to suffer.

February 1974

The boy is a ward of one of our northeastern states. He is mad. He
stared at me across the desk.

"Anybody can see my name is Speedracer. That's why I wear this
car around my neck." His name is Mark. "Sometimes I like to be
called Mark, but not John. John is the name they gave me when I
was born, but I figured that if I didn't earn that name I shouldn't use
it John doesn't mean anything." Maybe someday it will.

Mark (the car) was over a foot long, a crudely made, mostly white, racing model. It hung around Speedracer's neck on a length of heavy bicycle chain. As long as he was with us Mark-the-car never left its privileged position. Speedracer ate, slept, and showered with the car. He had, after all, worn Mark around his neck like some grotesque necklace since he was eight years old. He is mad.

Speedracer told me his story, almost casually, and with much insight and pain: his earliest memories in institutions and hospitals, increasing medication, physical restraints (we used to call them straitjackets), the periods of remission during which his madness receded for a while and he was permitted to leave the hospital for short periods.

When he was around fifteen he would run away—escape—from the hospital and hitchhike around the country until the recurring madness would leap out of his darkness and clutch him by the mind again. Then heavy medication and restraint would be necessary to leash his private demons for a while.

"When I lose my temper I can't control myself. I break things, I hurt people. I know what I am doing, but I can't stop. Please don't send me back. The hospital is okay, but I hate the medicines, the drugs. They mess up my head. Can I stay here? People are good to me here. People like me here. Mark likes it here, too." He stroked the car and kissed it.

"If I let you stay here, will you hurt my kids? How do I know that you won't? Will you listen to our doctor and take medicine if he says you should? Otherwise you can't stay. If our doctor says it is okay for you to stay, please stay."

He wouldn't agree to take any medicine. We told him he had to go, and his mad eyes blazed at me. "You're not being fair!" he screamed. "I want to stay here, I like it here. You're not fair. You're like everybody else."

I moved a paperweight and ashtray out of his reach and slid a letter opener on my desk into a drawer. "You might hurt my kids. How can I take the chance?"

"I'll be good. If I get mad I'll talk to one of the counselors. I'll go for a walk. You're not being fair."

"You can't stay unless you'll take the medicine, I'm sorry."

He stormed out of my office, which is on the fifth floor. By the time he reached the second he had changed his mind, bounded

cheerfully back up the stairs, laughing, to tell me he and Mark were
going to stay.

Our kids were great—and very wary. They carefully admired
Mark. Speedracer wasn't a bit of trouble for two weeks, taking his
medication, seeing a therapist. We liked him a lot. About a week ago
Speedracer appeared with a second car, also a foot long, hanging
around his neck (he called it Mark II). It was a young and innocent
car—hadn't been around very much—and he and Mark were teaching it things. Speedracer's imaginary world, and his skinny chest,
were getting crowded.

We tried but could not hold him in our world. The violence began
surging and bubbling beneath his placid, mad exterior, and then a
couple of days ago Speedracer refused to take his medication, exploded over a minor incident, and tried to attack one of our kids.
Our staff, alert and expectant, intervened, restrained and calmed the
boy. He agreed to go back to the hospital in the state that calls him
its ward and try again to re-join our world. He left us, or they left us
(Speedracer, Mark, Mark II, and Bikey—a fourth "person" had
joined the group on his chest).

His real name—the one given Speedracer at birth, the one he
hadn't done anything to deserve—was John. It is the only name he
needs. It means beloved of God.

April 1974

I found Mike in, of all places, our backyard, last Thursday. We
have a small garden behind our offices on Twelfth Street, and I've
gotten into planting seeds and trying to make flowers grow. (It sometimes takes my mind off things.) He was actually working for our
neighbor as an all-around handyman and yard boy.

The man in him had told my neighbor he was nineteen, in automo-
tive school, needing a part-time job. He saw me wrestling with a
large stump in my half of our small garden and came over to help. I
think he felt sorry for this aging, bald, getting-thick-about-the-mid-
dle man, muttering under his breath about stumps. The boy in him
took about two minutes to tell me that he was really only sixteen, a
runaway from Pennsylvania.

Mike the man/boy (on Mondays, Wednesdays, and Fridays he's
nineteen, the other four days he's twelve) can't go home or he'll be

arrested for running away from an unbelievably bad situation (his mother is an alcoholic, his father insane, his brothers and sisters retarded). He ran away two years ago when he was fourteen and has survived, somehow (you wouldn't want to know how). He works incredibly hard, trying to prove something. He feels better when he's hurting from working too hard. About the only things he likes to eat are hamburgers and Coke. He's desperate to live somewhere good, to go back to trade school. He didn't cry when he talked, in a matter-of-fact way, about his mother. He's beginning to believe me when I tell him that I can keep him, and I carefully explain that the law of the open range entitled any cowboy to claim and brand as his own any wandering calf.

He's the One
I Love the Most

"Keep on doing what you're doing,"
the doctor said.
"When you stop doing it, he will die."

Yesterday our man at the intake desk, Father Dave, took in seven kids—two more than we had beds for. We put one girl on the couch in the living room of our house on Fifteenth Street and bedded down the fifteen-year-old runaway boy from Nowheresville on some cushions on the floor.

Dave really shouldn't have taken the kids in, I guess, because everything gets really overcrowded and we know from experience that we can handle only just so many. "But, Bruce," he said, "that last kid was only fifteen. . . ." Dave has the hardest job in Covenant House. He has to turn the kids away every day when we don't have any more room, when all our beds have filled up.

He doesn't speak too often about it, but he's always pushing quietly (sometimes with desperation and anger in his voice) for us to open more houses to put kids in.

Dave never saw those seven kids before yesterday. All but one (whom we found on the street at ten o'clock last night) were referred by phone—just a voice calling and asking rather hopelessly if we had room. Dave never asks for psychosocial case studies or histories of former placements. Nor does he ask for documents or medical reports; the kids never have them.

The rule we've asked Dave to follow is "the rule of the empty bed." We don't believe in waiting lists, or in screening our kids to make sure we get the "good" ones. Our policy is first come, first served; if one of our beds opens up, the first kid to come or call gets it. We call this enormously difficult policy our "open intake." It places huge burdens on our staff, who never know just who will walk through that door except that the child will usually be quite young (fourteen to seventeen), sometimes in great need, and with overwhelming problems.

October 1974

Let me tell you about Timmy. Of all my kids he's the one I love the most. He's not supposed to be a sophomore in college, getting all A's and B's. He's supposed to be dead. Four years ago his older brother brought him up the stairs to my apartment. Timmy could barely walk. He was sixteen, a five-foot-ten-inch, 110-pound, black-haired, blue-eyed speed freak who had left a comfortable middle-class home when he was thirteen to wander and drift up and down the East Coast, wherever fancy and an incessant need for drugs would pull him.

Timmy lived any way he could, anyplace he could, pouring his life out daily through the hollow point of a needle. He swallowed or shot up anything he could find. (Once, almost in disbelief, he described how when he couldn't cop any drugs at all, he and a friend injected oven cleaner into their veins.)

I would wake Timmy every morning. He was crashing, depressed, semi-comatose from the speed he had obtained the day before, too weak and lethargic to move. I had to pull him up to a sitting position on the bed and sometimes even swing his feet out onto the floor. Sometimes I would hand him his socks and pants and shirt, and sometimes, because he just couldn't do it, I would have to dress him and haul, push, and cajole him to the breakfast table and make him eat. He would put five and six teaspoons of sugar into his coffee (speed freaks lust after sugar).

On that quick energy Timmy would leave the apartment, cop some speed, shoot up, and come back flying, excited, energetic, happy, smiling, ecstatic—only to crash and collapse six to eight hours later in a puddle of profound misery and hopeless depression. We surrounded him, as much as we could, twenty-four hours a day. We planned our own days to include Timmy. If Jerry had to go shopping, Timmy went along, and then Jerry would hand him over to Mike, who needed company while he picked up the laundry, who gave him to Bruce, who needed company on a trip to Manhattan College, who gave him to Pat and Adrian across the street, who fed him and made him laugh, who gave him to Mary, who wanted to read a book with him, who gave him back to Jerry and Bruce, who would make sure he was in his half of the bunk bed in cockroach heaven.

We all lived this way for a couple of months, Timmy and I and my friends. Timmy would always escape to cop some speed. One night he came home, gave me a bright-eyed, all-teeth-showing, infinitely sad glass smile, went into his room and swallowed thirty sleeping pills. We and he were lucky, or blessed by God, rather. He didn't die, though he wanted to. We redoubled our efforts, placing Timmy in a protective human cocoon. He always escaped us.

In desperation I took Timmy for evaluation and examination to one of the major New York medical centers, where a research program in methedrine (speed) addiction was being carried out. Over a period of two weeks they gave him every test possible in their huge ultramodern facility and then asked me to come for their diagnostic conference.

There were seven doctors, psychiatrists, psychologists, and social workers present. The eminent doctor leading the conference stated that in all his experience he had never encountered any boy who had so heavily abused so many different kinds of drugs. He asked the other experts to offer their own evaluation and prognosis of what was, in their judgment, the possibility of survival. On a scale of one to ten they all gave Timmy zero chances to make it. Very upset and shaken, I thanked them all and appealed to them for help: What can we do for Tim? The doctor simply said, "Keep on doing what you're doing. When you stop doing it, he will die."

Thanksgiving 1974

Tim didn't know the doctors said he was supposed to die. I never told him. It didn't matter much. He had already decided, chosen, wanted to, knew he would. My friends and I were afraid to stop trying to hold Timmy away from the edge of the cliff in his mind—

we loved him too much. We continued to surround him for as many of the twenty-four hours every day that we could. Little by little, it began to happen. As the weeks passed, for one whole day even, Timmy would not shoot up some speed. And then it was three entire days without drugs, and then, incredibly, a whole week! We celebrated. Timmy said to me that night with an indescribable look of hope that I can still see on his face, "You know, Bruce, I think I might live."

It was getting along toward summer in that year, and I was afraid to keep Tim with me during the long, hot, boring days in the East Village—drugs were as available as candy and cigarettes. Some Franciscan friars of my order who knew Timmy's story took a deep breath, took a chance, and took him to their summer camp in the Adirondacks.

We expected the worst, but it didn't happen. Tim didn't touch a thing for three months. He chopped wood, painted, and learned to water-ski, discovering a close affinity with the forest and mountains and lakes. He also gained thirty pounds and grew some muscles for the first time in his life. I went to visit Tim in August. He was waiting for me on the dock, unashamedly prancing and leaping about, flexing his biceps. His face and eyes were intensely alive and he was bursting with pride. I never loved him so much as then.

I had a surprise all cooked up for Tim when he came back to the city: his senior year in high school. Some really great Christian Brothers who run one of the best high schools in New York took a flier on him. Brother Kevin and his staff gave Tim enormous support and encouragement, forcing his mind to come back out of the shadows and start working again.

So did some other dear friends, who took him into their home during that crucial year and gave him absolutely essential months in a loving environment. He needed a place to find out that a world without drugs could be a safe and invigorating place to be, and Pat and Judy gave him that chance to discover it.

Tim graduated—with honors! He treated me and his parents (he had become reunited with them over the past year) to dinner. It was a formal occasion. It was, he said, the happiest day of life. I think it was mine, too.

He's a sophomore in college now. It wasn't easy. Tim went through a lot of bad times: discouragement, just getting tired of being good. He got through it, though, and is getting A's and B's, talking of a career as a marine biologist.

Most of my kids don't make it. For every Tim there are a dozen or twenty Johns, Marks, Marys, Bills, Angels, Cindys, who never come in out of the darkness, who can't tear free from their vices, who can't extricate their feet from the quicksand. My friends and I are grateful for Tim. He's taught us never to give up on a kid too easily.

Tim has taught me a lot about God, too. I've told Timmy a hundred times that God is the reason he made it back, because God loved him that much and wouldn't let him go. Tim believes it. Kids like Timmy are a good reason to be grateful on Thanksgiving. Grateful above all to the Lord, but grateful, too, to all of you who were His loving and willing instruments of strength and goodness for all our Tims, even, and especially, the ones that don't make it.

Christmas 1974

This Christmas, priests all over the world—among the poor in Asia, Africa, South America—during the Christmas Mass will lead their hungry flocks in the Our Father. They will say to God, "Give us this day our daily bread," and He will not give them bread, and they will starve to death.

God gave His spirit and Son to us, to our flesh, in our flesh, to make our hands His. He has no other. Our unity with God and the poor is so absolute that a hungry child has a right to say to God, "Give us this day our daily bread," and a right to look for it in our— or His—hands. God can appear to a hungry man only in the form of bread. We can be God to the poor by doing what Jesus did—by feeding them, by going among them, by holding out, in our hands, comfort for them.

This is the only way a Christian can find Him, can make his hands Christ's hands. All else is vanity and compromise and untruth. Our hands must feed the hungry, touch and comfort the sorrowing.

All salvation somehow involves a reaching out, a touching. Salvation, like our redemption, is indisputably physical.

We Call Them Urban Nomads

These are not pretty kids.
They do not tug at your heartstrings.
They do not make you feel good
when you try to help them.

February 1975

Orlando spent two years on the street doing what he had to do to survive (use your imagination; you won't be wrong). He got tired of watching his life fall apart and go down the drain, and knew that it was just a matter of time until he went to jail, so he came to us one night. He's really a great kid. We got him a job at Nathan's, where they sell those oversized hot dogs, and he likes it a lot. He needed help fast, and we were able to give it.

Same with Frank. He's eighteen now. A friendly cop brought him to us late one night. Frank is one of those "only in New York" stories. He's been living in the Eighth Avenue subway for three years, a teenage panhandler right out of Dickens.

He came to New York from Trinidad when he was fifteen, as part of a steel calypso band that didn't make it. When the band disintegrated, Frank literally went underground in that teeming, noisy, steel-and-concrete burrow that snakes along beneath the asphalt skin on Manhattan's West Side. He's a pretty crusty kid, and pretty flaky. We were able to help him very fast, too, by giving him a bed to sleep in rather than a metal subway seat. But he's got a long, hard way to go.

July 1975

I preached this past Sunday in our parish in Seaside Park, New Jersey. The weather was sunny and hot, and the beaches and board-walk were crowded with thousands of vacationers enjoying the fine weather.

As usual on one of my "preaching Sundays," I talked at all the Masses, describing our kids—who they are, where they come from, how they live. And then I gave out Communion to all the beautiful children with their sunburned noses and freckles and their clear eyes and squeaky-clean faces.

I've learned a lot about why people give to help our kids. It's easy and cheap and cynical to think that they give to relieve their guilt at having such beautiful children with goodness and light behind their eyes.

I think the people who went to church this Sunday in Seaside Park helped our kids because they loved God and loved our kids. I didn't notice any guilty gratitude. The problem with guilty giving is that it doesn't do anybody any good. To give to the poor without love for the poor poisons both the giver and the gift. Guilty giving doesn't reach out to the poor to share with them our own goodness and riches; it just erects a wall between us and the poor over which we throw our gift to them because we don't want to feel their pain, to sense their closeness to us.

It's not always easy to love my kids. They are not to be loved the way a lost, friendly puppy or cute kittens are loved, because they're cute and because it makes us feel good about ourselves to love them. If we love lost and hurting kids that way, then when they grow up and develop sharp adolescent teeth and claws, we withdraw from their need, the way puppies and kittens, when they grow up and stop being cute and warm and cuddly, are abandoned and left to the life of a stray animal. Like our kids, who become strays. Only we call them nomads.

Our children at Covenant House are beautiful, too, but it takes a bit of looking. You have to hope a lot, and overlook the marks that pain and cynicism leave on a child's face. The eyes are too knowing, too watchful, engrimed, dirty eyes that have seen too much too soon. Not like the beautiful eyes of the kids to whom I gave Communion this Sunday.

September 1975

The hardest question I get asked by people who learn about Covenant House is, Does it work? How successful are you? The way I answer that question depends a lot on who's asking it. Professionals in the field of child care get one kind of answer. People who just care about our kids (without the scientific interest of a professional) get still another answer. Those who think that somehow all street kids are lazy, shiftless drifters and criminals get still a third answer. My staff gets still another and a different response.

Professionals like to see the data. They like to extrapolate from a lot of scientifically collected quantitative material to prove a substantive change in a human being. Most people, though, who just really care a lot about the kids are more impressed by the kind of anecdotal information that I put in these newsletters: true facts, true histories, stories that illustrate how a lot of kids do experience a real change in their ability to love, to be responsible, to speak the truth, and to increase their capacity and desire to be good people.

The others—and there are a lot of them who are down on street kids and who think that somehow they're all pretty bad—I can get pretty impatient with. With them, I talk more about the reasons why my kids are having such a tough time, why some won't make it, and I try to put in perspective our kids' inadequacies and weaknesses and show that with a lot of help, a lot of support, a lot of love, a lot of structure, our kids can become really fine, good, productive human beings.

For my staff, who have to live day by day with the kids and who have to suffer with them their growing-up pains, I point out how effectively they have worked with our children, how much they themselves have grown because they have permitted themselves to be used up and even abused for the sake of our kids.

People tell me that I say really different things to different people about the kids, and I answer that of course I do. It all depends on who you are and what your own needs are and what you really want to believe and how I can make you believe it. The truth about our kids is many different things, and the truth we will understand is the truth we are ready to understand and want to understand. Only God encompasses all of it.

We know that we help some of our kids a lot—it's easy to see significant changes in many. We know, too, that we fail with many

more than we succeed. We hope we succeed with that greater number in the middle, but we are not always quite certain.

Growth and progress are judged depending on where you start
from. If you start from the very bottom, then three steps up the
ladder is great progress. To be more concrete, if you start with a
seventeen-year-old kid who can't read or write at all, and get him up
to the fourth-grade level, that's real progress. If you start with a kid
who can't stay under the same roof more than two nights at a time,
and get him to stay around for three months or six months, that's
fantastic progress.

If you start with a kid who's learned to steal and exploit and
intimidate in order to survive, and get him to stop doing those
things, that's progress, even if he doesn't turn into the kind of boy
you would want to marry your favorite niece. Limited progress, par-
tial, incomplete, but progress.

And, most of all, maybe progress is just that for one year, two
years, three years, four years, we have given a boy or girl a good
place to live in, and good people to live with, and time to grow up
and become better. Maybe all we've done is just give God His time to
work His own grace and love through us. And maybe we will never
see the end of it.

Professionals in child care sometimes give me a funny look when I
tell them that God is responsible for taking care of our kids and that
if any really good things happen to them, He should get the credit. I
don't have any problem about using other values and standards to
gauge the effectiveness of our program, but I think we ought to get
our priorities straight and first praise and thank God for having
loved and helped our kids and for letting us help Him with the job.

October 1975

We call them urban nomads, but they're really just street kids.
They're not the young, poignant, attractive, sympathy-inducing, nice
runaway children that everybody likes to help. These are not pretty
kids. They do not tug at your heartstrings; they do not make you feel
good when you try to help them.

They can be sixteen, seventeen, or eighteen. They have in common
that rather hopeless quality that you can smell in a life without
purpose. They are teenaged Bowery bums. They're just not quite old

enough yet to make it on the Bowery, but to all intents and purposes that's where they belong and that's where they are going to end up. Unless somebody stops them. Like José. He's eighteen now. He ran away from home in Pennsylvania when he was sixteen because of conflict with his parents. He's drifted around the country ever since—Florida, Canada, deported from there to New York City, and wound up last night in the Holy Name Center for homeless derelicts. He was too young, so they asked us if we had a bed for him. We took him in.

There's not too much motivation left in José. We're going to try and grab what little is there and hang on to it, and increase it, and try to give him back some sense of purpose, some feeling of hope, some idea that he just might make it. But he's not a lovely kid.

Neither is John, who's also eighteen—a real drifter, not a wanderer, not a traveler, not a pilgrim. A drifter. Unmotivated, aimless, from Queens originally, out of an alcoholic mother and absentee father, John's been in every institution and shelter in New York City. At one time, he was on heavy drugs. At sixteen he ran away from home and has been drifting ever since.

John was hanging out in the park last night and asked somebody where he could stay and they said why don't you go to Covenant House. So he came, and we have him now. He's not a nice kid with rosy cheeks and an appealing eye. Everything bad has happened to him. The corrosion has bitten deep into his character; he is poor.

Like Miguel, who was raised in New York City under rather dreadful circumstances. His parents couldn't make it here, so they went back to Puerto Rico. Miguel didn't want to go. He never had any experience in Puerto Rico, and so his parents left him here in the city. Miguel is sixteen, he's been abandoned. He's not well educated, he doesn't have any family. He doesn't really care about much—it's a very painful thing to care, because if you care about something and you don't get that something, then caring about it just makes it worse.

So Miguel has learned not to care about anything or anyone.

That's How
the Game Is Played

He sat there, inspecting my jugular
with the guileless eye of the corrupted young.

January 1976

It's different now! But back in 1968 when I moved to East Seventh Street in the East Village, street life, and the kids who lived it, seemed simpler. They were good kids mostly, free-spirited, from middle-class, suburban families, caught up in a life-style at once exciting and dangerous, romantic and risky, irresponsible and irresistibly attractive.

By 1968 the first wave of early, now disillusioned, somewhat cynical, aging flower children had attracted a swelling horde of imitators who flocked to Haight-Ashbury and the East Village to invent and to follow what they thought were new and better life-styles, freer, better value systems. The kids were certain they could avoid the hypocrisies and compromises of our older, war-fascinated generation.

They talked, incessantly, endlessly of love and community, about getting their heads together and doing their own thing with a zest and a measure of innocence that cheerfully defied the prudence of wiser heads and, in the process, added dozens of colorful phrases to our vocabulary.

I would walk through Greenwich Village in 1969 and '70 and watch the shoals of bright, gleaming teenagers wash up and down the streets in search of their magic spawning place: those special people, the enlightenment and revelation that would give instant meaning to their lives.

Purveyors of every kind of exotic creed clutched at their minds. And the drugs, the violence, the degradation lay in wait for them like wild beasts.

Many thousands of them came to Covenant House. We tried to sort the kids out, sending some home, keeping the few we had room for, trying to find places that didn't exist for most of the others. We tried to keep it simple: food if they were hungry, a place to sleep, hard-nosed counseling always.

In 1976 the romance is gone. Middle-class teenagers have learned that New York City is not a good place to run away to. Street life is bitter and hard and the kids are nomads and urban drifters and damaged children. They are not looking for enlightenment, excitement, fulfillment; that quick, beautiful stream of flower children was just a vivid ripple in the history of the late sixties. They are not middle-class kids anymore. They are the children of the poor, and the game they play is survival. The rules are simple: Do what you have to do to somebody else first.

The kids, the children, are harder to help, harder to love. They are not so beautiful, and their needs are greater. They challenge our faith in the redeeming power of the Lord and confront our own convictions: If we are born again in love and in the spirit of Jesus, are these to be reborn through us? And if it does not seem to happen? How does one measure our joy in the Lord against the misery of children?

When we teach a starving child to say, "Give us this day our daily bread" before he dies of hunger, we are caught up in a darkness so profound that only the light of Christ can pierce it.

May 1976

In the jargon of the street he's known as "rough trade," and he plies his wares, himself, up and down the Minnesota Strip. He is fifteen and looks eighteen, and he's seen the elephant.

We faced each other across my desk, casually, relaxedly, while I carefully arranged my face and my eyes and my mind so that nothing I said or did or thought or felt for the next hour was spontaneous or unconsidered. He offhandedly, with the practiced skill that needed no explanation, probed for my weaknesses, inspecting my jugular with the guileless eye of the corrupted young. Slow waves of depravity and innocence washed in shadows of darkness and light across his face.

He used the shreds of his innocence with a kind of detached, hapless malevolence to evoke my sympathies. By turns he was cynical and callous, winsome and desperate—for knowing moments at a time, vulnerable. He drifted in and out of reach, in and out of touch, constantly probing, watching for the moment of advantage.

The Minnesota Strip is the slimy underbelly of Manhattan, a fifteen-block stretch of Eighth Avenue porno parlors, strip joints, pizza places, cheap bars, fleabag hotels, and thousands of drifters, hookers, and pimps. It parallels Times Square and intersects that block on Forty-second Street, where a dozen third-rate moviehouses crowd together in grimy brilliance. At night the crowds of castoffs and nomads and derelicts mingle with the crowds of affluent theatergoers from the high-rent districts and suburbs. A lot of kids go there and make their living there. Like the boy across my desk.

You don't say very much to kids like that. It's always much more a thing of vibes and perceptions and boundaries. The trick is to offer what he needs at the moment, and rarely is that a lot of God talk. It's enough if he knows why you do it. This kid's needs were simple enough: a place to live, some safety, some food. What complicated the essentially simple immediacy of it all was our "no strings" thing. He wanted to pay for it. That's what he always had to do. That's how the game is played.

We play the same game with God all the time. We don't like his "no strings" love for us either, particularly if the "us" includes a depraved innocent, a vomit-spattered derelict, or a pimp with a stable of children whom he rents by the hour. We try desperately to climb up out of the us by being good, by being better, by deserving more.

We demand that God love us because we are good, and we are good to make God love us. We have to pay for it. That's the way we've always played the game. And to know that God loves us not because we are good but to make us so is sometimes unbearable. Because as he loves us, so we have to love us, all of us.

And so I try to love the kid across my desk in a way he really can't understand at all. But grace does, and God working in a depraved and empty and terrified heart does, and maybe, just maybe, the innocence will return to that face and he will take his eyes off my jugular and stop pushing his toe into my foot under the desk. Maybe that child who was never a child will become like a child. Maybe. He is yours and mine. Like it or not, he is part of us.

June 1976

triage   (trē 'äzh) F, sorting, . . . to pick out **I** *Brit* a: the process of grading marketable produce b: the lowest grade of coffee berries consisting of broken material **2:** the sorting of and treatment (of) . . . battle . . . victims . . .
WESTER'S THIRD NEW INTERNATIONAL DICTIONARY

Surgeons separate the wounded into three categories: the slightly wounded who would recover no matter what you did, those so severely injured that medical help was useless, and the other seriously wounded who might live if helped immediately. The first two categories were left unattended and uncared for.

I met Peter five years ago when he was fourteen—a street kid—and hadn't seen him for over a year when he walked into my office yesterday. He was wearing skin- and muscle-tight brief cut-offs and a body shirt unbuttoned to the waist. We exchanged greetings—mine delighted, surprised; his muted and detached.

I hoped he was doing well. Peter gave a sad, wry smile. "Okay," he said. "Not bad," he said. "I think a lot of killing myself," he said.

"Do you need a place to stay?" I said.

"No," he said. "I stay at the Continental Baths. It's cheap. I kind of help out around there."

"It's a bad scene," I said.

"It's a living," he said. And then I think he remembered about dying because he started slightly, sat for just an instant of frozen immobility, then shrugged, and again gave me a faint, sad smile.

"Come back to Covenant House, Pete."

"No more programs, Bruce. I'm too old. I'm a male hustler, Bruce. I'm not gay. I'm bisexual. . . ." He stopped and his face twisted. He couldn't continue.

"Come on back, Pete, to our school. We'll get you a job. That lifestyle is going to kill you, Pete. It's rotten that you have to do that."

He didn't hear me.

I grabbed his hand, his arm. "We've got this really great place on Third Street, Pete, really good people."

He looked at me in great pain. "I'm a go-go boy, Bruce, in this bar on Second Avenue. I dance there. If the johns like me they stick a five-dollar bill in my jockstrap."

"Come back, Pete. We'll find you a place. It's not too late, Pete. This Monday, Gene, downstairs, will get you a job. He's an expert at it. It's Okay, Pete. I'm really glad you're back."

"Bruce, I'm a stripper in a male burlesque joint: four performances a night for a hundred bucks. I dropped out of school in the seventh grade. I worked a couple of girls for a while, Bruce."

He couldn't stop. He had to tell me the whole sad, sick story. It was almost as though he was afraid to leave out any details, like when you go to confession.

I went on patting his hand. "I'm really glad you're back, Pete. So are Gretchen and Steve and Dave. You've got to change your lifestyle, Pete. You're into a lot of things that make you feel pretty sick about yourself."

"Bruce, I don't have any clothes. All my stuff was ripped off. I had a stereo. . . ."

"Pete, you're not going to get out of that mess you're in without help."

"There's a warrant out for my arrest, Bruce. I pawned a gold bracelet for a friend. It turned out to be stolen."

"We can work that out, Pete. We've got a place for you and a job and school. We've missed you a lot, Pete."

Finally there was no more to tell; the small dirty puddle that was his young life spilled out between us. He relaxed and took a deep breath. "I think I'll go downstairs and talk to Gene about that job. Is it okay if I come back and talk to you again on Monday?" He looked down at his hot pants with some amusement. "I can't go for an interview in these."

Pete can make $400 a week, tax-free, on the street. It's going to be pretty tough for him to work forty hours a week for $2.50 an hour. It's going to be even harder for him to go back to school and learn how to read and write. He's a good kid. He came in to see me for a lot of reasons he didn't really understand very well.

He's not a Catholic and not a religious kid and he doesn't know

anything about going to confession, but he needed and wanted abso-
lution bad. Like most of us, he was about as sorry as he could be.
A lot of people drift into, slide and choose into, a life-style that
ultimately kills them. It might be too late for Pete. The Peters of this
world are refuse in our social sewers, to be inexorably flushed down
and out, drowned in a sea of garbage, human pollution to be coped
with and buried and dumped. Many honest, caring people think so.
One such, a good friend, sighed and murmured the word "triage."
Let them go, Bruce. Think of the others, the ones you know you can
help, the ones that still have a chance. He's already almost dead,
Bruce.

Peter is already almost dead, and I think maybe the one way he
feels he can reassert some control over his life is to end it. Pete is
most definitely one of the Lord's lost sheep. He is not the white,
cuddly, innocent lamb that just happened to wander away from the
fold. In biblical categories I think it fair to say that Pete is a sinner,
the kind over which heaven rejoices if they turn away from their evil
and turn back to God. Pete can't do that without God's help, nor
can we.

Pete doesn't really want to end his life, but he's not certain he can
begin it again either. Only the Lord can provide the massive life-
support systems he needs to make it, and—to carry through with the
metaphor—places like Covenant House must exist as the intensive
care units for these dying children.

July 1976

It had not been a good day. That afternoon I had been mugged,
and one of my kids stole the grocery money before splitting. I didn't
like any of them very much. They were not good kids, I finally
decided; they were not grateful for anything I did for them.

It was two in the morning, and I couldn't get back to sleep because
someone was pounding on the door. When I opened it, there were
two kids standing there, fourteen and fifteen maybe.

Are you Bruce? the one asked. Yes, I said. Do you take kids in? I
looked at the bodies lined up on the floor. Yes, I said. Can we stay
with you? he asked, hesitating. No, I said. We have no room.

He started to cry. What can we do, where can we go? he said. You can go back out into the street and look sad, I said. He stopped crying. I can do that, he said, his eyes never leaving my face. I never saw them again.

THE GREAT AMERICAN SEX INDUSTRY

1977-79

BEN·AMI

God never lets us see the pit He digs for our feet until we fall into it.

The turning point in the history of Covenant House arrived, like many turning points, I suppose, unheralded, unacknowledged—and unrecognized.

Ever since the incorporation of our agency in 1972, a certain inevitable process of assimilation into the child-welfare system began to occur. It seemed to me that little by little the mission of Covenant House to street kids was gradually being absorbed and colored and finally shaped by the system.

Our easy, no-questions-asked openness to any kid who came to our doors was being replaced by the intake criteria imposed by the city and state. We were told which kids we should take, how long we should keep them, even what we could do for them.

Despite this encroachment upon our flexibility and openness, between 1972 and 1975 Covenant House flourished and grew quickly into a classy little group-home program with ten residences for about 120 kids.

And I was getting bored—and frustrated. What started out as a model of openness and availability to any kid on the street was quickly becoming like any other agency, dependent on government funds, subject to government priorities. Covenant House in 1975 was crisply pro-

*fessional, carefully compassionate—and rapidly becoming indistin-
guishable from any other group-home program in New York State.
It was time for me to leave, I thought. Covenant House certainly no
longer needed me. Since I loathe sitting behind a desk, I couldn't
imagine that God would want me to spend the next ten years adminis-
tering a child-care agency.*

*God doesn't tell me very much. I've never had any revelations from
the Lord telling me what to do or what to tell other people. God speaks
to me—or, more accurately, I become convinced of the rightness of a
decision or a choice by a reflection on my experience, on what has
happened in my life, on what is going on in my life. If it seems to me to
make sense, to be necessary, to be right, to be something that God
would want to happen, that with God's help I might be able to accomplish, that is enough for me.*

*I've never worried very much about failure. It is simply unimportant
to me. I've never worried very much about success. It doesn't count for
very much. But I am very competitive! I hate to lose, and when I think
I'm going to lose I can work very hard. It's not that I care very much
about winning. It's the not-losing. . . .*

*Making sense out of my life is important to me. The only thing that
really makes sense for me is to do what God wants, what pleases him.
Nothing else really matters to me. I do what I do because of God.*

*Maybe that's why, when I found myself in Times Square—Eighth
Avenue and Forty-second Street—one sultry July night in 1975, about
1:00 in the morning, I became very afraid. I don't remember now why
I was there. Perhaps I had gone to the theater with a friend.*

*The streets were awash with people: drifters, nomads, hustlers,
pimps, street people, gawkers from the suburbs. The violence, the foreboding—the air of malevolence—was actually palpable.*

*Standing on the corner of Eighth Avenue and Forty-second Street I
became aware of this very powerful, gut-wrenching conviction that if I
remained in child care I was going to wind up in Times Square with
these people. I felt as though I had been kicked. I decided on the spot
to resign from Covenant House.*

India was the answer. I would go to India!

*I set about preparing myself for a new ministry. I had my successor
all lined up: Sister Gretchen Gilroy of the Franciscan Sisters of Syra-
cuse, the leader of the first group of nuns to come to Covenant House
and the founder of our group homes for girls.*

I also learned to fly—in two months flat from the time I took my first lesson until the time I got my license. My idea was to get a plane cheap and fly it to India, where I would undertake my new ministry. It was not a particularly bright idea. In fact, it was downright crazy. I was not the world's best pilot!

I made appointments with four bishops in India and I was due to fly over there to discuss a possible new ministry when God—probably trying to keep me from killing myself over the Atlantic Ocean— messed around in my life again.

The Times Square Community Planning Board, because of its great concern for the hundreds of kids who were being exploited, bought and sold up and down Eighth Avenue and all along Forty-second Street, asked Covenant House to open a shelter for runaway girls.

The American sex industry was in full flower in Times Square. Organized crime had realized how much money they could make on commercial sex and ever since the early seventies had poured tens of millions of dollars of venture capital into their sleazy enterprise.

The merchandise they offered, the commodities that were bought and sold, were young people. Nobody ever buys an old prostitute. Nobody ever buys an old hustler.

I welcomed the idea of setting up a residence for these kids. With the cooperation of the Times Square Community Planning Board and the local business community it was easy to accomplish, and happened quickly. The establishment of this house was going to be my last official act in the field of child care.

I am also, however, a very logical person. At least I think I am. And it seemed to me—I said to the local community board—that what you really need in Times Square is a crisis center for kids. Someplace they can come and get the no-questions-asked help they need twenty-four hours a day. What a great idea, they said. Will you help us?

I may be logical, but I'm not always smart, or maybe God never lets us see the pit He digs for our feet until we fall into it.

What you need is a feasibility study, I said. I'm going to India, but I'll be glad to do a feasibility study.

I walked every block and every street from Thirty-fourth Street on the south to Fifty-ninth Street on the north, from Sixth Avenue on the east to Eleventh Avenue on the west, looking for a site. There was one beautifully empty building ideally located: on Eighth Avenue between Forty-third and Forty-fourth streets. It was right next to the biggest

*pimp bar on the Strip and right across the street from a porno theater
and a massage parlor. You couldn't want a more perfect location.*

*The next day I called the owners of the property and told them who
I was and what I wanted. I listened to a startled gasp on the other end
of the phone. The voice belonged to a member of an organization
called the Christian and Missionary Alliance: a really super group of
about a thousand Protestant Evangelical missionaries stationed all
over the world. For many years those buildings on Eighth Avenue had
been their world headquarters.*

*After a tour of duty, the missionaries would return to the missionary
residence on Eighth Avenue for medicals and some R&R before returning to their mission field.*

*The neighborhood had gotten so raunchy, however, that the mission-
aries didn't want to come there anymore. So the Alliance built a new
world headquarters in Nyack, New York, outside New York City, and
moved their entire operation there, intending to pay for their new
headquarters by selling their Times Square properties.*

*And they couldn't sell them. It wasn't that they lacked for custom-
ers. There were plenty of customers: pornographers, who wanted to
turn the Christian bookstore into a porno bookstore, the missionary
residence into a massage parlor, and the beautiful 1888 chapel into a
porno movie theater. The Alliance could not and would not sell to
these wretched men.*

*They were getting desperate, said the unbelieving voice on the
phone. "We had just begun a prayer vigil this very morning, asking
God to send someone along to continue his work. You can have it for a
million dollars."*

*I didn't have a dime. In fact I was bankrupt. So I decided to fake it
and said I would look into it.*

*I went to see Cardinal Cooke and told him about the kids on the
street and the need for a crisis center in Times Square and waited for
him to say no. (I wasn't worried. By the time you get to be a cardinal
you're more famous for your prudence than your fortitude!)*

*"How much?" he said, and my heart went through the floor. "Fifty
thousand dollars," I blurted out. "Yes," he said, and I cursed under
my breath—I should have asked for five times as much.*

*"The Church should be there on Eighth Avenue," he said. "Yes,
Your Eminence," I said.*

Feeling something very akin to despair, I went to my Order. "Look guys," I said, "I think I've just killed myself. Will you give me a hundred and twenty-five thousand dollars for a center in Times Square?" They laughed at me. "We'll give you twenty-five thousand dollars and loan you a hundred," they said.

I went to some friends in the Culpepper Foundation. "Will you give me twenty-five thousand dollars," I said. "Yes," they said. "In fact, we'll give you a hundred and twenty-five thousand."

This all happened in ten days!

Well, I can feel the hot breath of the Holy Spirit as well as the next man. So I wrote the four bishops in India that I would be delayed a few years and moved to Times Square, on Eighth Avenue, between Forty-third and Forty-fourth streets.

It was July 1976. Almost eleven years ago as I write this.

My staff and I spent the next nine months with contractors and painters and plumbers trying to get the old buildings in shape and moving our offices to Times Square.

We opened the program officially on April 1, 1977. The cardinal came to bless the place and said something about keeping me there forever.

The kids began flooding in!

On May 1, the roof fell in. My director of finance came to me in something of a panic. "Listen, Bruce," he said, "if you can't come up with a hundred thousand dollars in thirty days, it's all over. We're bankrupt."

I don't think I've ever been closer to despair than I was at that moment. I didn't know what to do, where to go. I had used up all my friends, all my credibility. . . .

I was in the process of writing a letter to the cardinal explaining what a dope I had been to think I could pull off such a venture—a letter very much along the lines of the man in the Gospel who had started to build and could not finish because he had not planned well and lacked the resources. I mean I was sick with disappointment and shame.

I mean we had just celebrated our grand opening a month ago!

I never got a chance to mail that letter.

Two days later, on May 3, Bill Reel walked into my office. I had never heard of Bill Reel. I had never read his column in the New York Daily News. Bill told me that he was going to write a column about Covenant House in Times Square and ask for help.

In two weeks, more than two thousand people sent in twenty-five thousand dollars. I was overjoyed. Bill was overjoyed. He wrote a second column. In the next two weeks another two thousand people sent in another twenty-five thousand dollars. The head of a New York foundation walked into my office a day later and put a check for ten thousand dollars on my desk.

And a little old lady from Trenton, New Jersey, got on a train and came over to see me. She didn't have an appointment. She hadn't called. She just walked into my office. "My name is Julia," she said. "Like you, I don't have any children. I just retired after thirty years with General Motors and I have a good pension. God will take care of me. You need this more than I do," and she placed on my desk a bankbook with her life savings of forty thousand dollars.

I had the hundred thousand dollars with about five minutes to spare. God never seems to give me much lead time in these matters.

Those thirty days in May were probably the most critical in the entire history of Covenant House. I could do nothing to save it. Nothing at all. When I learned that bitter lesson, one more time, God did.

Maybe you can understand now why I have this absolute conviction that God loves these kids so much.

I changed. Times Square changed me.

Covenant House changed, radically, back into what it should always have been.

My newsletters changed. You'll be able to see that as you read on.

The X-rated Children

"Take this one," he said.
"You'll like this one.
His name is Nandy. He's eleven."

August 1976

I live on the Minnesota Strip—Eighth Avenue between Forty-third and Forty-fourth streets. It's a sick, festering pus-filled boil of a place where the corruption and violence and exploitation of a diseased society burst into the open. You can find all the sadness in the world here.

I left my place yesterday morning at seven-thirty to go down to my Covenant House office. I stepped over a puddle of vomit in the doorway, said good morning to the prostitutes hanging out there, and walked down Forty-second Street to the Seventh Avenue subway.

There was a blond kid, about fifteen, leaning against the wall of a porno movie theater. Next to him was an overflowing garbage can. He gave me that unmistakably, speculative, inquiring look. The boy was still there when I passed back the same way six that evening. There was a drunk stuffed in the garbage can.

I went out again about two in the morning to get a bite to eat, and stepped over the drunk in my doorway; there were seventeen (I counted them) prostitutes across the street, moving slowly back and forth. It was a warm night, and the streets were crowded with hundreds of the night people, washing up and down the littered sidewalk. There was an indescribable sense of violence and electric ten-

sion, a fascination, the anticipation of something about to
happen. . . .

The boy was still there. We nodded at each other. I walked down
Forty-second Street and saw seven kids just hanging about by one of
the porno bookstores. The oldest was sixteen—obviously a runner
for a pimp. (A runner is a kid who works for a pimp as a negotiator.
Johns don't like to talk directly to pimps. They're afraid of pimps.
It's easier to make the deal with a runner who will negotiate time,
place, price.)

The older kid, the runner, touched me on the arm. "Which one do
you want?" he said. "You can have any one you want for twenty
dollars."

I said I wasn't into that, but he didn't believe me. He called over
one of the kids. "Take this one," he said. "You'll like this one. His
name is Nandy. He's eleven."

Sermons on sin are usually abstract statements about abstract of-
fenses against a God who is also conveniently abstract. Sin, in the
concrete on Eighth Avenue and Forty-second Street, is sin in the
X-rated lives of children, in their X-rated eyes and X-rated faces and
their X-rated bodies. The kids are sinners. We are, too. But they are
children who need finding and reaching out to.

They're good kids, mostly. They really are. When you're fourteen
and fifteen, and you can't read or write very well, and have no place
to live, and it's cold and you're hungry and you have no marketable
skills, you market yourself. They are children who desperately need
help in an area where there are no services for them and where
there's no place to go for help.

That's why Covenant House plans to open a multiservice center
on Eighth Avenue. It will be open twenty-four hours a day, seven
days a week. The center will be called Under 21 and offer no-questions-asked help to any kid who needs a bed, food, safety, a way out
from a degrading lifestyle. Jobs and school too and medical help and
just comforting and self-respect, so the kid who hangs out by the
porno theater won't have to make his living there anymore.

I've got this great place on Eighth Avenue, all kinds of space,
including a church! And a residence, and a walk-in center and offices
and stores . . . I have enough money to pay the rent, utilities, and
maintain the place. I don't have enough money for staff. I need either
thirty full-time volunteers or $250,000.

I extend a serious invitation to anyone who would like to give a year of his life to the Lord and to work with us and the kids on Eighth Avenue. We can provide free room and board and pocket money and insurance and a chance to practice the corporal and spiritual works of mercy.

Volunteers would be expected to live a strictly ascetic life in union with the worshipping Church (that means a lot of prayer, fasting, meditation, above all, the Eucharist, and other practices designed to nurture and intensify your spiritual life). This religious commitment is not only a survival mechanism—which it surely is—but also an indispensable means of bringing the Lord's grace and presence into the lives of these kids . . .

Thanksgiving 1976

It's easy and uncomplicated—on Thanksgiving—to thank God for giving us this chance to praise Him and glorify the Lord. It's easy to thank Him for His endless mercies and gifts. Words like "duty" and "obligation" shouldn't be uttered with the same breath that speaks of praise and gratitude.

But then if I write to you on Thanksgiving about my kids—the endless stream of the forlorn, helpless, burned-out kids: the Bills and Dianas and Tonys and Marys and Mikes and Jills and Bobs and and . . . The misery of children confronts the terrifying mystery of God's providential love for them.

The mind boggles, our faith strains, and giving thanks on Thanksgiving right away gets mixed up with duty and obligation, and a bit of guilt maybe (we do have so much, after all). Our love for God and a simple desire to help kids gets all messed up with a need to justify ourselves before God.

We don't like having our guilt chords plucked and strummed like a banjo even in the best of causes. The simple implied suspicion that we are helping needy kids out of guilt or our own needs fills us with resentment. Who, on Thanksgiving, wants to feel defensive about something as dear to us as our very love for God and for children?

That kind of guilt poisons and destroys love. It has nothing at all to do with authentic sorrow for our lack of generosity. The repentance we are led to feel for our niggardly commitment to the poor is

the very love of God Himself drawing and impelling us to love them
more totally, more wholeheartedly.

That kind of repentance evokes gratitude and love, not guilt and
remorse, for love is joyful and gratitude is joyful and helping the
poor out of love is joyful, and that is what Jesus said loving Him and
the Father is all about.

And yet we know with a rueful certainty that our good and bad
motives lie entwined together in an uneasy, writhing tangle, a welter
of jungle undergrowth in our souls. We all have to learn to live with
our mixed motives. Part of the infinitely painful process of growing
up is learning that our hearts are far from the simple "yes, yes" and
"no, no" of the Gospel.

So I invite you to help my kids, out of love, on Thanksgiving.
Accept the gratitude and joy that is a believer's right. And the peace.

And maybe a dim, beginning, shuddering understanding of our
inescapable role in the reaching-out, terrifying mystery of God's
providential love for the children of the poor . . .

January 1976

Our new year begins on a note of equally great promise and uncertainty. We have an opportunity, given us by the Lord, I'm sure, to
accomplish something really fine, even memorable, in child care in
New York City. Our twenty-four-hour walk-in center in Times
Square on the Minnesota Strip will open around March 1. If our past
is prologue to our future, we can look forward to another year of
severe testing.

She was fourteen, in New York only a couple of weeks, an
out-of-state runaway. Pretty and headstrong, she was convinced that her parents, being relics of the Ice Age, couldn't
understand. I don't think she wanted them to. She came to
Covenant House, stayed a few days (her parents knew), and
left without warning to live with a friendly young couple to
work as a baby-sitter. She paid a bitter price for her freedom:
Both husband and wife raped her, induced her to dye her
hair, provided a false I.D. saying she was eighteen, and got
her a job as a stripper on Eighth Avenue. The girl escaped—

she was held prisoner—and returned to Covenant House. Our staff called the police, who arrested both the man and woman. They are being held at high bail; the girl is in protective custody. The damning evidence: the diary of the woman, who kept a sick savage account of what they did to her.

Sometimes it seems that accomplishing God's will means overcoming the staggering deficits that beset us every month. I moan a lot and cry to my staff that I was not ordained to be consumed with anxiety about red ink and how to pay the rent and buy shoes for a hundred kids with dirty feet, or worry about a staff of ninety who are not supermen or -women, who get sick and quit at inconvenient times and make mistakes because they work too hard too many hours.

She was eighteen, from a southern state, in New York for only a day, lost, with no place to go. She found a nice friend who offered to put her up, then raped her repeatedly and wanted to put her out on the street to make money for him. She refused. The pimp beat her severely and shot her full of heroin. She escaped and called the police, who arrested the man and then brought her to Covenant House. The judge charged him with third-degree assault—worth ninety days— and slapped a stunning fifteen-year jail sentence on him for breaking parole.

The girl was threatened with death for testifying and, terrified, fled. She keeps calling, afraid to tell us where she's hiding.

Anger and rage can crowd out and do in the gentler emotions. It's hard to be clinically detached about your hating what happens to these kids and the people who brutalize them. My spiritual tranquillity is off somewhere crouched in a corner along with my inner peace and objectivity.

He is sixteen, or maybe fifteen, or fourteen, small, skinny, a throwaway kid with some ugly scars on his body. He came in from the suburbs, running from an alcoholic, punishing mother and harsh, domineering father. There's a long history of gross abuse and neglect and rebellion and pain. Too scared to talk much, he forced out the grisly details in a soft, grief-laden monotone. He walked around the streets for four days in New York City's bitter cold before, in total despair, he tried to sell himself to a passerby for five dollars so he could eat. God was good, and he made no sale. The man brought him to us instead. He sits there grinding his teeth down hard, jaws clenched against his tears.

"If You Really Knew What I Was Like, You Would Love Me"

The younger ones haven't learned to be hopeless yet.

April 1977

Our crisis center in Times Square is open, and as we promised, twenty-four hours a day. In less than a month, over five hundred kids came in needing help.

It's just beginning. Over a hundred were just homeless, needing a bed and shelter. They were all hungry. Most needed something a lot harder to supply than a bed and food: a future.

I just need a job, man, a chance, man. Nobody will hire me, man. How can I live, man? Behind the stark questions is, unvoiced, an even starker terror. Am I going to make it? Is it all over for me? They're sixteen and seventeen and eighteen and very much alone.

A really nice walk-in kid, Mike, fifteen, has been with us for about a week. We contacted his parents in the city right away. They showed up five days later. Snippet of an overheard conversation: Mike: If you really knew what I was like inside, you would love me. Mother: You mean the fact you you are lazy and won't go to school and—and—

They just walked out and left him. He's ours.

Paul, small, shrunken, heavy-eyed—pure street—walked/fell into our door today. A scroungy kid. He had been stripped naked on Ninth Avenue by a gang of five kids. Paul dug an old pair of size-44 pants out of a garbage can, slept on the street, in a doorway, curled

up inside his beltless Talon-zippered tent. A cop brought him to
Under 21. The kid went into the bathroom, and when he didn't come
out in ten minutes we checked and found him sleeping on the floor.
Diagnosis: not drugs but exhaustion. Twelve hours later he is still
sleeping. The who's, what's, how's, and why's we don't know
yet. . . .

He's sixteen, and exists almost outside the range of normal human
communication. In some private hell of alcoholic misery, he comes
back two or three times a day for some food, to abuse and seduce our
staff, to rip off, trying desperately to make contact, I think.

She is seventeen, her baby twelve weeks old, on the street, thrown
out by her teenage husband.

He is fifteen, blackened eye, cut and bruised face. He is from California, a nowhere kid, really bright, watchful, drifting.

The younger ones haven't learned to be hopeless yet. More bewildered and outraged than bitter, they hurt more. The young drifters
are the hard ones. Teenage midnight cowboys by the hundreds, adolescent hustlers, and prostitutes whose eyes glaze in disbelief when
you talk about a change in life-style, a job, school. The incredulous
"Who, me? Do you really think I can?" In their eyes, failure and
despair and cynicism and, sometimes, the smallest glimmer of hope.

For them, "youthful opportunity" and "career choices" mean how
many johns tonight, how many tricks today. Planning for the future
means only, Where will I sleep tonight and what can I do tomorrow
to forget what I did today?

June 1977

I owe a lot to Bill Reel of the New York *Daily News*. Both he and I
know that it was God working through him to save our kids. But I
still owe Bill Reel a debt I'll never be able to repay. I owe God most
of all. Bill Reel knows that, too. But the thing about depending on
God is that He means it. Sometimes I wish He wouldn't always let
me go right to the edge. Those cliffhangers play hobnob with my
blood pressure—but they do wonders for my faith.

You see, at the beginning of May, Covenant House and Under 21
were just about at the end of our financial rope. No kidding. Three
days later, on May 6, and then on May 20, Bill Reel wrote a column
that changed our history.

A lot of people became interested in the sad plight of the hundreds and hundreds of kids trapped in this sewer on Eighth Avenue. Many, along with their checks, wrote outraged letters telling us to "hang in there," not to get discouraged, hoping that "something could be done" to purify the sordid heart of this great city. They promised their prayers, and to help when they could.

I am no crusader, and I hate tilting at windmills. I mistrust and fear fanatics almost above all else. I do not like using violent language to condemn people, but there comes a point when not to condemn and cry out is in itself a sin. Surely few issues are more clearly drawn than those around the grubby, slimy problem of the grubby, slimy men who market children for money. They are evil, make no mistake about it.

I think we make a mistake in seeing this wretched trafficking in kids as just another intractable social problem like decaying housing and unemployment and the "welfare mess." I think their sin—let's name it for what it is—cries to heaven for vengeance.

The horror stories are literally endless: A boy came to Under 21— he was fifteen—a very good-looking kid, a runaway from Connecticut. He was approached in Port Authority Bus Terminal and offered quite a bit of money to star in a filmed sex orgy.

A girl, also fifteen, a runaway from Queens, was wined and dined and almost persuaded by a so-called "fashion coordinator" who just happened to run a model studio on Forty-ninth Street to pose for photographs, and to join him and some friends at a "party" for some filmmaking.

Before that, a girl who came to our program for help had accepted a similar offer, did pose, and was then raped.

Before that, a boy of seventeen, a go-go boy who danced on a bar on Second Avenue—if the johns liked him they would stick a five-dollar bill in his jockstrap. He was also a stripper in a male burlesque house on Eighth Avenue, four performances a night. His performances were filmed.

Before that, a fourteen-year-old girl, a runaway from out of state, was seduced, raped, held prisoner by a friendly couple in the neighborhood, who got her a false I.D. saying she was eighteen, and got her a job as a stripper on Eighth Avenue.

It shouldn't be happening to them. Just because men can make money buying and selling children. It shouldn't be allowed by any-

body. Our society has permitted to develop an enormous sex industry that we seem powerless to do anything about.

Under the protection of the First Amendment we are witnessing
an almost "anything goes" explosion of exploitation and abuse that is
destroying thousands of young people every year. Our political leaders, our law-enforcement agencies, the judiciary, blame each other
and point accusatory fingers elsewhere. We permit thousands of voy-
eurs to crowd our porno bookstores and theaters to be educated in
depravity, buying books that teach them how to seduce a young
child and watching films showing preteens engaged in all kinds of
sexual activity.

Many good people shrink from doing something about it precisely
because it does stink to heaven. My ancient Mother is still fond of
warning me: He who touches pitch will be defiled by it. A lot of us
recoil with a kind of instinctive horror when we are confronted by
this filth. Has anyone ever willingly cleaned out a cesspool or finished the job smelling like a rose?

Most of the legal efforts to establish safeguards for our children
seem to run afoul of the First Amendment guarantees of freedom of
speech. Surely no right-thinking person can hold that the First
Amendment was written by the framers of our Constitution to protect pornographers and the sex lords that prey upon children to
make money.

The First Amendment does not give anyone the right to cry "fire"
in a crowded theater. And it does not give anyone the right to abuse
sexually and exploit children either. It is inconceivable to me and to
many Americans why our Congress and our legislators cannot and
do not pass effective legislation.

The time for pious rhetoric and expressions of concern is long
past. Is it wrong to be outraged? Did we not see this coming long
ago? Has outrage become too unsophisticated for us? Are we incapable of saying very simply that this abuse of our children is wrong and
we will not tolerate it any longer?

America's "Untouchables"

He had a warm, open smile.
"Hi," he said. "My name is Larry.
I sell people."

August 1977

There's a mystery here, in this story, of grace and sin. I wish I understood it better than I do. Let me tell you what happened so you can try to understand it, too. I never met him, although he tried several times to see me, just dropping over, taking a chance I'd be in the center and I never was. My staff tells me he's a big man, inches over six feet. A couple of times he sent over runaway girls too young to work for him, and once a really sick youngster.

He owns and operates the newest and raunchiest peep show and brothel in town, just across the street: BEAUTIFUL GIRLS—25 CENTS A LOOK. Over a dozen prostitutes work the place (average time with a john is seven to twenty minutes. For twenty dollars). The place is open about eighteen hours a day.

Last week at about three in the morning he came over again, carrying a milk bottle filled with quarters, dimes, and nickels. "This is for your kids," he said. "We like what you're doing. I'm in a bad business, but I don't like kids getting hurt. We collected this money from my girls and their johns for your kids." He handed the milk bottle filled with money to Peter, the young and by now bug-eyed, slack-jawed staff person on duty and walked away. "God bless you," he said. It came to $84.20.

The next morning my staff told me what happened. I was furious,

I was outraged. I also laughed till I cried. "Take it back, right away," I said. "Tell him no thanks. Thanks a lot, but no thanks. Tell him we appreciate the thought, but no thanks. Thank him for sending the kids over, though."

I thought that was the end of it, just a bizarre incident to add to the many hundreds of others. But he came back the next day dressed in a beautiful white silk suit, grabbed a broom to help Peter sweep the sidewalks. "He didn't have the right to do that, that priest. He didn't have the right to refuse a gift to God. I don't hurt anybody. I've got four kids. I got to make a living. I cleaned up my place, made the girls stop stealing and ripping off the johns. I go to church. I tithe. I gave the money to another church." He went back across the street, got into his gold Eldorado, and drove away.

The more I thought about it, the more the inexplicable mystery of sin and grace and love, of lying and caring, oppressed and obsessed me. I think he tried to do a good thing. Yet what he does across the street is clearly evil. "God bless you," he said. He gives 10 percent of his "income" to charity. He runs a low-class brothel and cares about runaway kids and people who help them. And he wanted very much to be understood.

I can't get that "God bless you" out of my mind. I couldn't have said it back to him; the words would have stuck in my throat. I hate what he does. I'd do my best to close him down. But I have this awful suspicion that he was sincere. I wouldn't worry so much if he were quite clearly a flaming hypocrite. But that "God bless you" . . . I think he really meant it. And my mind reels, and I can't understand.

I know a lot about mixed motives. I'm the world's expert on mixed motives—my own—trying to disentangle the good from the evil, to unravel the knotted skein of my better self . . . the weeds growing with the wheat . . . and suddenly I am overwhelmed by my kinship with this man, for we are both sinners hoping in the mercy of God and His forgiveness.

September 1977

"Let me stay here. There's nothing for me out there. I'm going to die out there. Don't send me away. I'm seventeen and never got through ninth grade. What kind of job can I get? I wanted to be

smart. I wanted to go to college! I wanted to be somebody. What's
going to happen to me? I'll probably die out there. Let me stay here.
I'll sleep on the floor. There's nothing for me out there. Don't send
me away."

And then he rang his dismal leper's bell as he had learned he had
to do—to warn me: "I'm a hustler," he said, and watched me carefully with a total awareness that made me afraid.

I liked him a lot. I mean, I really liked him. I felt the electricity,
the chemistry operating between us. He knew it before I did. Jeff is
on the small, skinny side, a black kid, with helter-skelter features,
eyes, nose, and mouth all slightly askew. A nice-looking kid with an
old man's face. He spoke with a quiet, strained intensity that chal-
lenged my disbelief. I believed the incredibly large tears that ran
down both cheeks. I believed in his misery and aloneness and the
darkness that consumed him. I believed he wanted to mean what he
wanted me to believe.

I believed in him, but I didn't believe *him*.

Jeff's a hustler up and down Forty-second Street. That's been his
life for the past three years, since he was fourteen. A seventeen-year-
old leper, an integral member of the flotsam and jetsam society that
exists along the grimy fringes of the Great White Way. Mother Teresa of Calcutta called the Times Square hustlers America's untouchables. In St. Francis's day the untouchables were lepers.

"Stay around," I said. "Stay here tonight. Maybe we can talk
tomorrow. I'm glad you're here. If you're serious about school, we've
got this great place. I'll tell Karl it's okay for you to stay with us
even though we're way too crowded."

Jeff stopped crying and pulled himself together. "I need twenty
minutes," he said, "to tell my sister I'm okay, that I've got a place to
stay. She's worried about me."

"Be back in half an hour," I said.

"Be back in half an hour," he said.

He came back four hours later at two in the morning, drunk and
stoned out of his mind, abusive, ugly, threatening because we
wouldn't let him in. Come back in a week, sober and straight, my
staff said. You're welcome here when you're sober and straight.
You've broken the covenant.

I think he'll come back. Where else can he go? I want him very
much to come back, this teenage midnight cowboy who maybe is a

potential Mary Magdalene. I think I understand him pretty well. I
don't think he's that hardened and blinded sinner of the Gospel who
is already dead inside but just hasn't stopped breathing yet. More
than anything else he needs your prayers and your love and your
acceptance and your belief. He needs mine, too.

I am very disturbed by the fact that I didn't believe him, and that
he saw my unbelief—he saw everything—and that maybe my sympathy and compassion and understanding weren't enough. Maybe I just
know too much about hustlers for my own good, and what Jeff really
needed was just my believing him—not *in* him, but *him* (I shouldn't
have said *"if* you're serious." I should have had faith in the boy.) I
guess maybe I didn't embrace that particular leper. Instead I used
some dumb cunning distinctions to help me not to.

What St. Francis said to us friars bothers me a lot:

> For whenever anyone, whether noble or commoner, entered
> the Order, among the other instructions given him, they were
> told that they must humbly serve the lepers and live with
> them in their house, as was laid down in the Rule: Seeking to
> possess nothing under heaven except holy poverty, in which
> they were nourished by the Lord, with food for body and soul
> in the world, and in the life to come, will attain the heritage of
> heaven.

Does anyone want to come to New York and help me do it right
the next time—help us all do that? We've got a really great bunch of
people here. You just wouldn't believe how great they are. We need a
lot more.

P.S. Thanks for all the letters about that "guy across the street"
and the milk bottle full of coins. The police closed his place last
week.

October 1977

Eric Life and I have had some really hard times together. He was
sixteen and a hard-case graduate of just about every penitentiary for
kids in New York State. His last stint was eighteen months in Go-
shen Training School, at the time a kind of maximum-security prison

for incorrigibles. I was living in our old tenement on East Seventh Street trying to cope with the flood of street kids when the tides of fate—I mean God—washed him up on my doorstep.

Eric was pretty down and out and mean as a snake. He allowed us to give him a place to stay, but he made it clear that there were no strings attached. He was a proud kid with a sense of elemental justice that was implacable in its eye-for-an-eye ferocity.

We fought all the time. Eric thought I was easier on the other kids, that I favored them more than him (to tell the truth I probably did—getting close to Eric was like getting close to a cactus). In one of the few times when we weren't fighting with each other, Eric confided in me that his real name was Baez, not Life: "Bruce, I had to change it. It didn't make any sense not to. Ever since I was a kid it's been really bad for me. I used to ask my mother why everything was always so rotten for me and she used to say, 'That's life, Eric, that's life,' and I thought, Bruce, that I had just better change my name to Life."

Eric had a fierce desire to better himself. He struggled awfully hard to make it in the local high school, laboriously learning how to read and write, to study, to do homework. He did his chores better than the other kids. He made his bed neater.

I found it hard, I know now, to praise him enough, to appreciate enough his need for encouragement and support. He worked incredibly hard, and I just took it for granted and expected more. Eric always tried to give it. I understand now how hard he was trying to please me.

I forget now what our final blowup was over—something inconsequential, I'm sure—and it was a doozy. It ended with Eric in tears threatening to carve my anatomy in all the right places. For just a few minutes I saw the boy of the maximum-security cell blocks. "You just don't love me, Bruce," was all he said. We patched things up afterward, for a time, but Eric had had it. It was somehow never the same.

He left us to join the Air Force. Periodically word would filter back that Eric was doing well, adapting to the discipline, enjoying the structured freedom of the military. He also became the Air Force Ping-Pong champion.

He came back last week to see me, after three years. "Bruce, I went to church last Sunday, and the Gospel was about ten lepers that had been cured and only one came back to say thanks, and I thought I'd better come back and say thanks."

Just once in a while a story has to have a happy ending, right? I mean, I've been sending pretty gloomy epistles your way, until you must think that nothing good ever happens to our kids. This is the kind of story that keeps us going at Covenant House Under 21. Eric was not supposed to make it, but he did. We're going to meet a couple dozen Bills and Jims and Marys and Janets today, and we know now that they can make it back because Eric did.

Eric Life was not a churchgoing kid when he came to Covenant House, and we never tried to make him one. But he went to church last Sunday and listened to a Gospel about the mercy and healing and love of the Lord and he came back to say thanks, not to us, but to the Lord.

Thanksgiving 1977

There were two absolutely beautiful kids. Anna was a pretty little blonde, thirteen years old, from New England. Mike was fourteen, a good-looking kid from Delaware. They had some problems at home, but more than that, they wanted some excitement, some action! They wanted to stand near the edge of the cliff and look over; they were beautiful moths, flying, dipping, swooping around the bright lights and candles of the Minnesota Strip.

They were good kids, but kids, and they didn't *really* know that guys like Larry existed. Steve and I met him one night down the street from our place, about 11:30. We had been out walking around, getting some fresh air and looking for kids and were standing just watching the crowds when he walked up to us.

He was tall, imperially slim, impeccably dressed. He had a warm, open smile, he shook our hands warmly, he looked us straight in the eye. "Hi," he said, "my name is Larry.

"I sell people," he said. "Would you like to come around the corner to my hotel? We have a suite on the fifth floor. We have a live male sex act first and then a live female act. We specialize in women: white, black, Spanish, Oriental. No sadomasochism," he warned, and gave us that disarming smile again. "Come around the corner," he said. "I'll take you in the first time, and then we make you a member of the club. We're open twenty-four hours a day, seven days a week. It's only twenty-five dollars for half an hour." Steve and I said no. We were, shall we say, nonplussed!

In the meantime, back at the center, Anna and Mike were anxious to begin their new careers as cliffhangers and moths seeking candles to burn up in. Anna was approached by at least six pimps. We discouraged some.

Larry, who sells people, wanted and needed some new merchandise, and since he was too old to get into Under 21 he sent in a runner named Bobby to "get" Anna. Bobby was a smooth, fast-talking eighteen-year-old. We stopped him, too.

Mike, in the meantime, had met some *really* good friends. He didn't *really* know they were hustlers. They were wanderers, he said, travelers, he said, and it would sure be nice to move around the country with Kevin. Kevin was, even at seventeen, a pretty unsavory kid. Not a bad kid, though. He made a fairly substantial income hustling gays down the street.

It was about time, I thought, for me to do my own thing. I leaned very heavily on both Mike and Anna, told them about the facts of life on the Minnesota Strip. We put Anna on a plane and Mike on a bus and sent them home.

A Certain Kind
of Sadness

*"Bruce, I'm not going to make it.
I'm going to die out there."*

Easter Sunday 1978

Thousands of kids have walked into Under 21 on the Minnesota Strip since we opened our crisis center exactly one year ago. Many of them come to escape the billion-dollar Times Square sex industry that rules the lives of thousands of young people in a ten-block area around Under 21, to escape from the degradation and danger and the dying.

We stay open twenty-four hours a day—we never close—and boys and girls can come in at any hour of the day or night, on a no-questions-asked basis, to get help: food, clothing, shelter, a bed, protection from their pimp, a chance to go home again, to get a job, to go back to school, to begin to think that they might live.

A boy said to me once, "Bruce, can you give me one good reason why I should not jump off the Brooklyn Bridge?" And I had a very hard time finding a reason. He's seventeen years old, can't read or write. He's been a hustler for the last three years; ever since he's been fourteen years old, he's been selling himself up and down Forty-second Street. He's jumped in a thousand cars; he's slept in a thousand beds; he's an alcoholic—he drinks every day in order to forget what he has to do in order to survive. And I said, "I'm glad you're

here. Stay around. Don't go away. Maybe we can find a reason together."

A sixteen-year-old girl called me at 4 A.M. She desperately wanted
to leave her pimp, who beat her a lot and kept her high on drugs all
the time. She was afraid to leave him, afraid to stay, afraid to come
in. In one of the saddest voices I've ever heard, she said, "Father
Bruce, can you make me eleven years old again so I can go home?" I
said, "Come stay with us."

A boy said to me, "Bruce, I'm not going to make it. I'm going to
die out there. The street's going to kill me." And I said, "Come, be
one of our kids and we won't let it happen."

Death and dying have become a way of life on Eighth Avenue in
the heart of New York City's Times Square. Organized sin is literally
the life-style of thousands: chosen by a few, forced on many. Outside
our Under 21 chapel on the Minnesota Strip every day is a Good
Friday, where every day the carnage of Our Lord's passion and death
is reenacted and where every day Pilates and Herods wash their
hands and mock, where crowds jeer and deride goodness and condemn the innocent, where children are scandalized and corrupted,
and young people by the thousands are bought and sold.

There is very little hypocrisy and moral ambiguity on Eighth Avenue. The evil and sin are all out front, all very straightforward:
Greedy men make money out of other people's lusts for the bodies of
young people. The Lord is nowhere more present, nowhere more
available, nowhere more merciful.

A girl said to me, "Why do you and your friends run this place?
You must be very rich." And I said no, I was always broke and we
did it because of God and we cared about her and would probably
love her if she stayed around. And she said, "Can I come to church
and pray with you?"

A boy (a street kid, a hustler) said to me, "Bruce, give me ten
thousand dollars. Bruce, you must be a millionaire to run this place."
And I just laughed and said I didn't have any money and he asked
me where I got it and I said I asked people for it. And he laughed
and said unbelievingly, "What do you say?" I said to him, "Well, if
you had money and I asked you for some of it to help a bunch of
really good kids who had no place to stay, wouldn't you give it?"
And he said yes and started to cry. I think because it had been a long
time since someone had called him *good*.

You see, the goodness is all around us, too, here on Eighth Avenue, in the beautiful kids who come to us. It's not always easy to love my kids, to see the goodness. Our kids at Covenant House are beautiful, but sometimes it takes just a bit of looking for. We have to hope a lot and sometimes overlook the marks that pain and cynicism leave on a child's face.

Our kids are beautiful. They wouldn't like to hear me call them that. They would snort unbelievingly and say we were crazy or weird, and why did we think that? And that it just wasn't true, that would mean that we loved them, and there is no way they can believe that. *No way.*

That's what makes it so hard to believe in the Resurrection. Not that Christ physically rose from the dead—that's easy to believe—but that He did it for us, because He loved us totally, unreservedly, because we are so important to Him. Because we are beautiful to Him. We don't like that no-strings love for *us,* particularly if the us includes a depraved innocent, a vomit-spattered derelict, or a pimp with a stable of children whom he rents by the hour. We try desperately to climb up out of the us by being good, by being better, by deserving more. We demand that God love us because we are good and we are good to make God love us. And to know that God loves us, not because we are good, but to make us so is sometimes unbearable and is what Easter and the Resurrection are all about here on Eighth Avenue.

It is not always easy to see the Lord's Resurrection on Eighth Avenue. Outside, the prostitutes and hustlers still sell themselves. The massage parlors and porno bookstores did not close on Good Friday, and the brothels and burlesque houses still attract their customers today on Easter Sunday, and a hundred kids will come into Under 21 today who have never heard of Lent or Easter or the Lord or their need for resurrection. Their need for shelter and protection and a bit of comforting take priority.

It's the street kids, the utterly desolate and despairing sixteen- and seventeen- and eighteen-year-olds who wash back and forth, up and down the street, who hurt the most. It's those kids especially who teach me what Holy Week and Good Friday are all about. The inexcusable, unnecessary suffering and despair of these children relive every day on Eighth Avenue the Passion of Christ.

Easter is a happier time, at least in our hearts. We know by faith that the Lord is risen, in us and in the world, and in a way that I believe but do not understand, I know that the Resurrection will happen today on Times Square and Forty-second Street. Not too many people will see it, and fewer will believe it. Most of the people who stood by two thousand years ago and cheered the death of Christ did not see or believe His Resurrection either. Pilate didn't, and Herod didn't, and those responsible for oppressing the poor didn't, and the public officials who let evil happen didn't.

They *are* coming to the Church; they are coming to find God, to experience the Lord's power in their lives. They may not know it or see it that way. It may take most of their lives to understand that, but we understand it. We know that the Church should be here on Eighth Avenue. Perhaps more than any other place it should be here, accomplishing the Lord's will to draw all men to Himself. To lift us up with Him and to raise us to His life. We need your help.

Covenant House has taught me that faith is a place just over the edge of a cliff where you hang by your fingernails, to a root, and listen to the ground crumble beneath your kicking feet while you devise clever and fantastic strategies to rescue yourself, thanking God all the while because it proves, I guess, that you love *Him*.

August 1978

"Thanks, Bruce, for running this place. Because you were here, I didn't have to sell my tail to eat today." The voice welled up out of the darkness of the boys' floor of Under 21. (We had just put the kids to bed—thirty-two boys downstairs, twenty-three girls upstairs, nine more boys on the fourth floor.) I had stopped in about 11 P.M.

It's one of my favorite times to be in the center, to witness the magical transformation of dozens of street-wise, Times Square drifters, wanderers, midnight cowboys, and potential Mary Magdalenes into a gaggle of sleeping, very vulnerable children.

The boy made no attempt to whisper. He said it loud and clear. He wanted to be heard. I wanted to cry. What he meant was he didn't have to sell his body that day. I didn't cry. I just kicked the kid gently in the leg and said I was glad he was here. I walked around a bit, stepping over a dozen kids, kicking them if I thought they wanted to be kicked, grabbing a few hands that rose up out of that dark floor to block my path for a moment.

"Will you hear my confession, Bruce?" This time it was a whisper from a kid huddled in a corner. I did.

The kids quieted down real quick that night. It's almost magic the way sixty assorted Times Square wolflings can turn into children again. "Unless you become as little children . . ." It was an extraneous thought from the Gospel drifting into my mind that I quickly banished.

October 1978

It's about one-thirty in the morning on the Eve of the Feast of St. Francis, and my teeth hurt. (Last Friday, my dentist informed me that I had cracked my two upper rear molars. "You grind your teeth, Bruce." "I don't grind my teeth," I said. "You do, when you're asleep," he said. "It's a way of working off tension and anxiety.")

I've got to get this newsletter to the printer today, and, as usual, I've waited until the last minute. It's been a busy weekend for me and for Under 21.

I walked into the center last Friday night just as the police brought in Jimmy, an eleven-year-old runaway boy they found wandering the streets. A really nice kid—scared to death, but trying not to show it. He had successfully fended off a couple of johns who tried to pick him up. We got him home Saturday morning, safe and sound.

My staff was also trying to comfort seventeen-year-old Jeanie, who hadn't been so fortunate. She had been picked off by a pimp in the Port Authority Bus Terminal. Her grim story was all too familiar: Jeanie had been held prisoner for a week, drugged and raped repeatedly before she escaped and came to Under 21. The next morning, Saturday, her pimp actually came to our door and wanted "his" girl back. She was, after all, worth about three thousand dollars a month to him—tax-free.

We told him to come back later that day. My staff was arranging for a suitable police reception as I left Saturday afternoon to preach at all the masses in St. Catherine of Sienna parish in Mountain Lakes, New Jersey.

Sunday afternoon, after my seventh sermon at St. Catherine's (the people were really good to my kids), I drove to Baltimore to preach once again at St. Casmir's Church (it wasn't a very good sermon, since I hadn't much time to prepare), and I drove back to New York early Monday morning.

There had been a lot of activity in the center. Mark, only twelve, was there. Blank-eyed, haunted, and quiet, his body bore the unmistakable signs of severe child abuse. We reported the case immediately to New York City's Children Protective Services.

Dorothy was there, too, a pretty and pregnant sixteen-year-old who ran away from home because her mother wanted her to have an abortion. She wanted to keep her baby. My staff had already arranged for her to stay in a maternity shelter.

We still had not resolved the situation of sixteen-year-old Terry. New York City and Westchester County had been fighting for three weeks over who had financial responsibility for the boy—neither wanted it. (All Terry knew was that nobody wanted him!) So Terry stays at Under 21, confused and resentful. He sits there in a corner, crying, and I can't make him stop.

The situation of fifteen-year-old John was a little out of the ordinary. Brutally abused by his older brother, he had fled to us for help. What complicated matters was the fact that both John and his brother were foreign nationals attached to a diplomatic mission here in New York. His older brother contemptuously insisted that because of his privileged diplomatic status he was immune from prosecution. Our attorneys and the Bureau of Child Welfare are about to prove him wrong.

A small success story: Jeff has stayed with us exactly ten days now. Not bad for a kid who a year ago was afraid to stay in one place for more than an hour or two. Jeff has lived on the street for over three years—he's seventeen now—and he just didn't trust anybody. Jeff is one of my current crop of favorites, and, to the chagrin of my staff, he knows it.

It's about two-thirty in the morning, and my thinking is getting a bit unfocused. The prostitutes and pimps are out in full force. Outside my window just now I counted eleven prostitutes, their laughter drifting up from the street. I doubt that it disturbs the forty kids downstairs sleeping on the floor. They all look like angels now. (Yesterday we celebrated the Feast of the Guardian Angels. How do you thank forty guardian angels?)

I'm getting pretty tired, and I still haven't finished this letter to you. Tomorrow we celebrate the Feast Day of St. Francis and I've got to think up another sermon. I'm not sure what St. Francis would think of my ministry. There are not too many similarities between the beautiful Umbrian Valley and Times Square. We do have lots of lepers around, though, and a church that needs rebuilding, and one of the great things about being a Franciscan is that it really doesn't take much talent to be one. . . .

Sometimes, like about two forty-five in the morning, I resent Francis a bit. He sets an impossibly high ideal for me. I think of all my vices masquerading as virtues and wonder how I ever let myself get trapped like this.

January 1979

I noticed one of my kids sitting alone in a corner of our center. It was about 9 P.M. Oblivious to the other kids, he was totally preoccupied, using one of our red canvas cushions as a writing desk. In his absorption, he had sucked the business end of his ball-point pen and smeared his lips with green ink.

A certain kind of sadness has a smell about it somehow. At least I imagined I could smell the boy's sadness. The center was filled with kids, about fifty of them, and I was just circulating around. I became aware of the boy's somber, direct gaze leveled at me across the room. He had finished writing his letter. When he saw me returning his stare, he got to his feet in one quick and easy flowing movement of incomparable grace that only a sixteen-year-old can manage and handed me what he had written. There was no salutation. I read it in snatches—the center was very busy. Here it is, as he wrote it. I didn't correct or change a single letter.

I don't know where I am going. I have a general idea for which I am not sure of, to turn too. I sometimes feel depress, —for I usually don't know why. I wonder why I refuse people's help. A lot of things make me feel happy for awhile but I am jealous of other things such as people who have more than I do.

I really like this kid. He wouldn't win any beauty prizes: about five feet nine or so, lanky, with hair in his eyes, a crooked left eyebrow, and a practiced smile. Just your typical skinny run-of-the-mill Times Square nomad. I had a tough time reading his letter because of the interruptions. Sharon grabbed my arm and said she wanted to talk to me about her mother. Fifteen-year-old Dave, a budding philosopher from California, asked me why God could permit all the evil outside on Eighth Avenue. I gave him my thirty-second treatise on the nature of God, good and evil, and freewill. He was too smart to be satisfied. I went back to reading Billy's letter.

All throughout my childhood I been getting into trouble in school, home, and mostly everywhere I turned to be heading. In a way I admitted I have so called sticky fingers. A lot of people throughout the years asked me—"How do you feel?"—Now a few years later, I answer with truth I don't really know. People try to help me and I jam it up their————, I admit I caused some difficulty at home, and allso at school and other places. I allso feel that my father has problems, that he can't handle. And I felt I was used for a scrapgoat. I did a lot of things for attention, for which if I told certain people I feel that wouldn't understand me. But it would allso break their heart."

I looked for the boy and saw him watching me read his letter. I don't know what he saw in my face. A couple of volunteers who work in the center on Thursdays were eager to share with me their encounter with Val and Becky, our latest teenage Romeo and Juliet. Seventeen-year-old Jeff came up to me and demanded his rights to my company. He tells everybody that he's my favorite kid, and he might be right. I lost sight of Billy and went back to his letter.

Last January 1977 I had to go upstate New York to a home. People say I had a lot of potential to do certain things. But now these days I am not to sure of myself. Is it wrong just to want certain thinks in life, and find yourself reaching for them, but in a way they ain't there. I just wish that I didn't do certain things that I did. I could honestly say I don't really

know whats it like been loved or to give love. I did at certain
situations, but I guess, I really didn't.

I had a lump in my throat. I hoped he had seen love in my face
when I looked at him last. Nobody ever sees a lump in your throat,
even though it feels as big as a house. They, the lumps, disappear
pretty quickly, though, particularly when a couple of more-than-
usually-raunchy street kids (good kids, though; not nice, but good)
called upon me to exercise my Solomon-like judgment to settle a
"misunderstanding" between them and one of my staff. They didn't
like the judgment. So I offered them amnesty instead, which they
gladly took, what they really wanted in the first place.

Billy was nowhere in sight, and I went back to reading his letter. I
guess the kids must have seen my face, because nobody bothered me.

Once again today I blew my mind again, I went into a tantrum
for no reason. I started threating certain people for no reason what-so-ever. It's now a few hours later. I am thinking to
myself, what's my life coming to. I am faced with a hard
decision for which could be a good factor in my life. But I just
can't make up my mind. I been thinking lately should I throw
in the towel or keep on fighting and try my best, at what I
could do best.

That's it. Word for word. Misspellings and all. Kids like Billy talk
about suicide a lot, and sometimles they do it. Billy hustles johns
over on Third Avenue and Thirty-second Street. They drive by in
their cars and then they slow down and then they circle the block
and then they stop. Billy has seen the inside of a thousand cars. He's
a bright kid, and, as he says, he has a lot of potential.

He is still a pretty intact kid, wanting all the things that most of us
take for granted. He's not a particularly attractive kid, or even an
especially appealing one. His sixteen-year-old face isn't really sixteen
anymore. He's a bright youngster who doesn't even try to fool himself anymore, or not very much anyway.

The Billys of this world can run through your fingers like water.
At times like this I'd rather be a heart surgeon, knowing that some

tired heart pumps and leaky valves are just too worn out and it's not your fault if the patient dies. Billy needs a heart surgeon though, and I, with relief and some dread, commit him to His care—and yours. You own him, too. He is your son, your brother, your cousin.

RUNNING FOR THEIR LIVES

1979-82

*"Call me back in one hour
and tell me why you haven't done it today,"
Governor Carey said.*

*I don't even like to think about those first three years on Times
Square. The smart money said we would never make it. The drugs, the
violence, the street pimps, the organized-crime goons, the white-collar
pimps who actually ran the business . . .*
    *I hated living there. It was like the East Village scene all over again,
only a hundred times worse.*
    *But the kids were there. By the thousands and thousands. Derelict,
wasted, abandoned, hurting. Dying . . .*
    *They were great kids. They really were. Look, I'm not a sentimen-
talist about my kids. I'm no Father Flanagan. I've met some bad boys.
A few anyway.*
    *You shouldn't think they're bad kids. If you knew them you'd know
how good they are and how brave they are and how much they want to
make it back off the streets.*
    *About two days after our center on Eighth Avenue opened, I knew I
had a problem. A major problem.*
    *This may sound arrogant, but it's true: I had cornered the market
in street kids! Thousands of kids began coming into our small store-
front between Forty-third and Forty-fourth streets. I didn't turn any*

*away. You know why. I did it once before, and I have been haunted by
the faces of those two kids ever since.*

*When we didn't have any beds and cushions left, the next thirty
kids slept on mats on the floor. When we didn't have any mats left, the
next wave of teenage nomads slept on the chapel floor, curled up
under the altar, stretched out in the pews.*

*My once understanding and appreciative neighbors began to take
another look at the monster growing on their doorstep. The community planning boards, the theater organizations, the mighty New York
Times, had no real idea of the magnitude of the problem of thousands
of homeless, unemployable, and savagely exploited kids. They had
given their blessing to a small program to help nice kids. . . .*

*Instead of a few middle-class kids from the suburbs there were
literally thousands of forlorn street kids with peach fuzz on their
cheeks and despair in their hearts coming into Covenant House.*

*So when I desperately needed to expand our services—to open a
small medical clinic on the corner of Eighth Avenue and Forty-fourth
Street—my once friendly if skeptical neighbors turned hostile. I can
understand it better now. At the time I was pretty self-righteous about
it.*

*"They" (my "enemies" of the moment) threatened to have me
closed down, and with just a flick of their wrist they made enormous
problems for me at City Hall.*

*I countered with a threat to open a soup kitchen on the corner of
Eighth Avenue and Forty-fourth and serve hot, nourishing meals to
any derelict of any age. The hours of my soup kitchen would coincide
with the times of the Wednesday and Saturday matinee and the evening performances. My heart rejoiced at the thought of a couple hundred Times Square derelicts lined up in the lobby of the St. James
Theatre. . . .*

*"Peace," the mayor cried. "Let's find a bigger place for Bruce at a
different location." Everybody thought that was a great idea, and everybody said they would help me find a new site. It was a great idea—
and nobody did.*

*Once again I was desperate. In my heart of hearts I recognized the
justice of my neighbors' complaints. By this time, in 1979, almost ten
thousand kids were jamming themselves into our center on Eighth
Avenue. At times it seemed as though all the misery and fear and pain*

and loneliness—and sometimes the violence and the viciousness—of Times Square were coming through our doors.

Once again I walked every block, looking for a new location to expand to: from Fifty-ninth on the north to Thirty-fourth on the south, from Sixth Avenue on the east to Eleventh Avenue on the west. I checked out every empty warehouse, every half-standing shell of a building. There was nothing. Absolutely nothing.

I had given up. There was simply nothing left to look at. As I was returning to my office, I noticed a large, solid, eight-story building that occupied the entire block between Fortieth and Forty-first streets on Tenth Avenue. It looked very quiet. I couldn't see any activity around it. "What's that?" I said to a member of my staff. "Let's check that one out."

It turned out to be the Manhattan Rehabilitation Center. Owned by New York State, it was actually a jail for drug addicts—almost six hundred of them. Over the years New York State had built about thirty of these facilities around the state. It was supposed to be the answer to the question of what do we do with all the junkies on the streets. The program was poorly conceived, never worked in the first place, and New York State had closed all the other facilities and was in the process of closing this one on Tenth Avenue.

"Let's go for it," I said. So I wrote to the General Services Administration (this office handles all New York State property) and asked if I could please have their building for my kids. A polite letter back informed me that the building in question was hotly sought after by other state agencies and that under the law they must be given priority.

Despair again. I didn't know what to do—except maybe appeal to Governor Hugh Carey.

I didn't know the governor. I really don't know many important people, but I knew he had a close friend named Dr. Kevin Cahill, and I knew that a friend of mine, Monsignor Jim Murray of Catholic Charities, knew Dr. Cahill! So I called Jim and asked him if he wouldn't mind helping me meet Dr. Cahill, for maybe ten minutes. I figured if I could convince Dr. Cahill he might talk to the governor. It was a long shot, but I didn't have any others.

It was Holy Thursday 1979. Eleven years before that, also on Holy Thursday, I moved off campus to celebrate Mass in my East Village apartment and to begin my new ministry. Holy Thursday has always been important to me.

My appointment was set for 10 A.M. I wasn't late. Right on the stroke of ten, Jim Murray and I walked into Dr. Cahill's office. Dr. Cahill was very pleasant. I never had a chance to talk to him.

Governor Carey walked into Dr. Cahill's office! It wasn't a setup. It wasn't planned. It wasn't, either, a coincidence.

Instead of pitching Dr. Cahill, I pitched the governor. I told him about the thousands of kids in Times Square and my desperate need for a new building.

The governor looked at Dr. Cahill. New York City Department of Corrections wants that building, he said, but it will take the city years to get its act together.

The governor picked up the phone and called somebody in Albany. "I'm thinking of letting Covenant House use the state facility on Tenth Avenue. How long would it take to transfer the property?" He listened for about five minutes to the voice on the other end of the phone, and then he took the phone away from his ear for a moment, placed his hand over the mouthpiece, and said to Dr. Cahill, "They say they can do it, but that it will take a long time."

The governor looked at Dr. Cahill in silence for a moment. "It's Holy Thursday," he said. "Let's do it." He turned back to the phone he was holding in his right hand: "Call me back in one hour and tell me why you haven't done it today," he said, and then he hung up the phone and looked at me.

"We'll do what we can to help, Father," was all he said. I thanked the governor, thanked Dr. Cahill, thanked Monsignor Murray, and walked back to my office across town. It took me about twenty-five minutes to get there. I wasn't really sure if I understood what had happened in Dr. Cahill's office, but I was praying pretty hard.

My secretary was very excited. "You have two phone calls from Albany, Bruce. The man said it was very important and to call him right back." I held my breath while I dialed his number.

"Can you come over today and pick up the keys for the building on Tenth Avenue?" the voice on the phone asked. He seemed pretty excited.

"Yes," I yelled. "Just tell me where."

It was April 1979.

That's a true story. Word for word. Not an ounce of exaggeration in it.

It gets worse or—I should say, better!

Here I had this huge building. It actually turned out to be three large buildings, with dormitories, libraries, classrooms, a gym, a kitchen that would turn a professional chef green with envy, and plenty of office space.

Turning a jail into an attractive center for thousands of street kids was going to be a headache I didn't want and didn't really know how to handle.

I also didn't have any money. I was broke, as usual.

Being preoccupied with my new problems—the buildings and how to go about renovating them—I really didn't want to keep a lunch date with a man named Don Wilderman who, two weeks before, had invited me to have lunch with him at the Plaza. Don's daughter had heard me speak in her high school and told her father about our kids. Don wanted to have lunch because maybe he could help our kids in some way.

Lunch was great. I had never been in the Plaza before, and Don, who looked like a very successful lawyer, was a great host. We talked a lot about our kids and how great they are. Don was a real doer, and a real optimist.

"By the way," I said, "just what do you do anyway?"

"I'm President of NICO," Don said. "We're the biggest retrofitting company in New York."

"What's that?" I said.

"We renovate old buildings. Give us an old thirty-story building and we'll gut it and rebuild it in six months."

I poured half a cup of coffee down my left lung, coughed for about five minutes, and was finally able to say to Don in a somewhat strangled voice, "Let me tell you my problem."

I told Don about my block of buildings that needed renovation fast. "No problem," he said. "I'll have a dozen of my engineers and architects, plumbers and electricians there this afternoon."

"Are you kidding me?" I asked.

"No problem, Bruce. When do you need the building?"

"By September," I said.

"That's four months away. No problem," Don repeated. "We'll get it done for you. We're specialists in first-class, rapid renovation. No problem!"

We moved in in September 1979.

The money I didn't have? It came. I really don't know from where.

Don would send me a bill and there would always be money to pay it. Although at times I would get pretty anxious and my director of finance would go into his bathroom and have a quiet fit of hysteria. True story. Word for word. No exaggeration.

By January 1980 we were routinely housing over 250 kids a night, and we were jammed to the rafters. And, of course, we were always broke!

"Then They Sold Me to the Corporation"

*"I'd appreciate it
if you didn't lay any God talk on me."*

Marge had that special look on her face that warned me she meant business. "I think you ought to see this kid, Bruce." She said it with a no-nonsense deadly seriousness that was almost a command.

I always listen *very* carefully when Marge talks. At sixty-one, she's the oldest member of our volunteer community, the resident grandmother of Under 21, and a very wise lady—with that special wisdom that comes from raising her own family right down to a passel of beloved grandchildren that she spoils outrageously. (She spoils my kids, too.)

"Sure," I said. "I'll go downstairs in a few minutes." It was about 9 P.M., the tag end of a very hard day, and I sure wasn't looking forward to another heavy conversation.

I never got that few minutes. Another member of our community just "happened" to come by my room. Peter, a summer volunteer, is forty years younger than Marge and also blessed with a special wisdom about people. He is, I think, a very holy person. He hasn't learned to mask his feelings very well yet, and the urgent concern in his face alarmed me. There's this kid in the center, Bruce. He's pretty bad off. . . .

I didn't waste any more time. I went downstairs to the center. "My name is Bruce," I said.

"I'm Mark," he said. "I'm from ———." He named a large southwestern city. "I saw you on '60 Minutes' and had to talk to you, so I hitchhiked two thousand miles. I was afraid to take a plane or bus." He was nineteen, a good-looking kid, with a lot of black hair falling over a pair of the most watchful blue eyes I had seen in a long time. A slender, coiled-spring body moved restlessly all the time we talked.

"I ran away when I was fourteen," he said. "My father and mother were alcoholics." Mark stopped for a moment and looked at me searchingly. "I've got to tell you this," he said, with a small, rather uncertain smile. "If you don't mind, I'd appreciate it if you didn't lay any God talk on me."

He began again. "I met this guy. He gave me a lot of affection and a place to live. I needed the affection real bad. He taught me a lot about sex, and, I guess, he put me to work. I didn't mind it so much after a while.

"I was young and pretty, so he sent me out to my customers dressed like a girl—a transvestite." His face twisted a bit. "I lived with fourteen other boys in this big house. We were all pretty young, and pretty scared. He made all of us watch a kid get beaten, with a hanger. It was bad. That's what happened when you tried to leave. The next time you're dead."

Mark lit his tenth cigarette of the hour. His hands were shaking slightly. "When I turned seventeen and got some muscles, and my beard began to grow, I went butch—I didn't have to wear girls' clothes anymore—and then I got old enough and they made me join another group, Man-to-Man. It was a call service. Pretty high-class customers . . ." His voice trailed off. "Then they sold me to the corporation."

I've never seen a kid look so desolate and forlorn. He suddenly appeared a lot older than nineteen.

"I had a company car and an apartment and took care of corporation clients. They would fly me all over the country. The corporation had a representative that would take a portfolio of the kids in their stable, both boys and girls, to their clients. We didn't have any clothes on in the photographs. The clients could pick anyone they wanted. I was pretty popular. . . . They would come to my apartment."

Mark named the corporation. It's one of the Fortune 500. "I'm afraid," he said. "They don't like you to leave them. I left the car and just started hitchhiking. What can I do? I don't even know if you can help me, or would want to. . . ." His voice trailed off again. He tried not to cry, but couldn't manage it very well. "I can help you a lot," I said. "Stay around for a while. We'll work something out." I took Mark over to Carl, who was supervisor on duty that night. "This is Mark," I said. "Let him stay as long as he likes. Don't discharge him without seeing me." I grabbed Mark's hand and held it for a while. "Just stay around," I said. "You'll be safe here. I'll talk to you tomorrow."

He was gone the next morning. Nobody knows where or why. Probably because he just couldn't trust anybody that much, that soon. I never got a chance to use any God talk on him. I pray a lot for Mark. I don't think he will come back. Programs like Under 21 can't help the Marks of this world. People like Bruce can, if he weren't running programs like Under 21 and had the time for that total investment of caring that can reach out to a kid like Mark.

October 1979

October was very tough month for us here at Covenant House. Father Phil Treanor, who was on our staff for over five years, died suddenly of a heart attack while on vacation. Phil was loved by everybody, most especially our kids. (At our memorial Mass one kid walked up to the altar and stood there, tears streaming down his face. He could hardly talk through his sobs. "Phil taught me to be a person, not just a street kid. I loved him, and I love all of you for what you're trying to do. . . .")

Phil was only thirty-nine. It's easy to get cynical, to withdraw from our kids—they're not always the grateful, lovable kids that we would all like to work with. Life on the street damages and distorts our kids' hearts and minds. Phil loved them all. He never got tired of loving them.

I envied Phil a lot. His job as director of intake put him in daily touch with dozens of kids. Mine keeps me moving around, giving endless talks and sermons to raise the money we need. We miss Phil a lot.

Last week we buried Louie, too. He was sweet, shy kid who

thought he was street-wise but wasn't. He tried to defend a girl
insulted by a passerby on Forty-second Street. It was over quickly. A
knife flashed, and Louie was dead. A casual, senseless murder on the
street they call Forty-Deuce. Louie played the starring macho role in
the pitiful little drama called his life to its bitter conclusion. No one
came to his wake in the seedy funeral parlor, and only a tiny handful
of people showed up for his funeral in the big, gloomy Romanesque
church on a desolate Brooklyn street. He was a good kid.

We don't know if Maria jumped or was pushed, but she's dead,
too. Maria had been destroyed by Forty-Deuce long before she went
out that sixth-story window. We were never able to reach her.
Maria's anguish and despair were a palpable thing, and she hit out at
anybody and everything she could. She was only sixteen and had
been making it on the street for three years. I never once saw her
smile. I don't know any redeeming features about her life except that
the Lord loved her. She is infinitely better off with Him.

The night we buried Louie I got a call from another kid. He was
really scared and crying hard. A runaway at thirteen, he had been
into making porn films for three years. Now sixteen, he wanted out
real bad but was afraid he would be killed if he left, afraid he would
be killed if he stayed. He didn't talk very long. . . .

February 1980

"A lady should never get this dirty," she said. She stood there
with a quiet, proud dignity. She was incomparably dirty—her face
and hands smeared, her clothes torn and soiled. The lady was eleven.
"My brothers are hungry," she said. The two little boys she clutched
protectively were eight and nine. They were two of the most beautiful children I've ever seen.

"Our parents beat us a lot," she said. "We had to leave." The boys
nodded dumbly. "We had to leave," one of them echoed. The children did not cry. After living on the street for two weeks they did not
cry. I struggled to manage part of a smile. It didn't come off very
well. The littlest kid looked back at me with a quick, dubious grin. I
gave him a surreptitious hug. I was all choked up. "I would like to
take a shower," she said.

I was over in our new center on Tenth Avenue—the one Governor
Carey gave us, God bless him—just checking things out, talking to

the kids. It's brand new, you see, and the kids have only been in the place for a few weeks and they're still getting used to it. They like the new center a lot. What's more, they appreciate it.

A few minutes ago a kid who would never win any beauty prizes walked up to me, a typical Times Square hugger-mugger nomad, the kind you would never want to meet in a dark alley and the kind you'd like to have beside you if you had to walk down one. He was a big kid with lots of muscles hanging on him.

"Bruce," he said, "this is a really nice place," and he began petting me on the shoulder. "Thanks a lot," he said. "You must have a soft spot in your heart for us kids," and I said I did, and he said, "Bruce, why did you make it so beautiful?" and I said, "Because you're beautiful." And he smiled at me. I got more choked up—close to tears, in fact.

I can't cry—it's bad for my image—so I was glad when another kid walked over and he punched me on the arm and he said he really liked the plants and the flowers, and his friend who came with him said it was better than the Holiday Inn, and then this little girl said, "Come see my baby, Bruce." He was six weeks old and lying in the middle of one of our comfortable lounge chairs. He was a cute little kid. She was sixteen.

The new center, I reflected ruefully, was a dream come true, and just maybe also the beginning of a nightmare. You see, we had decided to move the kids in by stages: to open our first dormitory of fifty beds, move the kids in, and then work out the programmatic kinks before we opened the other sixty beds. It made good sense to do it that way. The new dormitory is beautiful: small, attractive single rooms, really grand toilet and shower facilities, a comfortable lounge, a dream of a dining room—cafeteria-style.

We had over seventy kids sleeping on the floor in our Eighth Avenue Under 21 last Monday when we ceremoniously moved fifty kids over to the new dormitory. The kids were ecstatic, and I was relieved and happy. Not only because the kids had a new beautiful place to live in, but because there were just twenty or so kids left sleeping on the floor, and I was confident that in a couple of weeks—when God sent us enough money—I could open the other sixty beds.

Then something terrifying happened. In twenty-four hours another 50 homeless and abused youngsters appeared like magic and slept on that vacated floor. Now we have 120 kids instead of 70. I am really scared that when we open our last 60 beds another 60 kids will appear out of the night and fill up the floor again. There's got to be an end to them. There's got to.

I thought back to a conversation I'd just had about an hour before with our director of finance, Bob Cardany. Bob works tremendously hard, is loyal, dedicated, really loves the kids, and is a man of great faith. He came to my office trailing yards of computer printouts. The look on his face told me it was bad news.

"Bruce," he said, "do you know that we've spent our entire food budget for this fiscal year in the first five months? Did you know that?"

I said that I'd suspected it because of the enormous number of kids. (You see, we feed about three hundred kids a day, which is a lot of kids.)

"Bruce," he said, "we're way over the budget in all categories. We can't go on spending like this."

"I know," I said. "We have to," I said.

"Where are we going to get the money?" he said.

"That's *God's* problem," I said.

Our problem is, of course, that we don't turn any kids away. I've told my staff that I'd fire them if they turned a kid away. I used to, before I knew better. When we just didn't have any more room I would say no. But I can't do that anymore. I know now, too well, what happens to a kid when he stays on the street.

I also can't do it, quite honestly, because no matter how hard I try, I can never forget the faces of two kids that knocked on my door very late one night. One boy was fifteen, the other fourteen.

I can still see their faces. I can still see the tears on that boy's face. Since then I've ordered my staff never to turn a kid away.

They must take them in. Regardless of how many knock on our door. So many kids come in every night now that I've had to tell my staff to sleep the kids in our chapel: the ten, twenty, thirty, forty extra overflow kids will sleep on the floor of our chapel on Eighth Avenue on the Minnesota Strip under the altar, in the sanctuary, and the aisles.

When you think about it, a church is not a bad place to sleep kids in. The company is great, and besides, people have been sleeping in church for a long time, especially on Sunday!

Last night 230 kids slept in Covenant House: 70 of them on the floor, 40 of them in our chapel.

I went down last night to check things out. About one-thirty. There were just a couple of lights left on. My staff was there on duty. The flickering sanctuary lamp cast large soft shadows on the copper sculpture of the young Christ crucified in Times Square. I stepped quietly over the bodies of a couple dozen sleeping children and wondered for the thousandth time why it had to be that way and when it would all end and when people would stop buying and selling kids.

There was an article in today's paper about a bust the cops made last night at the Club Sansouci, an after-hours joint a couple of blocks from Under 21. They auctioned off kids there, to pimps, to the highest bidder, for money, drugs, and guns. The pimps—the buyers—could check out the merchandise—the kids—before they bid on them. The average price for a kid was ten thousand dollars. The auctions have been going on for years. According to police reports, hundreds of steady customers used the place as a central market to buy kids.

"Thanks, Bruce, for Running This Place"

Something happened to his face that was absolutely terrifying.

Lent 1980

No matter how old we get, we all like beginnings: birthdays, New Year's, anniversaries—and Ash Wednesday. The beginning of something is always a promise of newness, of being able to walk away from failing again toward the hope of making it this time.

Ash Wednesday is one of my personal favorites, a very comforting time for all of us sinners who hope in the mercy of God. It's a reminder that sorrow and repentance can, with God's help, be real again and change our lives again, that we can say yes to him again. I've always liked Ash Wednesdays—probably because I've always needed them!

Jeannie was too ecstatic to be thinking somber thoughts about Ash Wednesday. She spied me the moment I came walking into Under 21 that afternoon and came charging over; an ear-to-ear grin split her very lovely seventeen-year-old face. "Look at these keys," she yelled. (Rather startled, I took a hurried look. Thank God, they weren't the lost keys of an Under 21 supervisor. I breathed a sigh of relief.)

"They're my first keys to my first apartment," she said. "I'm on my way."

"Fantastic," I said. A nice way to kick off Ash Wednesday—with a touch of promise and hope, I thought.

Benny is a pimp and he doesn't know much about Ash Wednesday and repentance, but he sure knows a lot about sin and evil. He appeared at Under 21 just before midnight, all 200 hostile pounds of him, menacing, insistent. He wanted to see Julie, and right away. Our supervisor, Winston, explained that Julie was upstairs asleep and didn't want to see him. Julie was seventeen and wanted nothing to do with Benny. Benny got even uglier; he demanded to see her and tried to force his way in the door. Our staff stopped him. (I have a very gentle staff, and quite a few of them are big and gentle. It took a lot of bigness to gentle Benny.)

Benny went berserk, screaming in rage and anger: "I spent a lot of money to put clothes on her back. It's time she got on her back and made me some money. I'm gonna come back here with a gun and blow you all away!"

We called the police, as we always do when the pimps just won't accept the fact that Under 21 is a sanctuary for kids. I thought about Benny and the Crucifixion, and was suddenly deeply ashamed that I just didn't like him at all and had very little love, if any at all, for him. Maybe Benny doesn't know much about Ash Wednesday, but only God knows what twisted pain helped make Benny what he is.

It still was not quite midnight and Ash Wednesday was just about over when Todd rang the bell. A really nice-looking kid with wide-open blue eyes. He comes from one of America's best-known families. He had no place he felt he could go, he said, and he just walked in because the sign said Under 21.

Father Ned Murphy, one of the super Jesuits on staff (even if I am a Franciscan), talked to him for about eight hours. Todd cried off and on through the night. He had just turned twenty and no one had yet told him they loved him. Ned did. Todd has already lived a long Lenten loneliness. Maybe Ned started a small resurrection that first night of Lent.

It didn't get any better Thursday morning. I got a call about Mike, a very young sixteen (like maybe thirteen going on sixteen), a kid from outside New York who had spent a few days in Under 21 before Christmas. Mike had been picked off and was now being held, with a few other kids, in a fear- and drug-induced servitude in an uptown apartment by a notorious pimp. His friend who called was really scared: "Whatever you do, Bruce, don't give them my name."

I called the New York City Pimp Squad and gave them the address and apartment number. They said they would do what they could. Mike is a good kid and a bright kid but awful young. Too young to understand how bad it could get. I hope and pray that he makes it. So many don't.

It was a relief to get into my car Saturday to drive out to Woodcliff Lakes, New Jersey, to preach at all the Masses in Our Lady Mother of the Church and ask the people to help my kids. (That's the way I inveigled most of you to go on the "list.") It's a great little parish and the priests and people were absolutely super and the U.S. hockey team beat the Russians and there was this little kid—couldn't have been more than ten—an absolutely beautiful kid, who stopped me after Mass and said, "I like your sermon. God bless you." I came back to New York feeling just swell.

Today is my birthday and I'm fifty-three and I hate it. I will never grow old gracefully. I have to finish this newsletter, and I'm already a couple of days late, and my long-suffering printer will be tearing his hair out tomorrow trying to get it ready for mailing. Have a good Lent.

Jesus said that we must lose our lives in order to find them, that we must take up our cross and follow Him if we would be worthy of Him. If we have a good Lent, maybe we can be a little sign of resurrection for Todd and Benny and Mike, and for each other. Our dying to sin may be their only hope of life in Jesus. Maybe Benny might become a Dismas.

As always, I beg you to keep us in your prayers. Your compassion for my kids is one of the really beautiful things in my life.

Holy Week 1980

Without preamble he launched into it: "Thanks, Bruce, for running this place. It helps a lot of kids. If this place had been around five years ago when I ran away (I was thirteen then), maybe I wouldn't be where I am now. It's probably too late for me," he said matter-of-factly. But then, almost as if the brutal finality of what he said was too much for him to bear, he continued without pausing for breath. "I've got to get my act together," he said.

I had stopped downstairs to have lunch with the kids—it's one way of keeping in touch—and I picked an empty chair at a table with a kid who hadn't quite completed growing up yet. "My name is Bruce," he said.

"Mine is, too," I said.

He smiled. The kid was an almost tall, kind of an almost finished kid, just under six feet. A cane hung on the back of his chair. Chicken pot pie was on the menu, and he made suitable compliments to our chef as I sat down.

"I live mostly on the subways," he said. "It's got so that I like the noise. Can't sleep anymore without lots of noise. My leg got hurt on Forty-Deuce. Stomped," he said. "I can't really work because of this leg. Never finished the sixth grade, although they kept passing me to the ninth grade although I wasn't never there. I can't read, Bruce. I would like to get a job, but I have to panhandle most of the day to get food money. I have to get my head together," he said.

Then something happened to his face that was absolutely terrifying. Something that went on inside and crawled out through the flesh, seeped through the skin around his mouth and eyes, mushing the dozens of tiny muscles that held his face together. "I don't like to hustle johns," he said. "Besides, it's harder now. I'm not so pretty anymore. I'm what they call rough trade, Bruce. Thanks for running this place. I'm eighteen," he said. "I'm going to get it together," he said.

The boy with my name understands very little about what happened in a grove of trees in a garden called Gethsemane, where the life of a man named Jesus fulfilled its cosmic purpose with a passion and fire and totality that we simply call the "Passion." I thought back to another conversation with another kid who understands a lot more about it.

"Hi," he said. "My name is Tommy. I'm from Indiana. I'm here to be a volunteer." He was a great-looking kid.

"That's great," I said, "but you look awful young."

"I'm eighteen," he said, proudly and a bit apprehensively.

"That's awful young," I said. "How did you hear about Covenant House?"

"I read about it in the newspaper," he said. "I gave my boss two weeks' notice, quit my job and told my mother I was coming east to work on Eighth Avenue."

"How did she like that?" I said.

"Not very much," he said, "but anyway, my mom and dad gave me a farewell party, I got on a bus, and here I am."

"Why didn't you write or call or something?" I said (because if he had I would have said, "Thanks a lot but no thanks, you're too young").

Tommy looked at me and he said, "I thought if I just came you would see that as a sign of faith in God."

What do you say to a kid like that? I said what we adults always say when we don't know what to say. I said, "We'll see." He's still here. A really super kid. A little young for this work maybe, but a super kid with great convictions.

Because we generally choose it, there is little of passion and fire in our lives. The mores of our civilized world cause us to look askance at strongly held convictions and burning commitments. The Church (our holy Church, our passionless, anciently wise, prudent, and careful Church) thrusts upon us once more the events and passions of Holy Week with its zealotries and hatreds and convictions, the relentless loves and rivalries, the soaring worship of the man from Nazareth, and the grimy, hopeless betrayals. Sin stands forth present, ugly, naked. So does, too, the passionate love of the Father and the Holy Spirit, expressed through the passion of Jesus.

None of this right now makes much sense to our kids, and none at all to the kid with my name. He's had his own share of personal Good Fridays and precious few Easters. Yet in some way the mystery of his salvation and redemption is inextricably conjoined to my own. To our own.

June 1980

I used to be a male chauvinist priest. I admit it. But a thousand bloody encounters with dear friends who delight in pointing out my limitations (everybody should have friends like mine) have practically turned me into a radical supporter of women's rights.

I almost lost my credentials as women's advocate altogether yesterday when I went down to the center to greet last night's crop of kids. I had been away for three days giving a series of talks and speeches—actually just trying to raise some money before we went broke—and I was anxious to see my kids. There was a game of cops and robbers going on in one corner, cowboys and Indians were whooping it up in another, and a gaggle of kids were playing hide and seek behind some cushions by the windows. "What's going on?" I yelled. Ten kids under six stopped making like banshees and looked at me solemnly. I gaped at six more kids under two who didn't know enough to be aware that The Man (that's what the kids call me) was around. My staff didn't pay any attention to me at all. A whole bunch of my senior staff were gathered over in the corner cooing over a twenty-eight-day-old baby. They all had real goopy looks on their faces. I immediately surmised that a severe epidemic of maternal instinct was breaking out in Covenant House.

"Look at this adorable child, Bruce." Sister Gretchen had the goopiest look of them all. "Isn't she cute?" she said. I allowed that the slightly wrinkled infant was semi-cute but had a long way to go and that kids were even cuter once they were out of diapers, and what had happened anyway? Covenant House *is* a child-care agency, but this was ridiculous.

Sister Gretchen kept hanging on to the littlest one while she filled me in on the events of the last three days. All but two of the kids had young mothers with them, victims of abuse and abandonment: Eight young teenage mothers came to Under 21 for help. (The twenty-eight-day-old baby had an eighteen-month-old brother who had been beaten badly by his nineteen-year-old father, and the seventeen-year-old mother of both children took the two of them and ran away from him to Under 21.)

In the meantime, the war parties got all mixed up: The cops became Indians and the robbers turned into cowboys before my very eyes. I moved over to a quiet corner where two older golden-skinned kids sat looking scared and trying to make sense of Under 21. They weren't succeeding very well. Kenekong and King Vorarvat were Laotian boat people who had gone adrift in the concrete bays and rivers of Manhattan while on their way to their American sponsors in Connecticut. The police brought them to Under 21 and asked us to locate their new home.

Sharing their somber solitude was a beautiful little girl. "Hi," I said. "I'm Bruce."

"I'm Celeste," she said defiantly, "and I'm fourteen and I'm pregnant."

I sat down next to her for a moment, but she moved away.

I wasn't alone very long. A really beautiful kid, nine years old, came up dragging his sister, who was six. "Hi," he said. "I'm Samuel. This is Arethea." His little sister climbed up on my lap. "It's great that you're here," I said. "Why did you come to us?" The little boy looked around, got up, and put his lips right into my left ear. "Because my father was beating her," he whispered. "So I took her and ran away."

I just hugged them both.

I saw Mary Beth—one of our community members (with a master's in special ed.)—talking to Ralph over by the TV, which for a change was not on. I knew what the conversation was about. It is *always* exactly the same. Ralph is fourteen, and a very disturbed, infinitely sad street kid who I don't think is going to make it. He hears voices a lot. Every now and then his voices tell Ralph to kill himself, so he comes to Under 21 to find Mary Beth.

"It's time for me to go to the hospital again," he said. "It's my voices. Can I have a tuna fish sandwich?"

"Ralph, you don't like tuna fish sandwiches," Mary Beth said.

"Yes I do. Can I have one, please?"

Mary Beth got him a tuna fish sandwich and Ralph took a couple of bites and put it aside.

"You're right," he said. "I don't like them. Can I go to the hospital now?"

Sam and Arethea got tired of being hugged and ran off to join in the general pandemonium. Chris, also from community, stopped over. "Glad you're back, Bruce," he said. "How was your speaking tour?"

"Great," I said, "but my voice is going fast. And my sanity." I just looked at all those little kids. They really were kinda cute.

Chris wasted scant sympathy on me. He was really happy. "Bruce," he said, "do you remember that really nice gay kid? The one with four rings in his ear—the go-go boy who danced on the bar down the street and who ran away when he was fifteen and has been into hustling for three years? He's off the street, has a job and a bank account, is back living with his parents, and has a girl friend! I think he's going to make it. He stopped to tell me that he was doing just great."

I went upstairs to my office and looked with undisguised loathing at my desk piled high with paper. But then I thought of what was happening downstairs in the center and felt really good and glad and happy that God had given us this work to do for him. I mean, it doesn't make living on Eighth Avenue a joy—you'd have to be crazy to enjoy it—but the kids and our great staff make it all worthwhile. Last night, driving back to the center from Princeton—I had given a talk to a really great bunch of students at the university—I turned on the ten-thirty news just in time to hear a spokesman for the mayor's office declare that prostitution was under control on Eighth Avenue and that the situation had dramatically improved.

Thirty minutes later I parked my car in the Forty-fourth Street garage half a block from the Eighth Avenue center. Nearing the corner, I had to stop for a few moments while four prostitutes guided their johns into the Globe Hotel. I rounded the corner and counted eight other prostitutes working the street by the Cameo porno theater. The triple feature that night included *Inside Young Girls* and *Baby Face*. The next morning I got up at five-thirty for prayers with my community of volunteers and counted, from my window, seven more girls still working the street.

I don't know where that spokesman got his information about prostitution getting under control. I think he must be talking about another planet. I would concede a slight improvement over the last four years—the mayor's Midtown Enforcement Project under Carl Weisbrod has been trying really hard. The situation has improved from the absolutely horrendous to the merely terrible.

"I Get Ten Dollars Apiece for You"

*The word on the street is,
johns prefer chickens.*

August 1980

Linda was eleven, still a virgin, when her pimp took her. Peter was dancing on bars when he was sixteen, Martha was fourteen when her pimp dyed her hair, got her a phony I.D., and put her to work in a massage parlor. Tony was only fifteen (I personally checked his age with the Bureau of Child Welfare) when he finally fled, in terror, Paul Abrams's call-boy service. Annie was still only fifteen when her pimp went to her mother's house in upstate New York, waited until her mother left for work, and took a very unwilling Annie back to life on the street and a near death.

There are many reasons why we have a sex industry in Times Square—and now, all around the country. It is one of the "growth industries" in the United States. None of the reasons are very mysterious. The simple, undeniable fact is that we want one. There are literally millions of customers—almost 100 percent male—who patronize this multibillion-dollar business.

Millions of customers! Who have to believe the bizarre myth that prostitution is a victimless crime. Who have to believe that prostitution is nothing more than a commercial recreational transaction between someone who wants to buy something and someone who wants to sell. Millions of customers who choose to believe that sex is entertainment and that it's okay to pay the entertainers. We have, in our liberated society, chosen to identify sex as entertainment and to scoff at the notion that there is something sacred and deeply personal and profoundly private and intimate about sexual experience.

The sex industry here in Times Square is not only geographically contiguous with the entertainment industry (that great gathering of fine theaters and restaurants that has justly won for Times Square the title of entertainment center of New York City); the sex business, dominated and controlled by organized crime, has actually formed a continuum with the entertainment industry. It has almost become impossible to distinguish between some aspects of legitimate theater and the sex industry. And we seem to want it that way.

If you wanted to spend a sophisticated evening at the theater, and had twenty-five dollars to spend, you could, for your twenty-five dollars, buy a front-row seat at *Oh! Calcutta!* the longest-running (over twelve years) erotic musical in New York. For your twenty-five dollars, in your front-row seat, you can watch a dozen young naked bodies, male and female, sing and dance and tell you jokes while they simulate sodomy and intercourse on the stage.

If you don't have twenty-five dollars, but you do have twenty-five cents, you can take your quarter to the peep show just down the street from Under 21 on Eighth Avenue. You can drop your quarter in a slot, and for ninety seconds a screen will flip up, and you can watch one naked young lady dance. She won't sing. She will tell you some very filthy jokes, and she will invite you to masturbate.

There is no ethical or moral or qualitative difference between spending that twenty-five dollars to see *Oh! Calcutta!* for your sophisticated evening at the theater, and spending that twenty-five cents at the peep show owned by members of organized crime, or watching the action at a West Side hangout on West Forty-fifth Street run by Matty "The Horse" of a certain organized crime family, or enjoying the entertainment at the Pussycat, another sexual supermarket owned and operated by Micky Zaffarano, the top pornographer of them all, located right in Times Square. It's just sex as entertainment, and very big business.

Hundreds of thousands of New Yorkers and out-of-town visitors patronize the sex industry and make a lot of very unwholesome people very rich. There's no mystery why we have a sex industry. The

reasons have always been the same: greed and lust. Their greed and
our lust, and our inability to care enough about what happens to the
young people who, every year, become enslaved by the industry to
satiate our appetites.

Because we tolerate and patronize this very sick and savage business that treats young people as commodities, as merchandise (the
pimp functions as middleman; he provides the merchandise), we
have made places like Under 21 necessary.

This year we expect at least another ten thousand beautiful kids to
come through our doors. Most of them will have been involved, on
some level, with the industry. Most of them call it making a few
bucks. I have never met a young prostitute, girl or boy—and I've met
hundreds—who wanted to be one. I've never met a young prostitute,
girl or boy, who did not start out as a runaway. They have very few
options.

One of my boys put it for me very directly. "Bruce," he said, "I've
got two choices: I can go with a john [a customer] and do what he
wants [his actual phrase was "sell my tail"], or I can rip somebody
off and go to jail. And," he said, "I'm afraid to go to jail. I wouldn't
make it through my first shower. I can't get a job, I have no skills, I
have no place to live." He is sixteen. I do not know what I would
have done if I were sixteen and faced with that impossible choice.

That's why we run Under 21, and that's why we keep it open
twenty-four hours a day, to give these boys and girls a third alterna-
tive, an option that leads to life and not death.

We have almost lost the ability to protect our children and, God
help us, the will to do so. Until the citizens of this country decide
they don't want a sex industry, and that it is not okay to buy and sell
children and young people, the Lindas and Marthas and Tonys and
Peters and Annies will continue to be placed in harm's way, their
lives destroyed, their spirits damaged irrevocably. Because we want
it that way.

You see, the word on the street is, johns prefer chickens—kids.
Because of greed and lust, and our sloth and fear. Who, after all,
wants to take on organized crime? Our politicians certainly don't.
Our law-enforcement groups can give you a thousand reasons why
they can't either. Our prosecutors and our judiciary tell us they have

their hands tied. And everybody has a finger to point at the other guy.

Who wants to take on the well-organized, well-financed pressure groups that worry more about the civil liberties of pimps and criminals than those of their victims? Who wants to be held up to scorn and ridicule as book burners and fanatics because they see pornography as a degradation of an entire gender and a classroom for rape and seduction?

All the kids I mentioned above are still alive. Most of them just don't stand a chance of making it out. Veronica and Gayle and Alicia and Helen and Harry and Eddie and Marguerita and Red Devil and Ramone are all dead. These are kids who came to Under 21 for help and did not make it. Murdered kids.

Maybe they're not the nice cuddly lambs that just happened to walk away from the fold, but they are good kids. And, God knows, they are certainly sinned against. They are also, God knows, the lost sheep of the Gospel that Jesus said we must go out and find; they are the prodigal sons not yet returned to their fathers, the young Magdalenes not yet aware of their need for forgiveness.

They're good kids. Not good maybe the way your kids are good, and not nice maybe the way your kids are nice. But good kids. What happens to them should not happen.

September 1980

Unsavory, bum, derelict, malevolent, con artist, raunchy, dangerous—these were the words that, unbidden, and with surprising urgency, surged up out of my memory banks. He had reached out a tentative arm and stopped our slow progress up Eighth Avenue.

"Hi," he said. "My name is Jason."

I groaned inwardly and mentally scrubbed my mouth out with soap, once again aware of how easy it was for me not to see God in him. I wished for the hundredth time that month that St. Francis had never embraced that leper and wondered when I was ever going to grow up and climb down out of my spiritual high chair.

It was about ten-thirty on a warm, muggy Times Square night. The Democratic convention was in full swing, and New York was jammed with visitors. The predators and jackals along the Minnesota Strip were out in force stalking their game.

He spoke to us with that fawning candor older street people use when they begin their hustle and seek to disarm their wary prey. We were, to Jason, just two slightly paunchy, bald and balding fiftyish, out-of-town visitors looking for some action. My friend, another Franciscan priest, Father Douglas Lawson, from our headquarters in Union City, New Jersey, had come to visit.

I was going to brush by him impatiently, but then I thought Doug should hear it, so I stopped.

"Would you gentlemen like to come to our place on Forty-eighth Street? It's just off Eighth Avenue." He paused. "I get ten dollars apiece if I bring you in."

"What's the place all about?" I said.

"It's a bar," he said. "Cheap drinks. Straight business. Live sex acts, lesbians, everything. You don't have to buy any girls. Just sit and watch if that's all you want to do. We have twelve girls to pick from—fourteen to twenty-one. Forty-five dollars for an hour, sixty dollars for four hours, a hundred dollars a night. The girls have to do what you want," he said. "We have six places. We'll give you a membership card and you're welcome at any of them. They're run by ————." He mentioned his name. (You would know it if I said it.) "I get twenty dollars if I bring you in," he said.

I thought Doug had heard enough, so I broke into his monologue. "No thanks," I said. "We've got to be moving along."

He followed us for almost a block, repeating his offers, making his pitch, selling his merchandise. Some of the merchandise was only fourteen years old. "I get ten dollars apiece for you," he said.

I saw Father Douglas off on his bus at the mammoth Port Authority Terminal on Forty-second Street and walked slowly back to my room at Under 21 on Eighth Avenue. Despite our brief encounter with Jason, I was really quite happy. We had a really great bunch of kids—all 176 of 'em—the center was operating as smoothly as a twenty-four-hour, no-questions-asked crisis center smack in the middle of Times Square's virulently poisonous sex industry ever could or would. . . .

Other dreams, visions, speculations, filled my mind that hot night. I thought of all the little kids seven and eight years old sleeping on newspapers on the streets of Guatemala City. Last month I had been invited to give a paper on Under 21 at an International Conference on the Family in Latin America.

After my presentation, many people from half a dozen Latin American countries begged us to help their own street kids—the *gamines* in Bolivia, the *niños de la calle* of Costa Rica. Members of my Covenant community are anxious to volunteer their time and their lives in Guatemala. I have such a strong conviction that God wants us to help these kids. But then I worry about money and all our kids here, and our bills. And then I remember something a very wise man said to me once: "God never ordered anything He didn't pay for!"

October 1980

Hot Friday nights in Times Square are the worst. Forty-Deuce pulsates with an almost palpable malevolence, the simmering violence barely beneath the surface. The police patrols are beefed up, and cops move slowly and carefully in watchful groups of three and four up and down the block, keeping the lid on.

On Eighth Avenue—the Minnesota Strip—action is not quite so frenetic. The streams of street people have learned that they and the more transient rivers of theatergoers do not flow together easily. The two groups eye each other warily; light-years of culture, education, and deprivation separate the haves and have-nots.

The pain, the despair and hopelessness of America's underclass are masked somewhat by Friday night's frantic carnival gaiety, the alcoholic mists and drug-induced euphoria that anesthetize hundreds of the young and not-so-young people that wash up and down Forty-Deuce and the Strip.

Friday nights are bad for me, too. Almost invariably I'm working late in my office trying to clear away some of the paper that threatens to overwhelm me. It's especially important that I get to the most urgent things before the weekend, since I'll be away Saturday and Sunday preaching at all the Masses in some parish. Telling the people about my kids and asking for help, asking them to join our mailing list.

It's how we survive mostly. (We just couldn't make it without that consistent support that you provide each month—or whenever you are able.) I was thinking of that last Friday about 1 A.M. Actually it was Saturday morning. I was hating my office with a passion and finally decided I either had to stop work or burn my desk, so I decided to return to our community on Eighth Avenue. Maybe somebody might still be up.

As I went downstairs in the elevator I was thinking of a couple of letters I had just read, one from a kid in Dorchester, Massachusetts, and another from a small town in Montana. They're great letters, and I thought you might like to read them, too, exactly as written.

Dear Father Bruce,

My name is Dianne and I'm 15. About one-and-a-half years ago, when I was 13, I ran away twice. The first time to Boston, where I stayed at ——— House. The second time I ran to Los Angeles. I was never involved in the sex industry like most of your kids, but I easily could have been. A guy approached me in the bus station and asked me if I'd like him to show me L.A. This was at 3:00 A.M. If I didn't have an uncle there in L.A. maybe I would have gone with him. It would have been better than starving. Maybe I'd be walking the streets right now, or maybe dead. I thank God I didn't get into it. I ended up going home. Although everything isn't perfect here, I know now that's better than it would have been out there.

I don't know why I wrote, maybe because I know now how much kids need people like you. Maybe I want to thank you for being there for us. Even though I'm not one of your kids but you are helping all kids. And I'm a kid so you're helping me. And maybe I want to tell you that there's at least one kid that you're not going to meet, one who's not going to be mentioned in your newsletter, or in the obituaries. And I thank God for that.

> With much love,
> Dianne

That letter made me feel pretty good. It should make you feel pretty good, too, because Covenant House is just a lot of really good people helping in all kinds of ways for kids like Dianne to make it.

The other letter was from Annie in Montana.

Father Bruce,

I saw you on the T.V. today and I heard you talking about
the kids which come to your place for sanctuary, and I
admire you for being there when needed.
I myself had been thinking about running away from
home. But when I heard you today I realized that I have it
better than I thought I did. I only wanted to leave home
because my parents always want to know where I'm going
and whom I'm going to be with. I suppose that's not much
for them to ask, it just gets on my nerves. Maybe it would
be easier if I were a boy.

I would love to help you, but I am only 14 and I really
don't have a stable enough income to be able to provide
you with much money, so I can only pray for you and your
kids, and hope the good Lord answers my prayers. I need
to go now it's getting awfully late.

With much admiration for a job well done,

Annie

I got off the elevator really anxious to get back to the community.
There was a small knot of people in the lobby. A couple of adults had
just brought in three kids. The older girl was eleven. Her younger
sister about ten. Their younger brother couldn't have been more than
eight. Really beautiful kids. All three were crying. At one-thirty in
the morning Covenant House can look big and scary to a bunch of
little kids. I grabbed the eight-year-old (his name was Danny) and
hugged him while I heard the story. The parents of these kids had
simply abandoned them, walked out on them and moved to Miami.

"They said they didn't want us," Danny said. "They didn't want
us."

I thanked the two good Samaritans who had found the kids on the
street and brought them to us and directed my staff to prepare a
bedroom where the kids could all sleep together. I couldn't make the
kids stop crying.

I had to fight really hard to maintain my composure. I can never
get used to it. I wanted to yell all kinds of terrible things at those
parents. I walked back to Eighth Avenue feeling pretty rotten, but

glad that we were there. The streets had quieted down a lot. The theatergoers had all gone back home, and most of the street people were beginning to disappear to wherever they disappear to.

Nobody was up in the community when I got home, so I went up to my room overlooking the Cameo porno theater thanking God that prayers were at 9 A.M. instead of the usual six-thirty or seven.

There was another letter on my desk in my bedroom. Some kid had written to me directly at my community residence. . . .

Dear Bruce,
I'd just like to express my most overwhelming thanks to you. I'm also happy to announce that I'm back at home in Texas with my family. It's places like your's that can help a kid like myself stay out of trouble and to be safe and off the streets.

You did so much for me, I just don't know how to thank you. Like your counselors said, "It will be different when you get home, because now they know that you are serious, and they'll see you as a human being," and that's exactly what is happening.

It takes people with a big heart, and an extreme amount of patience to run a place like Covenant House–Under 21. And you all handle it beautifully. Once again thanks for *everything* and may the Lord Bless and keep you. I turned 16 today.

                                                                        Reuben

That was a good letter to read before falling asleep.

"I Guess That Means
You Love Me, Too"

"I wish you well in your work, Father," he said.
"I wish you every failure in yours," I said.

May 1981

SEX IS A GROWING MULTIBILLION BUSINESS, screamed the head-line over an article in a recent edition of the New York *Times*. Reporter William Serrin wrote how a former "Wall Street trader" had become a successful executive in the business of porn. He had nine retail stores and sales that approached, he said, ten million dollars a year. He sells sexual paraphernalia.

The *Times* story conveyed a sense of corporate legitimacy: "He worked long hours, generally employed his own capital, or returned company profits to his business and paid close attention to detail. . . . The sex industry is a rapidly growing, still immature industry, a significant part of New York and the nation's economy."

Reporter Serrin noted the sex trade has "a large work force, high-salaried executives, brisk competition, trade publications, board meetings, and sales conventions."

Trade publications? We know of one newsletter catering to the sex trade, called *The Adult Business Report,* that gives helpful hints on how to run a successful porno bookstore—let the people browse, don't wrap the books in cellophane—and how to avoid prosecution under obscenity laws.

And, as if we Americans weren't merchandising sex correctly, the

Times reports that a West German sex firm soon will be doing business in the United States. Owned by a sixty-one-year-old woman, the business had $48.6 million in sales of all kinds of explicit erotica last year. "We're a good, a nice company, and we treat people well. We think we are strong and courageous and idealistic enough to go into America and not get dirty," she said.

U.S. News and World Report, in its March 16 issue, indicates that a vast middle-class market has opened for the sex trade: X-rated videotapes outsell other videotapes. Two thousand parties were held last month in middle-class homes in nine eastern states; the object: to sell sexual products in a "safe, comfortable atmosphere."

I've said it time and time again: We have a sex industry in this country because we want one. There's simply no other reason. The saddest aspect of it is this: that the sex industry swallows thousands upon thousands of kids. It brutalizes them, physically and psychologically. And the more we adults look upon sex as just another form of entertainment—the more legitimacy we give to porno shops and theaters, and topless bars, and escort services, and massage parlors—the more it will become okay to involve kids.

Reflecting that sense of "legitimacy" we have given the sex industry: A Family Court judge here in New York who dropped charges against a male adult who had had sexual relations with a fifteen-year-old minor, and had been arrested. The judge said what had happened had to be considered a "mere commercial recreational transaction." No harm done!

I hope that as you read this you don't think this is happening only here in New York City. It's a national problem. One U.S. government report says there are six hundred thousand female and three hundred thousand male teenage prostitutes in the country. I think that's a somewhat exaggerated figure, but I have no doubt that teenagers by the tens of thousands are involved.

Given the right circumstances, where you find teenage runaways, there you'll find teenage prostitution. Not 100 percent of the time. Not 100 percent of the kids. But, whatever the percentage, it's too high.

In the last few months, concerned people from nearly a dozen metropolitan areas and a dozen foreign countries have come to us for help. People know that what we do to help kids we do well. They want us to open crisis centers like Under 21 in their cities. Their stories have a tragic similiarity: The problem of homeless kids can no longer be thought of as something hidden that's going to go away. And, with no options open to them, the kids fall prey to the hustlers, the pimps, the johns. The rest of the story you know.

June 1981

Mr. Herald Price Fahringer looks like a benevolent, pink-faced grandfather who dotes on little kids. He wears four-hundred-dollar suits and has a really sweet smile. He makes a lot of money defending very rotten people who sell films showing little boys engaged in homosexual activity.

Soft-spoken and kindly, Fahringer is a very successful attorney. He even managed to convince the New York State Court of Appeals that Paul Ira Ferber, who sold the films, should not go to jail because he has constitutional rights to show little boys that way. It's legal.

Fahringer is the top smut lawyer in the country. His fees are enormous. His clients, the porn merchants all over this country, can well afford to pay him from the huge profits they make from the sale of this garbage.

I did not want to debate this man. I don't even like to be in the same room with people like that. But when David Hartman of the "Good Morning, America" show called me late Thursday afternoon and asked me to appear on his Friday-morning show to present my views, I felt I really had to do it. I'm no constitutional lawyer, but somebody, I felt, had to speak for the kids and, God knows, we've met scores of these sad and destroyed youngsters at Covenant House.

We each had about three minutes to present our position. My contention simply echoed the cogent, forceful position of the dissenting and defeated minority on the Court: that the First Amendment is not an absolute and that its slight impairment under the disputed law was justified by the compelling right and need of the State to protect its children from this merciless and mercenary exploitation.

I added that what was being protected was not the First Amendment but the right of some very greedy and unscrupulous men to make a lot of money exploiting the innocence and inexperience of young children.

We left the studio together and by happenstance found ourselves sharing the same ABC-TV limousine provided to take us back to our offices. We had an unpleasant and very frank conversation. He got out first. "I wish you well in your work, Father," he said. "I wish you every failure in yours," I said.

The New York papers all reacted strongly to the New York State Court of Appeals decision. The New York *Daily News* and the New York *Post* lined up strongly on the side of the kids; the New York *Times* lined up with the pornographers, its editors no doubt ruefully reflecting that its noble search for truth put it in bed with some pretty slimy company.

Very few of you have ever seen child pornography. Even fewer, I'm sure, have ever met the kids who "starred" in it. We meet those tragic youngsters all the time.

Like Debbie: She left home at age fourteen—after being raped by her brother. Since her father wouldn't believe her, she got into prostitution to get back at him. She is now seventeen and wise in the ways of the street beyond a hundred lifetimes. Debbie carries and flaunts her own pornography pictures of herself in the nude taken by her pimp.

The New York *Times* thinks it should be legal to show those photographs around unless they could be judged legally obscene. They can't, they couldn't, and they won't. The photographs of naked Debbie suddenly have a life all their own—protected, says the New York State Court of Appeals and the New York *Times,* by the Constitution. Debbie is not protected.

Nor is Nancy. She's older now, and she works in a peep show on Broadway. That's a place where you can drop a quarter in a slot, which makes a screen flip up so you can watch Nancy dance naked. She'll tell you some very filthy jokes. She's been into porn since she was fifteen. Her naked picture has been displayed in the windows of a twenty-four-hour-a-day sexual supermarket called Show World. It's run by members of organized crime. Nobody is going to prosecute that crime family, and Nancy's nude display is not legally obscene.

Or Billy's. He's seventeen and lives with an older man in a plush apartment. He works for a thinly disguised call-boy operation and poses for his protector, who is into photography. He was on the street and into porn before his fifteenth birthday.

The New York State Court of Appeals and the New York *Times* think that it is perfectly legal to merchandise these kids' photographs, that your right to possess and view these horrors is more important than the moral and physical destruction of the kids who made them.

What about the kids? Who protects them from the exploiters and the users? The law that was gutted by this obscene decision of the New York State Court of Appeals was a good law. It was designed to protect children under sixteen from sexual abuse, and it worked!

Four years ago you could walk into dozens of Times Square bookstores and buy films and books showing kids engaged in bestiality, sadomasochism, homosexuality, and every kind of sexual activity. The New York State law, passed in 1977, did something very simple: It banned films or performances of any sexual acts by a child. It worked! Child porn simply disappeared from the shelves. Now it will surely come back because the New York State Court of Appeals said you couldn't ban child porn unless it was declared legally obscene— and, given the laws that protect obscenity in this country, that is for all practical purposes impossible.

The issue is, at its heart, a moral one: our right to protect and safeguard our children from this vileness. It is not preeminently a legal issue, a First Amendment free-speech issue. Paul Ira Ferber may not, and cannot, in any decent society, be permitted to sell dirty pictures of little boys and get away with it. Those who would exalt and defend our personal freedom at the expense of little children do indeed worship an obscene deity: a naked emperor. Maybe his votaries at the New York *Times* will eventually be able to hear the cry of our outraged and violated children. He's not wearing any clothes— and we would like to keep ours on!

Bob Morgenthau, Manhattan's D.A. who lost the case, has vowed to appeal the decision to the U.S. Supreme Court. He might like to hear of your support. If the Supreme Court upholds the decision, then more carefully formulated legislation will no doubt be introduced in the New York State Legislature that will withstand the pornographers. Cardinal Cooke, who has voiced strong indignation over this decision, has also vowed to support such efforts.

Will you help us help our kids? Will you speak out? To your legislators, police commissioners, U.S. attorneys, district attorneys, governors, local branches of the ACLU and the New York *Times*.

July 1981

This little old nun with a man's stride—she can't be more than five feet tall—visited my kids at Covenant House last Thursday night. She came straight from lunch with President and Mrs. Reagan at the White House.

There were lots of TV and newspaper people around. There always are when Mother Teresa of Calcutta comes to call. I had never met Mother Teresa before. In fact, I've managed to avoid meeting her—it makes me very nervous to be around holy people. It always seems to me that they can size me up in a wink and nail me for the sinner I am.

But I knew that Mother Teresa was in the United States to meet the President, and at the request of Pope John Paul II, to publicize natural family planning. And, I thought, wouldn't it be just great if Mother Teresa would come and talk to my kids!

I happen to be very close to a good friend of hers who was coordinating her travel plans. I called my friend to see if she would ask Mother Teresa. Well, it seems that Mother Teresa had already heard about Covenant House and would be delighted. So another good friend rerouted from La Guardia to Newark the private plane that he had provided for her travel, zipped her through the Lincoln Tunnel, and she came.

Mother spent about fifteen minutes with the press, and then I took her over to our main lounge at Under 21, where our kids were waiting. Now, I've got some pretty tough kids. Good kids mostly, but not very many would ever win any beauty prizes. Intimidate or be intimidated, seduce or be seduced, get over on or be gotten over on, is the code they are forced to live by. Equality for some of my kids is won by a fist, a knife, a gun. Trust and faith and love are only words, useful to deceive by.

This little old nun, in a ragged sweater and blue-trimmed sari, ignored the adults around. She talked directly to my kids: "You are good, you are beautiful, thank you for the beauty you give back to us. Love each other, love Jesus, love God, who loves you. This center exists so that people can love you. So many people all over the world live in the streets. A place like this has one purpose: to radiate the joy of loving God and loving each other."

One bemused and startled Delilah of the streets murmured, "This is really heavy stuff."

I had my eye on another kid—a four-letter-word kid named Steve. He was about seventeen, a real hard-case drifter—"rough trade" in street parlance. That's a kid already too used up, too shopworn, no longer pretty or handsome or good-looking. Nobody wanted to buy this kid anymore. He couldn't even give himself away. You deal with kids like that with profound caution and a deep, deep sadness. Your sadness to match his bitter pain.

My kids sang for Mother Teresa. She loved it. They also gave her an "I Love New York" duffel bag and an Under 21 T-shirt. She really liked that, too. My kids were really happy, and happiness washes away a lot of grief from kids' faces and makes them beautiful again.

I couldn't resist leaning over to Mother Teresa and whispering, "I think my kids in New York are more beautiful than your kids in Calcutta." She just smiled and reached out and took from the arms of a sixteen-year-old mother a month-old baby who was squalling his lungs out. The kid didn't realize he was being crooned to by a tough-minded little old lady saint and kept right on bawling.

I broke things up pretty quick. It was obvious that Mother Teresa was very tired. The kids sang her one last song, and Mother Teresa went back to the South Bronx to spend the night with her sisters. The crowds dispersed, and the kids began going back upstairs to their bedrooms. Steve happened to find himself in my way.

"Bruce, does she really mean that stuff about loving us?"

"Yes, she does," I said.

"I guess that means you love me, too," he said.

(Heavy stuff, indeed!)

We need your prayers very much right now. Me and my kids. I have come to a decision, with your help, that God wants us at Covenant House to help these kids in other cities. I really appreciate the fact that several hundred of you responded to my request for feedback on this matter of expansion. Two or three thought it was a bad idea, a couple dozen thought it would be okay, but warned me about the risks of overextending, of biting off more than I could chew, but, overwhelmingly, hundreds of you thought it was something I should do.

Look, I'm not one of these people who has lunch with God and gets the word on His will for me straight from the horse's mouth. I know God's will more from the absolute logic of my own experience, and the suffering my kids endure, and the pain. From kids like Steve. I'm simply putting the whole matter, all the problems, all the anxiety, in God's hands. If it be His will, for His honor and glory, and for the good of our kids, He will help us accomplish this purpose. All my friends and I have to do is work our tails off.

My Kids Are
Scared to Death

*A hundred people know my first name
and it ain't really me, Bruce.
I ain't anybody somebody knows.*

August 1981

There was this little kid running stark naked across the lawn. He
was jumping and squealing and shouting with delight as he
flung himself, all parts of him flying, into the swimming pool. His
name was José Francisco Alejandro Luis Díaz. He was seven and a
half years old, and it was the first time in his life he had ever been in
a pool. José Francisco, etc., etc., couldn't have cared less how deep it
was.

"Get that kid a bathing suit," I growled to Jim O'Keefe, project
director of our new place in Guatemala. I didn't growl very loud—
it's not only bad for my image (I always have to play the role of the
kindly benevolent Father Bruce who wouldn't skin even Benny the
pimp down beneath his birthday suit)—I was too happy. My growl
was more like a purr.

You see, our little streaker, José Francisco, etc., etc. (who just
couldn't wait to find a bathing suit), was the first kid we took into the
Cortijo de las Flores, our newest Covenant House in Antigua, forty
miles northwest of Guatemala City. José was followed into the pool
almost immediately by his more modest twelve-year-old brother,
Gustavo Antonio Juan Santiago. He was more discreetly attired in a
voluminous pair of gym shorts borrowed from one of our staff.

Both boys had been conceived, born, and raised in a back-room

brothel in Guatemala City by their homeless young mother. Their
fathers are nameless. After their mother died, the kids drifted out of
the brothel into the relative kindness of the streets. A dear friend
who helped us open our place here found these children and brought
them to me. These kids have to be the first, I said.

Miguel was the third. An absolutely gorgeous kid, Miguel is
eleven. He's been living in the streets of Antigua since he was eight,
surviving by shining shoes, begging, and being accommodating to the
tourists who were captivated by his charm and intelligence. His
mother has fifteen children and simply cannot feed him. He has no
father he knows.

The Cortijo de las Flores—the name, appropriately, means Inn of
the Flowers—is, or was, a beautiful old small hotel. Some friends in
the United States and Guatemala provided the funds for us to purchase it to use as our first Casa Alianza—that's Covenant House in
Spanish. We will be able to care for 150 abandoned and orphaned
boys, six to twelve years old. (In twelve to eighteen months we hope
to begin taking in their little sisters in an expanded program.)

As I write this letter I've got this big dopey grin on my face that
won't go away. I've just returned from ten days in Guatemala, which
I spent in an endless round of staff meetings, official engagements,
and one very large rather unplanned fiesta. The people of the sur-
rounding villages and towns came to our new Inn of the Flowers to
celebrate with us the opening of our program. The bishop and his
priests came to bless the place. The mayors came. The poor came.
The wealthy landowners came. There even may have been a few
guerrillas in the crowd (Guatemala has been raked by political and
partisan violence for years).

"We are here to care for the children," I said, as plainly as I could.
"Homeless and dying children may not and must not be held hostage
to any political ideology, whether of the right, left, or center." I
think everybody understood where we were coming from.

Our staff, members of the Covenant House volunteer community,
has done an absolutely superb job in getting our new facility organized and open—exactly one year from the day when I stepped over
and around two young kids, not more than nine and ten, sleeping
under a pile of newspapers in a back alley in Guatemala City.

Look, boundaries on a map are lines on a piece of paper. Blue,
green, red, purple, orange are just colors designating pieces of one

earth that we call different countries. But the children are the same. Seven-and-a-half-year-old naked José Francisco, etc., etc., has the same parts and the same needs and the same hungers and the same rights as your Joeys and Frankies and Davies and Bobbys—and Marys and Alices.

September 1981

Sixteen-year-old Jenny watched the old yellow Cadillac with Texas plates drive slowly down the street in Baltimore. Classes in summer school were over for the day, and Jenny was waiting for a bus to take her home.

"Want a ride, baby?" The two men and two women in the car seemed friendly.

"Sure, and thanks," she said, and threw her school books in the backseat and climbed in. The date was July 9.

It happened that simply. Jenny, a really good kid, was on that day a not very smart kid. The car quickly turned north on Interstate 95 and headed toward New York City.

"Take me home. You've got to let me out. Stop the car," Jenny demanded.

Lenny and Pat and Joe and Carol just laughed. "There's a five-hundred-dollar charge on you, baby," Lenny said. "You've got to work it off. Don't make us any trouble."

The yellow Caddie stopped at a couple of truck stops on the way north. The incredulous schoolgirl, by now in a state of total shock, was forced to turn tricks with some truckers. Joe beat the reluctance out of her. Lenny kept the money.

The four adults, and by now benumbed child, arrived in New York City and checked into a seedy hotel on the Grand Concourse in the Bronx. Lenny and Pat and Joe and Carol split up. Jenny was forced to stay with Joe in the hotel. They changed rooms every day. Jenny was put out to work the streets in the Hunts Point section of the Bronx. (Hunts Point is the pits! There isn't any more dangerous, ugly place for a kid.)

Joe beat her a lot—Jenny was not a very willing and cooperative captive. She managed to escape in the middle of the night after Joe fell asleep. Jenny took fifty dollars from his pants and grabbed a cab to Manhattan's Lower East Side. Exhausted and confused, she checked into another cheap hotel.

Jenny poured out her story to a young woman in the next room. Toya was sympathetic and understanding. "I'll help you, baby. Me and my friend Blue Fly, next door." Blue Fly is a really evil, rotten pimp. He laughed at the girl. "Your mistake, baby, was telling somebody your story. For being so dumb, I'm laying a thousand-dollar charge on you. You can work it off on the Bowery. Don't try to escape again. The police won't help, and we'll get you, we really will. There's no place you can hide."

Jenny tried to refuse to work and was beaten. She didn't bring back much money and she was beaten again. The terrified kid decided that she had nothing to lose—being dead was better—and broke away and ran down the street, chased by Toya and Blue Fly. Jenny dived into a large parking lot, rolled under a car, and waited, panting convulsively, until Blue Fly and Toya ran past. Jenny got back on her feet in almost mindless, blind terror and ran and ran and ran and ran, down streets, around corners, across intersections, ignoring traffic and pedestrians . . . and then she saw a couple of New York City blue-and-white police cruisers parked outside the Fifth Precinct.

Her odyssey of terror and degradation was over. The police took competent charge. A car was dispatched to look for Blue Fly and Toya. The Runaway Squad and the Pimp Squad were contacted, and Jenny was brought over to Under 21. Our doctors gave her a thorough examination, treating her for shock, and bruises, and rape.

Her overjoyed parents were contacted and immediately came to New York to claim their daughter. The police are continuing their investigation, and they are looking to arrest Blue Fly and his friend. Jenny has agreed to prosecute.

Jenny will never forget, as long as she lives, her days of terror and horror in New York City. We shouldn't forget them either. Until we find a way to deal effectively with the hundreds of pimps that prey on children like Jenny, her story will be repeated over and over again. Only when we stop glamorizing and romanticizing pimps and mythologizing them as American folk figures will our law-enforcement authorities, our prosecutors and judges take our "outrage" seriously.

The fact is, of course, that pimps are an intrinsic part of our vast and well-organized—and well-patronized—sex industry. Anybody who picks up a girl on the street has to know that she is controlled by a pimp and is thereby contributing to her captivity, degradation, and shame—even when despairing young people themselves have gradually come to accept their life-style. We can't have it both ways. Pimps are just one of the slimy, evil, rotten messes formed by the sex industry. They feed on it. They gather around the porno bookstores and theaters, massage parlors, burlesque houses and topless bars, sexual supermarkets like Show World and the Pussycat, like flies around stinking carrion.

I hope the police are successful in bringing Blue Fly and Joe and Lenny and the others to justice. I am not a vengeful man, and I am sworn to being understanding and compassionate, but right now don't anybody ask me what I would like to see happen to Blue Fly. I would be ashamed to tell you.

October 1981

A bus driver found her in the parking lot behind Under 21. My kids kept sneaking over to look at her body. She was seventeen or eighteen. You really couldn't tell how pretty she'd been—her face had been mashed in, and she had been stabbed eight times. The autopsy put the time of death between 2 and 5 A.M. on Thursday.

Detectives were able to determine that up until the night before her death she had been living in a sleazy hotel on Forty-seventh Street. The hotel is used by a lot of pimps and prostitutes.

My kids all know her, but nobody knows her real name. They remembered she used to have a baby. The word spread through Under 21 like wildfire. The kids sat in stunned silence, or talked quietly. The older kids didn't bother getting angry or belligerent— casual, unexplained, anonymous death is a fact of street life.

That afternoon, Sister Alicia, our director of residential services, called our kids together in the main lounge. "Look," she said, "this is a dangerous and violent area. Out there, we can't protect you. In here, we can. You're safe in here. Look," she said, "we care about you. Don't hang out in the streets. Times Square is a sick place with sick people who will do this to kids."

Our counselors, heavily involved, trying to reach as many kids as possible, reported that the shock and fear were profound. Our kids are afraid of dying—they feel exposed, vulnerable, used. A curious, uneasy undercurrent of the discussion swirled to the surface repeatedly. We don't know her name. I can't use my name. Nobody knows who I am. We can't tell anybody who we are. A hundred people know my first name and it ain't really me, Bruce. I ain't anybody somebody knows.

All during that day we tried to calm and reassure our kids—and brace ourselves for what we knew would happen. A lot of kids did not go out that night. They stayed around, in the center, watching TV. The few that did go out came home early.

And then it began. The new kids, those we never saw before, began flooding in. Knowing they would be safe here. Our intake workers reported that a record number of kids came in that night and the next. More than eighty new kids. They came in small groups of twos and threes, afraid to walk alone, to be alone. We took them all. We beefed up our own street patrols. Put a twenty-four-hour street counselor outside.

We were right to be afraid. Late Saturday night they found the body of Cheryl in an abandoned warehouse on Thirty-third Street. She had been strangled and beaten to death. She was fourteen. Cheryl ran away from warm, caring parents, from a small town, from safety and security and a future, to the Big Apple, to Fun City, to the Great White Way, to Forty-second Street and the pushers and pimps and panderers and johns who buy little girls.

Cheryl had stayed at Under 21 for about five days back in June and then returned home to her parents. She ran away again and came back to New York—a tiny little moth—and flew directly into the flame. If she was trying to get to Under 21, she never made it. She was only blocks away when she was killed.

The police described her as simple, not sophisticated. She was known to hang around the bus terminal, often seen there in the company of a pimp.

My kids are scared to death.

Does Martin Hodas Know What He's Doing?

Ignorance might get a lot of people into heaven.
Does it keep everybody out of hell?

Thanksgiving 1981

Paradise Alley just reopened, gaudier, brighter than ever, this time with live nudes. For almost two years, this raunchy blight of a peep show had been closed by the effective action of the mayor's Midtown Enforcement Project, run by the capable and caring Carl Weisbrod.

Paradise Alley is right across from Under 21. The action on Eighth Avenue heated up right away. The girls are back working the street in front of our chapel. The pimps, hustlers, runners, johns, and assorted hangers-on are back. Paradise Alley is right next to the Cameo porno theater, which is right next to the Globe Hotel, the biggest hot-bed hotel on the block. From our Covenant community residence we can see the continuous action on the street below. The buying and selling of bodies, the commercial recreational exchange called prostitution that is one of the biggest—untaxed—industries in New York.

Martin Hodas lives at Harbor View West out in Lawrence, Long Island, 11559, an exclusive suburb of New York City. A lot of very wealthy people live there. Martin Hodas is the smut king of New York. He owns Paradise Alley. He lives far from the sleaze and grime and violence and exploitation and death of Eighth Avenue and Forty-second Street. But he makes a lot of money there.

Martin Hodas, who lives in exclusive Lawrence, out on Long Island, owns at least six other porno bookstores in New York City. What he retails is promiscuity, adultery, sodomy, fornication, sadomasochism, homosexuality, and all kinds of things we used to call perversion. He lives at Harbor View West. . . . The very address reeks of affluence and security and no garbage in the streets and no riffraff hanging around. There are certainly no pimps and pushers and prostitutes and johns hanging out in front of Harbor View West. The neighbors would complain. Property values would go down. Their children would be endangered and corrupted.

It's perfectly okay, though, for Martin Hodas to live there. I wonder if his neighbors go to his parties or invite him to theirs. Martin Hodas is a panderer. Webster's New Collegiate Dictionary, 1980 edition, defines "panderer" this way: "someone who caters to or exploits the weakness of others, a pimp." Does his wife know Martin Hodas is a pimp? Do his kids know their father is in such a dirty business? I wonder how he explains it to his children. I wonder if Martin Hodas out in exclusive Lawrence knows what he is doing.

Can you forgive a sinner before he repents of his sin? Should we? Is the answer always to cite the example of Jesus—"Forgive them, Father. They don't know what they're doing"—these unforgettable and troubling words whispered by Christ minutes before He died in agony, extending pardon to the men who tortured and killed Him?

Are there some who do know what they are doing and don't care? Men who act out of greed, a lust for money, by exploiting the darker side of our nature? If, after all, nobody really "knows" what he's "doing" or choosing to do, for evil or good, then the reality of freedom and choice and accountability flies out the window. There is no good and evil, no right and wrong, no vice and virtue. There are only different degrees of ignorance.

Ignorance might get a lot of people into heaven. Does it keep everybody out of hell? Is nobody there, because nobody ever knew enough about the evil he committed to merit punishment? Does Martin Hodas know what he's doing?

Christ said a lot of troubling things. Paradoxes. Scary things. Like "Judge not, lest you be judged." He unhesitatingly forgave Mary Magdalene because she was sorry for her sin. Christ forgave the sinner and said, "Go. Sin no more."

Maybe we could help Martin Hodas at Harbor View West become

unignorant. Maybe if you dropped him a line—don't rant and rave—and pointed out what a rotten, evil, corrupting business he runs, he just might listen. You know where he lives.

January 1982

January firsts and New Years' beginnings are heavy times for everybody. Especially for us eunuchs. There are lots of things I don't understand, but I really do understand now, so much better, what it means to become a eunuch for the sake of His kingdom. (Hey, please don't misinterpret, you guys. Read the Gospel of St. Matthew 19:12–15.)

For a while I thought I was going to beat eunuchhood. I mean, I had the best of both possible worlds: I really enjoyed being a priest, and I also had bunches of great kids that I loved. They were almost like my own, even if someone else had them first.

In the earlier days of Covenant House it was a lot simpler. I was just past forty, my worries were clearer, more straightforward. I worried about the junkies coming on to my kids when I lived in an apartment in the East Village (where Covenant House got its start). There was the acute daily anxiety of how I was going to feed the kids and pay the rent. My staff and I were close friends who cared a lot about a few kids that we all knew by name and size and shape and smell, almost.

I guess some people still think of Covenant House that way—a smallish kind of place where this noble priest sits, patting nice little lost kids on the head with one hand and fending off pimps with the other while he worries about rent and food bills and the kids who don't make it. That last part is still true enough, God knows.

But that noble priest? Well, he's a balding, fifty-four-year-old, sometimes anxiety-ridden (like yourselves) talking head, speaking hundreds of times a year about thousands of kids I don't know very much anymore. They pass through Covenant House at the rate of over a thousand every month. I'm lucky to catch an occasional familiar face. Now I worry about millions of dollars, not hundreds (your few bucks a month still mean everything to us!), and fifteen thousand kids, not a handful, and an agency with over four hundred on staff, not a few close friends who helped me with my kids.

It's a lot different now. It's still very personal with me, but it's become different. I'm an eunuch again, and I don't like it very much. The kids don't inhabit my personal space anymore, and I really miss that. There's an unavoidable distance now, and the anxiety is a lot greater.

But despite anxiety and distance—and maybe because of them— my vision (call it that, please. I think it *is* that) about these kids is much broader. I worry a lot now, just as much really, about the street kids in L.A. and Houston and Washington and Boston and Toronto. (We've been asked to help in all these places.) They all have the same faces: lips curled—forced—into a smile, a wary teenage insouciance, eyes that are watchful and scared—and brave, too.

Their eyes really get to me. They say it all so clearly: Like me, please don't hurt me, are you going to care about me? Why should you, you can't, you won't, you mustn't. In the meantime, there's always the transaction: You buy me with money, I buy you with . . . with what? Your need, too. I guess that's better than nothing at all. I have become a connoisseur of eyes.

The trick is, of course, to keep what Christmas meant in December alive in January: the Incarnation of God in Jesus as our permanent Hope and Wonder, the visible, touchable, and touching basis for —and test of—our faith in the promise of God's love.

I mean, if God loves us in December, He loves us in January. If God was Love-made-visible-and-touching in a stable on a hillside, He is present, too, and visible still, on our New York streets in 1982. Our love for our kids—yours and mine—is inextricably bound up with the conviction that as we love our kids, God does, and will love them. It's our covenant.

But tell that to a street kid with hurting eyes and the chances are downright excellent that he won't believe you. He's used up all his love language in a thousand lying encounters: Hey man, I really care about you. I mean, I wish we had time to get to know each other. Later, man. See you around. Thanks for the twenty bucks. . . .

It's better, safer, if the realization that you love him creeps up on him and surprises him, takes him by stealth. If he makes the God connection . . . but that is, I guess, a translation, something he does for himself with a little bit of help from a eunuch, some creative, fertilizing act of love and communion with a Lord he may come to know.

Lent 1982

Laurie is thirteen, a classic middle-class kid from a middle-class family. She was picked up by a Times Square pimp last week and raped and brutalized for a few days before being put out on the street last Friday to make money.

Early Monday morning Laurie had the wit and the courage to escape and come to Under 21, the crisis center operated by Covenant House in Times Square. After three days and nights of sheer hell, Laurie is safe now. We were able to place her in a temporary foster home outside New York City.

Tommy is not safe, and he remains at Under 21 because he is convinced that if he goes outside he will be killed. I mean murdered —wasted, as the kids say. Tommy is from New York City's teeming slums. He's eighteen now, and it's hard to say he ever had a family that counted in his young life. He's a very bright and talented kid and he knows it. Tommy even almost managed to finish high school before he went on the street. (His parents drowned themselves, and Tommy, in a sea of alcoholic cruelty.)

Because he was bright and talented and good-looking and in great need for love and money (or money and love), he found it easy to get both. From some very unscrupulous people who found a way to use all his talents. Put on the circuit between Boston, New York, Washington, and Atlanta, he was bought and sold, rented out and leased. He performed for individuals; he danced, naked, for groups; he also delivered lots of heroin and coke to some very important people. Tommy quickly found that, increasingly, he had very little to say, and then nothing at all to say, about what he did or where he went.

Kids who do what Tommy did get to know too many faces, too many places, too much about how the system works. Especially bright, talented, perceptive kids with good memories, like Tommy.

Kids like that also get older, and less good-looking, and less in demand, less marketable—out-of-date, on-the-shelf merchandise. And very expendable. Like Tommy. Because he's dangerous now. Not to anybody really important—the sick, evil, greedy people who really run and make huge profits from this enormous meat grinder, the American sex industry, are insulated from its daily death and dying—but dangerous to lots of other cruel and brutal people who tend the nuts-and-bolts operation and make it work.

But Tommy is, mostly, dangerous to himself. What he knows has

made him positively lethal to himself. His knowledge of what goes
down is a hand grenade about to explode in his pocket.
So he's afraid to go outside now. With good reason. I believe him.
You see, he couldn't know what he has told me without being extremely dangerous. I've heard it all before, too many times. I've told
Tommy not to testify or to bring charges—it would just get him
killed, and nobody would be exposed and brought to justice.

I don't think an eighteen-year-old kid should be a martyr because
of our greed and lust and apathy. I haven't totally figured out what
to do about Tommy yet. We've set up some special security precau-
tions to protect him.

Peter is only sixteen, and he doesn't know half of what he thinks
he knows about street life. He, too, needs love and money—or money
and love—and he's been asked by José and Marty, two Times Square
film entrepreneurs who swim around in the slime of Forty-second
Street, to make porno films. It's not a lot of money—only three
hundred dollars—but for a homeless, unskilled, poorly educated
street kid it's the difference between sleeping in a bed or on a subway,
between eating or not. (How do you like *those* choices?) Once you
turn sixteen, for all practical purposes it's legal to make a porn film
because, I guess, the American public wants it that way.

Laurie and Tommy desperately want out of the sex scene because
they *know* it's a meat grinder. Peter, only sixteen, doesn't believe me
when I tell him. He's only sixteen. Bad things only happen to other
kids when you're sixteen. "Bruce, it's my chance to make it! I'll do
anything they want, Bruce. I need the money." And then Peter
ducked his head and uncurled his tightly clenched fist, spreading his
fingers wide, inspecting each finger with minute care. Almost like he
could see his life slipping away between them, Peter looked back up
at me. "I need the money, Bruce," he said with finality, and got up
and left my office. It's legal to make porn films when you're sixteen
in New York.

I had an interview with David Susskind a couple of years ago. It
was a good interview, possibly the best discussion on national television of what Covenant House is all about that I've ever been part of.
Since I was David's only guest, we had plenty of time, well over an
hour, to really get into issues. (There's very little meaningful com-
ment you can squeeze into a five-to-six-minute segment on most talk
shows. Even twenty minutes barely gives you time to provide a con-

text to help people understand a very brutal reality.) David Susskind is, I think, the best interviewer on TV. His questions are thoughtful, honest, real questions, not disguised cues designed to produce an interesting show.

I didn't think David was a believer, in God, so I was surprised when he asked his final question. "Father Bruce, how can God permit these things to happen?"

Questions about the nature of good and evil and God's Providence and justice and mercy are, ultimately, unanswerable—especially with thirty seconds left on a nationwide TV show. I think I said, conscious that the clock was running down, that I did not know the answer. I still don't.

It's Ash Wednesday again. Lent begins once more: Jesus' answer to the fact of sin and evil, to offer His life in a total outpouring, nothing held back, of His Love. Maybe He never told us how to solve intellectually the great mystery of our evil free choices, but He told us what to do about it. Love is a mystery only to those who do not love or cannot believe in it.

May 1982

The predator at our door was about thirty, a dark, lank, straighthaired, bleached-blond, bitter-faced woman. Her quarry, fifteen-year-old Richie, was safe inside. "I want him," she said. "He agreed to work for me."

Our security people were not polite. "He doesn't want to go with you," one said curtly.

The bitter-faced woman turned to leave, malevolence incarnate.

Richie is a beautiful kid. He arrived at Under 21 begging Pampers and food for an eighteen-month-old baby, abandoned by her junkie mother and being kept by her twenty-year-old father in a cheap Times Square hotel. The room rent was being paid by six prostitutes who took pity on a homeless and incompetent young father. "The baby is hungry," Richie said. "She doesn't eat too often. I haven't either." We quickly provided Pampers for the baby and food for both.

When Richie came back to Under 21 later that day, our staff got a better look at him: a not-quite-finished kid, quickly losing the last traces of baby fat, the hard but delicate lines of lean adolescence

clearly visible in face and body. In another six months, Richie would
be a really handsome kid.

"I can't go home," he said. "My stepfather doesn't want me. He
won't let me in. I've been on the street for about a year. Mostly, with
some friends, I rip people off. But lately I've had to get some money
for the baby. She doesn't cry when I hold her. She's only eighteen
months old. Her father, Tony, is my best friend. Sometimes I have to
hustle johns to get money for the baby."

"Let's take care of the baby first, okay?" Our staff quickly convinced Tony and Richie to bring the baby in to our clinic. They were
both obviously totally committed to eighteen-month-old Lisa. Tony
reluctantly, but obviously relieved, agreed to take the baby to her
grandmother.

Richie stayed on with us at Under 21, and our staff began the
difficult and sensitive process of trying to help a young street kid get
his life back in order.

Richie's brief history—gave us an all-too-familiar glimpse into
that netherworld of Times Square: the smoking hell beneath the
bright glitter and the crowds. "I didn't like to rip people off," Richie
said. "I never hurt anybody. I didn't like to hustle the johns either.
Then this woman offered me five hundred dollars—he paused,
flushed and stammered a little, and dropped his head—"to have sex
with her and her daughter onstage in front of a lot of people. It's
pretty bad. You have to look happy when you do it. At least you
can't see the customers—the lights are too bright. I'm afraid of her,"
Richie said. "She wants me to work for her some more."

It's been a bad week for kids at Under 21.

Mary, seventeen, has a baby and no husband. Her sister supported
them both by working in a topless bar in Manhattan (that means her
sister was rented out by "Matty the Horse" Ianniello, the organized-
crime garbage who controls the topless-bar industry). Mary left her
sister's apartment and came to Under 21 because her sister's boss
wanted her to work the bar.

Beth, sixteen, very bright and pretty and very frightened, came to
New York City running from two pimps in Rhode Island. In Times
Square less than a week, she was picked off by another pimp, raped
at knifepoint, and inducted into his stable. Beth waited until he fell
asleep and fled to Under 21.

Anne came in last night, tired, cynical, desperate—older inside her mind and heart than any of us will ever get. She's seventeen now, has been a prostitute since fifteen. You might say she came by it naturally. You see, her mother was killed by *her* pimp. The apple doesn't fall far from the tree.

Sometimes people write me very concerned about the traces of anger or sadness that occasionally appear in my letters. I try pretty hard to control these feelings, but I'm not always successful. You see, it's their faces. Kids' faces are supposed to be happy and open and excited and alive. Their eyes should be filled with trust and innocence.

And the chances are downright excellent that Richie and Tony, Mary, Beth, and Anne will not make it. (All the girls have been threatened with death by their pimps.) I mean they will die. Quite young, deformed and made ugly by an industry that caters to our pleasures. Society (that's us) has been unable to protect these kids or punish their exploiters.

Meanwhile, quite literally outside our doors, roam—and wait— the predators, the pimps, and a bitter-faced woman. Five hundred dollars is a lot of money for a fifteen-year-old, soon-to-be-gangling Richie, and, unless he's careful, he just might get to like what he's been into. (All you have to do to start is teach yourself not to care too much.)

"I Wish I
Were Your Father"

*"Doesn't anybody stay in one place anymore?
. . . I sure hope the road don't come to own me. . . ."*

The dull New York State Thruway miles were unwinding monot-
onously at exactly sixty-one miles per hour. The song pouring
out the speakers and filling the car—I had the volume way up—was
a hauntingly beautiful ballad by Carole King: "You're so far away
. . ." It's a great song.

I've been on the road a lot these days. Spring is a very busy time
for talks, and we're also busy setting up Under 21's for kids in other
cities. Sometimes I think I live mostly in airports and behind the
wheel of a car. I've been averaging five different beds a week for
months. (Don't worry: My super-capable staff in New York runs
things a lot better than I ever could.)

I get pretty tired sometimes. Like this Friday, driving up to Sche-
nectady at 6 A.M. to give a bunch of talks at four high schools and
two colleges and preach at all the masses in St. Paul's Church this
weekend. I was "vegging out," as the kids say (i.e., assuming the
relaxed, unconscious, vegetable-like state of a turnip), no thought or
feeling, letting the music from the car radio wash over me.

I was really getting into the song: "Doesn't anybody stay in one
place anymore? . . . ." The next verse snapped me out of my reverie:
"I sure hope the road don't come to own me. . . ." Vivid memories

of a conversation I had with a bunch of my kids in our new Toronto Under 21 jarred me awake.

We had opened our beautiful new Under 21 for kids in Toronto February 1 of this year, and I was visiting there a couple of weeks ago—it was jammed, naturally, with over seventy kids—making sure that things were going well and checking out the new staff. It was about midnight, and I was sitting in our main lounge talking with a half dozen really great kids ranging anywhere from sixteen to nineteen. It was a very quiet, low-keyed conversation (the other kids had gone up to bed).

What happened was very moving. Each kid talked directly to me, each in turn shutting out everybody else in the group. Nobody interrupted or commented on anything somebody else said. We just listened—I mean, really listened—to each other.

Lance was the last kid to talk. A tall, quiet, good-looking boy. He spoke with the confident self-assurance of an eighteen-year-old who knew his own name. "I like to move around a lot, Bruce," he said.

"You're a traveler?" I said. "A wanderer?"

"Yeah, Bruce," he said.

"A seeker, maybe?" I said.

Lance nodded a bit uncertainly, his face suddenly wary and closing. "You're a drifter." I said it quietly, kindly, with a question at the end of my voice.

The other kids got real quiet, and our conversation ended pretty soon after that. One by one each kid said some final, terminating thing before they said good night and went upstairs to bed. I shook hands with each kid. I wanted to touch them.

Lance stayed around. We sat there looking at each other.

"I ain't no drifter, Bruce," he said. His lips twisted, and again that look of uncertainty and a brief touch of panic crossed his face. "I'm just . . ." His voice trailed off.

"It's better to settle down," I said. "It's better to stay around," I said. "It's better to find what you're looking for—at least once in a while."

Jesus, too, was a wanderer, a seeker, with no place to lay His head —like my kids. I hope they meet each other sometime, someplace on that road my kids call home. Jesus' own journey to the Father ended abruptly on a road on a hill overlooking Jerusalem: He ended His life as He began it—homeless, on the run, pursued by His enemies, no stranger to abandonment and loneliness, stripped and undignified, and finally, killed. I don't think the Lord has any trouble loving street kids. They've suffered so many of the same things—together. Lance doesn't see it that way yet. He doesn't know that yet. His Easter hasn't happened yet. He's still in the middle of his own crucifixion, and he's afraid of dying, and his faith isn't strong enough to cry out to the Father. . . .

Lance, too, got up, and stood for a moment indecisively, as if he wanted to say something else, something final, something that would sum up things, or maybe he couldn't shake the vision of what lay down that road (like Jesus couldn't, and was afraid).

"I sure hope the road don't come to own me, Bruce," he said.

"Pray for me," I said.

"Sure," he said. Lance reached out and touched my arm. "Good night," he said. "Pray for me, too."

Back in the car heading south on the New York State Thruway, I thought of Lance. The car purred along almost on automatic pilot at exactly sixty-one miles per hour. I passed a state trooper parked behind a clump of trees with his radar gun aimed squarely at me. I wasn't going fast enough for him to stop me, but I still slowed it down a bit.

I thought of the next six days and fourteen talks: Boston, Las Vegas, Steubenville, Fort Lauderdale, and Gainesville. "I sure hope the road don't come to own me," I said back to the music.

June 1982

It doesn't take long to murder a child, and there are lots of ways to do it. You can shoot them, OD them, stab and strangle them—push them out of windows and off roofs, run them over with cars. A lot of my kids have died that way. More surely will.

There's another kind of death my kids experience, that leaves them, for a while, still breathing in and out, but inside their heads where they live, a corpse.

Three months on the street is a very long time. Six months is forever. A year? Then they're just breathing in and out but dead inside. The poison works quickly. The girls' faces show it first. The boys can hide it a little longer.

In the beginning the kids can still argue with me: Hey, Bruce, he's no pimp—he's my boy friend and he needs me. . . . Hey, Bruce, I can stop when I want. . . . Hey, Bruce, I'm just trying to make a few bucks. In the beginning they can still make distinctions between what they are inside their heads and what they do with their bodies. But after a hundred or five hundred or a thousand johns it becomes difficult, and then impossible, to separate what you are from what you do. You become what you do. And you no longer care. Somewhere along the process a child dies. He's been murdered. Each john has struck a blow. Each john teaches a kid twenty bucks' worth of what street life is all about. The code is very simple: intimidate or be intimidated, seduce or be seduced, get over on or be gotten over on, do it to somebody else first—and make sure you get paid. Don't believe anybody.

For my kids, every simple human gesture becomes suspect: An offer of a cup of coffee becomes the beginning of a seduction. "Look, Bruce, it works this way. I see this john cruising Forty-second Street, like say near the arcade where all the kids hang out. He stops to look in a camera store near the corner. I stop, too. You got a cigarette, mister? (That means I'm available, Bruce.) If he gives it to me, the contact is made. We just have to work out the details. . . ."

God talk becomes extremely precarious, even risky. Let me tell you about "Our Father," Scott. Never mind that you never knew your own father, that he was never there for you. Our Father in heaven is different. He's always there. He sees you and knows you and loves you. You've just never met Him. . . .

The boy looked me right in the eye. He spoke quietly and courteously. "I'm too busy right now, Bruce. No offense, okay, but I've got to make a few bucks. Your God is okay, I guess, but He's sure not part of anything I've been into. I sure hope He can't see what I'm going to have to do tonight. I do *have* to, Bruce. I don't like it very much, but I'm afraid to hate it too much.

"Thanks for running Under 21, Bruce, but I can't stay. I guess I don't like the street very much, but it's where I live. You've got some rules here, Bruce, and I can't take the curfew. Besides, there's something going on outside and I'm missing it. Tell you what, Bruce. I'll just go out for a while. It's only two A.M. and I'll just a walk around the block a couple of times. See you later."

The kid paused a moment, his hand on the doorknob, the door pushed open a few inches to let in the street noise. Outside a fire

truck from the Thirty-eighth Street firehouse hurtled by. Its deep
bellowing klaxon drowned out his words, but I could still see his lips
moving. He waited until the truck had passed ". . . Your God has
too many rules, Bruce," he said, "and I'd rather have you for my
Father."

He never came back. I knew he never would. I keep wondering
and thinking that maybe if I were better, or smarter, or holier, or
worked harder, or prayed more, I wouldn't lose so many. Look, I
know the Scriptures as well as the next man. I've squeezed a lot of
comfort out of God's word, especially that statement of Christ's
about choosing the weak and inadequate of this world to do His will.

Right now I sure feel weak and inadequate, and there's precious
little comfort left in those texts. I guess what I'm trying to say is that
I mourn for this kid. I mean, he's still breathing in and out, but he's
almost dead inside. And I have to take what little comfort I can—
and it's not much—from the *fact* that God loves these kids infinitely
more than we do.

July 1982

I met a little kid today who I wish were my kid. I mean, really my
own kid. (Let me say right from the start that the joys of "spiritual
fatherhood" can't hold a candle to the real thing.) I've always known
that, of course—every priest does—but Father's Day makes it worse.

I was preaching at the nine-fifteen Mass in this great parish in
Clinton, Connecticut—St. Mary's. The weather was gorgeous (the
first Sunday in weeks we didn't need boats and life jackets to go with
our umbrellas) and so were the bunches of kids sitting all through
the church with their proud fathers. I was preaching at all the
Masses. I was sadder than usual. It had not been a good week.
Monday I buried one of my kids. His name was Danny, and I loved
him a lot.

And there were bunches of girls in deep trouble in the center: Lisa,
fourteen, kidnapped by a pimp in Baltimore and sold to another
pimp in New York, was being returned to a foster home. She didn't
feel wanted there, but she had no other place to go. Maryann, nineteen, and both happy and scared, was about to get on a plane to L.A.
and her mother, whom she hadn't seen for three years. Julie is seventeen and too scared of her pimp to talk much. There's no way she

wants to go back on the street or, right now, even outside. I mean, she's that scared.

And then I got this anguished letter from a woman on my mailing list that bothered me a lot. I've read it a dozen times. If you don't mind, since some of you may feel the same way, I'll quote from it.

Dear Father Ritter,

I am the mother of ten children, ages 8 to 25. We have 8 boys and 2 girls. My husband and I are teachers. Through the years I worked to help pay the bills. However, I either subbed or did part-time teaching. For many years I taught reading from 9 to 12. I was able to be home when the children were sick, go to their plays and games etc. and was always home when they came home from school. We sent our first 5 children to Catholic Elementary and High Schools. Out of that number, we have one who continues to pray and go to Mass.

The next two had 8 years of Catholic elementary school. One of them, our 16-year-old daughter, is currently in complete rebellion. She is the kind of child you talk about in your letters. She is on pot, alcohol, contraceptive pills, and is totally disobedient.

Do I sound bitter and fed-up? You bet. My marriage is in ruins, my mental health is in jeopardy, and my Faith is held together by a string. I am not alone. The city, suburbs, and even this lovely country, is alive with abused parents.

I am sure you are doing much good work. I'm sure you've been told how great you are. We were sending you money long before you became so famous and vocal.

However, your words annoy and bring to tears those of us who still read your letters. Let me just quote a few from this most recent letter.

"Never mind that you never knew your own father, that he was never there for you." Really? You want to bet on that? How many fathers have you seen who are reduced constantly to tears by rebellious children? Open your eyes

and give men like my husband equal treatment. You've
been blinded and deafened by the lies of many of these
youth.

What can I say? Nothing that will bring this anguished mother or
father any comfort. The prodigal son delighted *his* father because he
returned home repentant. Magdalene was forgiven because she loved
much and repented and the Lord rejoiced. But if the prodigal does
not return? The Magdalene does not repent? What then, except to
mourn them—and forgive them.

Let me tell you an allegory.

The world's *greatest* sinner was to appear before the throne of God
for judgment. He was an unspeakably vile sinner. No greater sinner
had existed, or would exist, in the history of the world. No man was
ever more alienated from God, no man more deserving of divine
repudiation. His vileness was such that the angels standing before the
throne of God fled in fear before the face of this sinner. As the man
approached to be judged, the very stars in the heavens fell and the
sun and the moon trembled in their orbits. Planets exploded in horror, and the mighty cherubim standing before the throne hid their
faces. The man did not slink into the presence of God; he did not
crawl up to the throne of justice. He strode through the courts of
heaven unafraid, his head held high, and looked God right in the eye.
God looked back at him and said in a terrible voice, "Do you have
anything to say before I condemn you?" The sinner lifted his head
higher and looked right back at God and said, "I appeal."

The seraphim and cherubim were startled and cowered at this
insult to God and stood forth to defend God's honor. The archangels
were angered. Even God seemed somewhat surprised. His face darkened, and God said, "To whom do you appeal? To what do you
appeal?" And the man said, "I appeal from Your Justice to Your
Mercy."

We may not be the world's greatest sinner, and surely we hope the
heavens will not tremble when we stand before the throne of judgment and see God. But I think our prayer will be the same. I think
we will appeal, all of us, from God's Justice to His Mercy. I think we
will all say then as we have said all our lives, "Lord, have mercy on
us."

Blessed are the merciful, Jesus said, for *they* shall obtain mercy. Sometimes our minds reel and sometimes we don't want to understand because we are afraid. And sometimes we ask dumb questions of God, like saying, "Jesus, what did You really mean when You said that?" Jesus said, "Well, the answer is simple. If you are pure of heart, you will understand. Blessed are the *pure of heart,* for you will *see* God."

And if you continue to pursue the Lord with dumb questions, we say, "Well, God, we really still don't understand: When did we see You, so that we can tell if we are pure of heart?" And Jesus will tell us, "You will see Me when you are merciful. When you feed the least of My brethren, when they are hungry, and you clothe the least of My brethren when they are naked, and shelter the least of My brethren when they are homeless, and when we forgive our children for their sins against us." I mean, if God commands us to forgive our enemies, why surely, too, our children . . .

And still unwilling, we might argue with God and say, "God, what comes first, a merciful heart, or a pure heart?" Jesus will say, "Mercy." Before understanding, before sacrifice, before justice—that very simple, elemental gift of ourselves in love to those who need us, through an act of mercy. "Blessed are the merciful," Jesus said. "They can appeal from My Justice."

So I had a lot on my mind on Father's Day, standing at the door of St. Mary's in Clinton, Connecticut, thanking the people as they came out of the church. I was smiling a lot, and I meant it, sort of. But to tell you the truth, it was a pretty functional smile.

And then this little kid walked up to me. I mean, he was beautiful. And I thought maybe I could kidnap this kid (nobody would believe a priest did it) and take him back to New York with me. And the kid kinda bent his head back to look at me and said, "Can I give you my lunch money every day for your kids?"

I fell apart. I dissolved. I grabbed this kid and said, "Look, you're seven years old, right?"

"No," he said. "I'm eight."

"Did you understand everything I said in church today?" I said.

"About half of it," he said.

"Blessed are the pure of heart," I said. "What's your name?"

"Grove," he said.

"What's your first name?" I said.

"That's my first name," he said.

"That's a beautiful name," I said. "I wish I were your father."

He's a Good Family Man, the Judge Said

"This ain't no damn circus we're running.
You know I'm a pimp
and I know you're a whore."

August 1982

We won! By a clean, decisive knockout in the final round. No TKO or split decision, no ambiguities—the victory was stunning in its implications and consequences. The Supreme Court had spoken!

You see, Paul Ira Ferber owned a dirty bookstore on Eighth Avenue. He sold child porn and made a lot of money doing it. He said the United States Constitution gave him that right. New York State said it did not, so our New York City cops arrested the sanctimonious Mr. Ferber for selling films showing kids under twelve engaging in explicit sexual activity. Paul Ira Ferber was convicted under a 1977 New York State law making it a felony to use kids in sexual performances.

The judge in the case, Justice Dorothy Cropper, could have given Mr. Ferber seven years in the state penitentiary. Instead, she sentenced him to forty-five days in city jail. For a felony. Despite two previous criminal convictions. (Oh, he's a good family man, she said; and she couldn't really see how pandering child pornography really hurt anyone.) Like her colleague, Judge Marks, who earlier gave the producer of some twenty thousand obscene films—some involving child porn—sixty days, Judge Cropper apparently thought she owed kiddie-porn promoters an apology because our legislature decided to make them criminals. Mr. Ferber certainly had the best lawyer his rotten money could buy.

Paul Ira Ferber never went to jail, of course. He appealed his conviction to the New York Court of Appeals, the state's highest court, saying the U.S. Constitution gave him the right, under its freedom-of-speech provisions, to sell child porn unless a jury had declared it legally obscene (an almost impossible feat, much like trying to prove how many angels can dance on the head of a pin).

Incredibly, the Court of Appeals agreed with Mr. Ferber. We were appalled. Covenant House immediately urged Manhattan District Attorney Robert Morgenthau to appeal this incomprehensible decision to the U.S. Supreme Court and offered our total help in the case. I put all the resources of the Covenant House legal staff and our research department at the D.A.'s disposal.

Covenant House attorneys (as "friends of the court") prepared two briefs, urging in the first that the Supreme Court hear the case and, in the second, arguing the case on its merits. We asked the Supreme Court to uphold the New York law against kiddie porn whether or not the material in question can be deemed "legally obscene."

The death rattle of the child-pornography industry echoed throughout the land on July 2, when Justice Byron White announced the unanimous judgment of the U.S. Supreme Court in *New York* v. *Ferber.* Paul Ira Ferber, convicted of selling two grotesque films involving children twelve years of age and under, should soon begin serving his forty-five-day jail sentence.

It was a stunning reversal. The Supreme Court threw out last year's decision by the New York Court of Appeals which had overturned New York's ban on child pornography on assumed First Amendment grounds. *New York* v. *Ferber* is a landmark decision not only for its contribution to our understanding of "freedom of speech" but also for its wide-awake awareness of the severe harm kiddie-porn merchants inflict on the children they use. All too often the welfare of these children has been forgotten in the theoretical discussion of the sex industry and its perceived protection under the First Amendment.

At Covenant House's Times Square crisis shelter, we have never been able to forget sexually exploited kids. Well over half of the two hundred or more kids we shelter each night have traded sexual favors for money, food, or a place to sleep, just to survive on the streets. Others have been forced to make pornographic movies. (The very first six runaway kids who knocked on my apartment door back in 1969 had just been forced to make a porn film in order to get some food.)

What the Supreme Court ultimately saw, which the Court of Appeals did not, was that the issue of obscenity was irrelevant in light of "a government objective of surpassing importance (prevention of sexual exploitation and abuse of children)."

The legal obscenity standard fails to take cognizance of the harm inflicted on child performers. As the Supreme Court noted, the making of a kiddie-porn movie is nothing short of sexual abuse, with the resulting film being a "permanent record of a child's participation," which can haunt the child for the rest of his or her life. Brooke Shields's efforts to suppress lewd photographs taken, with her mother's consent, when she was ten years old, are a classic example of what that "permanent record" can mean to the victim.

The horrors of the child-pornography industry thus fully justified the Supreme Court's decision recognizing and classifying kiddie porn as outside the protection of the First Amendment.

Manhattan District Attorney Robert M. Morgenthau and Assistant District Attorney Robert M. Pitler, who argued the case before the Supreme Court, deserve the highest accolades.

It is now up to the U.S. Congress to amend the federal statute to eliminate the onerous obscenity standard from its kiddie-porn law. New York's thirty sister states, which do not have statutes similar to New York's, should also consider amending their respective statutes to the full extent permitted by the Supreme Court's decision. And the age of consent to make a porn film should be raised to eighteen or even twenty-one. It is *legal*, heaven help our kids, to make a porn film in New York when you are sixteen. You can't drink, drive, or vote, but you can make porn films! As the New York experience proves, the market for child pornography can be crushed with strong-enough laws and law enforcement.

Even more important, though, is a growing national recognition that sexual exploitation of children—through prostitution and sexual abuse far more than pornography—is a daily fact of life in every part of this country. The one million children who run away from home

each year, along with many others who are simply pushed out by
their parents, have few options for survival.

Next month we will officially inaugurate the Covenant House In-
stitute for Youth Advocacy, which will provide the highest-quality
legal research and assistance to public and private groups on matters
of urgent concern to the youth of this country and around the world.

September 1982

You won't like what you are going to read. Before you let your
children read this letter, make sure you feel it is appropriate for them
to do so. What follows is a verbatim transcript of a taped conversation one of my kids had with a really rotten pimp, known on the
streets as Sweet Talk. I've changed the names and cleaned up his
filthy language and edited the text only where necessary to clarify its
meaning. Every year thousands of girls like Margie, and thousands
of boys, run away from pimps like Sweet Talk, fleeing for their lives
—and hundreds of these kids end up at Under 21. If you ever wonder why our doors stay open twenty-four hours a day . . . why I
will fire any staff member who turns a child away . . . and why I
insist that our entrances be patrolled day and night, seven days a
week by armed guards, this transcript will make it totally clear.

New York City Police Department, Precinct——, today's date
is 8-16-82 and the time is fourteen-hundred hours. This
investigation is being conducted under major case 04128
on complaint number 5847. The following is a recording of
a telephone conversation between the complainant, Margaret Steward, and the subject, Jerome Thatcher, a.k.a.
Sweet Talk.

My name is Margaret Steward and I live at 874 W. 29th
Street. I was born on April 6, 1965. The following is a
telephone conversation being recorded by Police Officer
O'Brien. This recording is being made with my knowledge
and I hereby consent to such a recording.

MARGIE: "Yes, can I speak to room 19?"
VOICE: "Just a minute."

SECOND VOICE (FEMALE): "Hello?"

MARGIE: "Yeah, Joy? Is Sweet Talk there?"

SECOND VOICE: "Uh, huh. He's sitting in the car, you want me to get him?"

MARGIE: "Yeah, please." *(pause)*

THIRD VOICE (SWEET TALK): "Hello?"

MARGIE: "Hello."

SWEET TALK: "Who's this?"

MARGIE: "Margie."

SWEET TALK: "What's happening? Where you at?"

MARGIE: "At the home." *(our Under 21 center)*

SWEET TALK: "That's that same joint?"

MARGIE: "Yep."

SWEET TALK: "Why'd you call?"

MARGIE: "Because."

SWEET TALK: "I want to know why! You had me thinking that you wanted to come back to me. . . . I want to know why you called!"

MARGIE: " 'Cause I'm scared to come back."

SWEET TALK: "Why's that?"

MARGIE: "Because look at all the stuff that happened to me. You broke my cheek, and screwed up my teeth. . . . You don't think I'm scared of you?"

SWEET TALK: "I know you is. Hey, hey, I tried to tell you all about that."

MARGIE: "If I come back, are you gonna send me to work? You know I'm sick. I just got out of the hospital. . . . It's not worth it. I'm out here busting my tail for you and you just act like you don't care."

SWEET TALK: "You know I do. I don't know why you even say that."

MARGIE: "If you care, why are you always running up to me and grabbing me? And why are you always threatening my momma?"

SWEET TALK: "Hey, I'm gonna tell you, girl, you ain't seen nothing yet. I'm telling you, you done got me to the point,

girl, where I feel like riding to your momma's and killing
everybody in the house. Because I told you, next time you
leave me you gonna pay, or somebody in your family's
gonna pay. I take this too g-dd-m serious, girl. You understand what I'm saying! You went into the hospital. You
came out, and now you just gotta go to work! Point blank!
What more can I tell you? Now it's time for you to sell your
tail."

MARGIE: "You gonna pimp me until I die, huh?"

SWEET TALK: "No, baby, uh-uh. I don't even want you to look
at it like that."

MARGIE: "You're starting to make it one of those 'pimp/
hooker' relationships. I mean, you're starting to whip me
and things like that. I mean, every little thing I do, you blow
up at me for. And you don't think I'm suppose to be scared
of you?"

SWEET TALK: "I don't know why. You're my woman, you're the
one who gets to sleep with me. I ain't scared of *you*. . . .
Come on back home, baby, come on back!"

MARGIE: "Sweet Talk, if I come back you ain't gonna whip
me?"

SWEET TALK: "I ain't gonna do a thing to you."

MARGIE: "I'm sick of selling my body to make money. . . .
What are you gonna do when you see me?"

SWEET TALK: "Probably hug you to death, and make you realize what's happening. Damn, I had so many plans for your
tail on the fourth and on your birthday. Could of made a
fortune."

MARGIE: "See, if you really cared about me, you wouldn't be
sendin' me out in the streets to do that stuff."

SWEET TALK: "Well, if I didn't, we'd end up in the street anyway." *(chuckling)*

MARGIE: "So you're saying if I come back it's gonna be the
same old thing? I gotta work all night. . . . Sweet Talk, *I*
don't wanna be out on the streets!"

SWEET TALK: "I ain't gonna mess with you, girl. I just want you go get through your mind that this ain't no cat-and-mouse game. This ain't no damn circus we're running. You know I'm a pimp and I know you're a whore. You know what I'm saying. Hey, we're trying to establish a man/woman relationship. . . . Anyway, how you doing now?"

MARGIE: "I'm doing better than I was. I'm not out selling my body all night for—"

SWEET TALK (INTERRUPTING): "What time is it?"

MARGIE: "I don't know. It's about time for me to go back up to my floor."

SWEET TALK: "What time you got to be in?"

MARGIE: "Nine-thirty . . . nine, I mean."

SWEET TALK: "Hey, I'm thinking about coming to pick you up, okay?"

MARGIE: "I'm already in the building. They ain't gonna let me out."

SWEET TALK: "G-dd-mmit, if you wanted to come out of there, you'd come out of there! Now, don't go handing me this crap across the phone! You hear me?"

MARGIE: "I can't leave now! Security's out there, and because—"

SWEET TALK: "Hell with security. Just tell them you're going home to your momma. What're they gonna do, tell you no, you can't go?"

MARGIE: "No, they're gonna tell me to wait. And they're gonna call her 'cause these people up here are scared to let me go outside."

SWEET TALK: "Say, baby, I wanna be with you just as well as you wanna be with me, but this across-the-phone stuff ain't gonna do it—"

MARGIE (INTERRUPTING): "I gotta go to my floor. I'll call you back tomorrow."

SWEET TALK: "You'll what? You don't want to be with me now?"

MARGIE: "I don't know, Sweet Talk—"

SWEET TALK (INTERRUPTING): "Answer me."

MARGIE: "I don't know, I gotta go."
SWEET TALK: "Dammit, answer me—now!"
MARGIE: "I gotta, I gotta go."

I feel almost like washing my mouth out with soap. I decided to let Sweet Talk speak for himself. I mean, this really happens every day to hundreds of kids all over the country. It's not a myth. There are, this morning, a half dozen girls in the center who have also escaped from this incredible type of slavery.

Margie made this tape—that is, she cooperated with the police in order to get Sweet Talk arrested. Because the word on the street was very simple, and very clear: Sweet Talk was going to kill her. He's in jail now, thanks to the Pimp Squad of the NYPD. I hope he stays there for a long time. It took a lot of courage to do what Margie did. I'm happy to say she's back home now, reconciled with forgiving and loving parents.

Because of you, we are able to be here for Margie and the thousands of other kids—boys and girls, young men and young women— entrapped and enslaved in this vicious industry.

More than anything else, I need your prayers for my kids, my casually heroic staff, and for myself. We also need your continued financial help. I think you now know why we need both so desperately.

I guess, too, I should ask you to pray for Sweet Talk. I don't want to pray for him . . . but I'll try. (I ain't a saint.)

THE MORAL MURDER OF OUR CHILDREN

1982-84

"You can go back out into the street,
I said,
"and you can look sad."

The innkeeper said, "No. I can't help you," he said. "Go away," he
said.
   It was late at night. The inn was very crowded. The young couple
was poor. The husband, frantic with anxiety, insisted and pleaded and
argued desperately. "Look, my wife is going to have a baby any min-
ute. Please, you've got to let us in." Clearly, there were no large tips
forthcoming to inspire the innkeeper's compassion and understanding.
You can't take responsibility for every pilgrim and traveler and
wanderer who knocks on your door, even if the girl is young and tired
and about to have a baby.
   After he turned them away, I wonder if the innkeeper ever gave the
young mother and her husband a second thought. Listen, I know
exactly how that innkeeper felt. Maybe he'd had a bad day. He wasn't
such a bad guy. You just can't assume he was an unfeeling, heartless
wretch and sweep him out of your mind like so much dirt. He must
have had his reasons. And besides, it turned out okay. The young
couple found a cave on a hillside where some shepherds stabled their
animals. The fourteen-year-old girl had her baby there. It turned out
all right.
   Two kids knocked on my *door one night. It was late and I had had*

*a bad day. I didn't want to wake up. I didn't want to answer the door.
I was tired and had gone to bed angry. There were a bunch of kids
bedded down on the living-room floor, and the six bunk beds were
filled. I had been mugged earlier that day and one of my kids stole the
grocery money—and I didn't like any of my kids very much. They
didn't appreciate me and weren't very grateful. . . . Playing the role
of noble martyr to the hilt, I opened the door.*

*Two kids stood there, uncertainly, obviously reading the look on my
face. One of the kids said, "Are you Bruce?" and I said yes. And he
said, "Do you take kids in?" and I said yes. "Can we stay with you?"
he said. And I said, "No, because we have no room." The kid began to
cry. "Where can we go? What can I do?" he said. And I said, "You
can go back out into the street, and you can look sad."*

*The kid stopped crying, and he looked at me. "I can do that," he
said. So he did, or they did. They both went back out into the street.
One boy was fifteen, the other was fourteen. I never saw them again.*

*I can still see their faces, just about as clearly today as I could that
night. I can still see the tears on the boy's face. I can see how the other
kid stood, and the way he looked at me.*

I wonder if the innkeeper kept remembering, too.

No Eternal Flames
for Joey

*"The films in this case represent a form of child abuse
as vile as any known to civilized society."*

"**R**on sent me," he said.

He had this big dumb grin plastered all over his face. "I heard the President mention Covenant House during his talk on TV. I was pretty hungry and I didn't have anyplace to go, so I found out where you were."

Every month more than 250 really great kids come into our Covenant House/Houston program for shelter and sanctuary.

This one kid was really special. He didn't look very special: just an ordinary, run-of-the-mill, nice-looking, gee-whiz kind of kid. He didn't have any special problems either. Nothing different from any of the other thousand boys and girls.

He's important. So are all our kids. The fact that President Reagan pointed them out last month will, I hope, make it impossible for Americans not to understand how needy they are, how good they are, how brave they are . . . and how much they need and deserve our compassion.

Let me tell you about those kids for a moment. Two thirds of them are boys. One quarter are fifteen and younger; another quarter are sixteen and seventeen. Almost all are local kids (most runaway kids never really run very far). Most come from abusive, one-parent, alcoholic families.

There are few mysteries about why these kids leave home. They not only lack any family ties but most lack any significant relationship to any caring adult, to any neighborhood, to any nurturing school system. Still others, who come from warm, loving homes, find themselves unable to cope with the ordinary and not-so-ordinary pressures of growing up.

Most of them are victims of social decay and family disintegration, caught up in a nightmarish struggle for survival before they have had a chance to grow into physical and moral maturity.

Their individual pain, their unique suffering, is only a symptom of a much deeper disorder in our society: the disintegration of families and the moral and ethical environment that traditionally sustained them. While the American family is still an awesomely strong and resilient institution, it has probably never been closer to collapse than it is now. At the very least it is in grave danger.

Over the last decade, the number of married couples with children declined, while the number of single-parent households doubled. The divorce rate has actually tripled since 1960. (Less than a quarter of our kids in Covenant House have been raised in two-parent homes!)

The instability in American family life is clearly evidenced by the mushrooming mobility of American society. Fully 45 percent of Americans changed their residence from 1975 to 1980. The kids at Covenant House once again illustrate the extreme effects of this new trend: Almost two thirds have moved at least once during the past year, and about 25 percent have moved four or more times!

Family life for many Americans has become an erratic, rootless journey from one faceless neighborhood to another. Is it so surprising that many of our children eventually take to the road as well?

When we look deeper, beneath the surface of family life in this country, some really ugly, really frightening facts emerge. From 1977 to 1980 alone the number of reports of child abuse and neglect rose by over 50 percent. (At Covenant House half of our kids have been the victims of repeated physical abuse.)

Nationally, over 25 percent of girls and 10 percent of boys are sexually abused. Over 25 percent of our girls have the courage to tell us that they have been raped.

Powerful economic and cultural forces at work in our society are seriously undermining the strength of the American family. Average income has continued to decline while the federal tax burden on those same families has increased. It is an incredible fact that today a single parent with two children can expect to pay higher taxes than a married couple with no children.

Raising a child is an expensive business. When you are unemployed, as millions of Americans are, it is well nigh impossible. Our government estimates that cost at about two thousand dollars a year per child on even the barest-boned budget. What's more, the cost of raising a child increases constantly as he or she grows. This rise in child-rearing costs is devastating, especially for families subsisting precariously at or below the poverty line.

Government statistics can easily document the accelerating deterioration of the economic underpinnings of the American family. Statistics can never be a fully adequate measure of the appalling and self-evident decline of the quality of life in our society, and of the social moral climate that supported and nurtured family life in the United States.

Ours has become a deeply materialistic, even hedonistic culture, a society of consumers. Certain companies—seemingly with our passive consent—carefully manipulate children to develop their consumer mentality, then cynically turn around to use children in seductive, sexually suggestive ad campaigns to sell products to adults. Surrounded by a culture that regards children more as objects than as developing human beings, it hardly comes as a shock that many parents treat them as objects, too. This dehumanization of children can lead to cultural perversions that are deeply humiliating to those who love the best in America.

Most of our kids here at Covenant House have suffered some form of exploitation on the street. A tragically high percentage of them become the casual merchandise in a massive, well-financed American sex industry. They have become the commodities, the merchandise in our sex-for-sale society, where it has become okay to pay for sex and be paid for it. That moral landscape gives little shelter to values that support and sustain healthy family life.

But let's be fair to American families. If it be true that we as a people are less faithful, less tender to our families than ever before, it is also true that many of these factors are beyond our control.

Whatever their origins, the effects of family disintegration and the destructive and deforming impact of weeks and months of street life on kids are agonizing to review. According to a recent Columbia University study, 82 percent of our kids at Covenant House suffer from extreme emotional depression. At Covenant House one third of the girls and one sixth of the boys have previously attempted suicide. Half of our kids consider suicide as their only option.

For a short-term crisis program like ours, the plight of these children presents an overwhelming burden. In the end we can only claim to succeed with a third—through either family reconciliation, provision of a full range of clinical and medical services, referral to a longer-term program, or helping kids get a start with a job. Of course, we try to do better, we try to do more. But as long as there are still tens upon tens of thousands of these infinitely sad, desolate, and eminently exploitable children on the streets of our towns and cities, we are not doing enough. None of us.

Broken families and homeless children present a searing challenge —the deepest ethical and moral challenge of our generation. Whether we respond to it will depend on the resolve and willingness of all of us to commit ourselves to the care and protection of family life. The time for repairing endangered families and rescuing their children is not after they have fallen apart!

That commitment, solemn and necessary, must begin with the acceptance of one great, if unpleasant, fact: The nature of "family" in our society has changed. We must face the new American family as it is emerging and evolving before our eyes. To leave behind fond reminiscences of days gone by, and to deal honestly and nonjudgmentally with the reality of what we have become: a nation that has adopted new social, cultural, and ethical mores; a nation with millions of latchkey children and one-parent families who demand our attention and support.

A lot of people asked me what it felt like, what it meant to me to be mentioned by the President in the State of the Union Address. I was amazed and delighted. I was really proud that Covenant House was singled out for praise by the President. It was a very special moment for me: To move from the status of maverick, renegade, instigator, and agitator to that of unsung hero was quite a trip—even if the journey did take fifteen years!

It had to be a very special moment, too, for tens of thousands of street kids, even though they didn't know it.

Lent 1983

A fire can only burn so long before it should stop. Eternal flames before the graves of heroes whom the next generation will never know have always seemed, to me, somehow pointless—only God is always. (Even hell was never forever until it began, because sin did.) I don't know very much about sin, and I don't like to admit it in myself. I'm more at ease examining the consequences of sin in somebody else's life.

Joey was killed Friday, a senseless, brutal murder. He was seventeen. The street killed him long before the stabbing knife put a brutal period at the end of the brief somber paragraph that was his life. I knew him pretty well. We liked each other a lot. I don't think Joey was a sinner, but sin killed him.

I think it's going to kill Maryann pretty quickly. She's seventeen, too, and works as a bookkeeper for a large brothel in Los Angeles. She can't really escape and doesn't really know if she wants to. I don't think Maryann is a sinner, but she'll die of it, sooner or later.

Billy is a mule for organized crime. He carries large amounts of drugs for some evil people in New Jersey. He is by turn both brave and cynical about surviving. Right now, today, he's very afraid of dying of that quick mandatory bullet in the back of his head. I don't think Billy is a sinner.

Lester is eighteen and makes porn films in Massachusetts. He absolutely hates himself and the people who made him a "star" in thirty films. We're worried that he may kill himself before the man who has threatened to kill him does so. What he actually hates is the effect of sin in his life, and he thinks that sin is himself. But he's no sinner, and sin is not him.

Neither is Angie, who, thinking it through and putting it all together and getting it all straight in her mind, accepted a job as a stripper in San Francisco for two hundred dollars a night to earn enough money to escape the life so she could marry her boy friend and live happily ever after.

All these kids, except Joey in the morgue, are in Under 21 today. There are also three hundred others. What they have in common is how good they are and how brave they are, and how *passionately* Jesus loves them.

We don't understand that passion any more than we understand sin. We're just not . . . ready . . . for it.

We have been overtaken again by Lent, an event that (would we but wish it so) could transform our lives. But, as so often before, we are not ready. Lent will slip away from us (and these kids) one more time.

We remember that parable—the five foolish virgins who missed the arrival of the bridegroom at the marriage feast because they weren't ready—and we tremble. We hasten to remind the Lord that His apostles weren't ready either, or His friends, or Pilate or Herod or Judas. And we, too, like most of that Passover throng, are unready strangers in Jerusalem. We meant to be ready. We had taken note of our past derelictions (we were not going to fall asleep in the garden again). But we did, and now we must make the best of it.

Sorry, Lord, again. At least I think I'm sorry. I would feel better about it, Lord, if I could feel passionately about my sins, at least a little.

We would almost regret, if we could or dared, that God became so passionately physical about loving us. Or that Jesus could so passionately love us, the passionless. We are not ready to face the passionate question: Are we really worth that much to Him? Can we really mean that much to Him, to Them? What can He really see in us except a vast desire and need to be loved that much?

None of this right now makes much sense to our kids. Joey and Maryann and Billy and Lester and Angie had their own share of personal Good Fridays and precious few Easters. But there will be no eternal flames for them. Only His passionate, enduring love. And in some very clear, simple way, the mystery of their salvation and redemption is inextricably conjoined to our own.

April 1983

Scott Hyman is twenty-six and lives at 66-10 Yellowstone Boulevard in Forest Hills, New York; Clemente D'Alessio is forty and lives at 10 Courtney Drive, Farmingville, New York. This past Monday, Judge Thomas Galligan sent them to jail for two to seven years.

Scott Hyman and Clemente D'Alessio were convicted on forty-three counts of distribution of child pornography. The trial lasted four weeks. It took a whole week for jury selection because so many prospective jurors simply refused to watch the horrifying films. The outraged jury took exactly three and a half hours to reach a verdict.

The nine films in this case involved fourteen children from seven to fourteen years engaging in explicit sexual activity. The children in the films all appeared to be poorly cared for. They were filthy, wore torn, dirty clothing, many had bruises and welts on their bodies. One nine-year-old boy appeared drugged. Another bewildered seven-year-old, two front baby teeth missing, stared vacantly at the camera. The films were supplied by Clemente D'Alessio and sold by Scott Hyman to an undercover police officer. The defendants offered to provide hundreds more. In a conversation with the undercover police officer secretly taped by the NYPD, Hyman claimed it was easier to obtain films of very young children than films of older adolescents because the older children start wanting a share of the profits.

Neither Clemente D'Alessio nor Scott Hyman showed any remorse at all for their vile behavior. D'Alessio laughed and joked during the testimony. During large portions of the trial, he adopted and exhibited an air of total indifference.

The defense attorney for D'Alessio, Marvin Kornberg, was stunned when Manhattan District Attorney Robert Morgenthau, asked for the maximum sentence. Kornberg stated:

"It is almost inconceivable that the D.A. is requesting a *savage* seven-year consecutive sentence for such a minimal transaction. This would be the moral equivalent of asking for a twenty-year sentence for a person selling a stick of marijuana. The request is unconscionable."

D.A. Morgenthau, in his Memorandum to the Court, responded:

In this case, society has every right to voice its moral outrage and indignation at the crimes committed by these two defendants and to demand retribution. . . . Children, many pre-pubescent, who appeared undernourished, wearing dirty, tattered clothing . . . in those films were real, flesh and blood children. They were not actors portraying characters in a screenplay; rather, they were young children between the ages of seven and fourteen who performed explicit sexual acts before the naked eye of the camera, and thus, were immortalized on film and exposed for all time.

The films in this case represent a form of child abuse as vile as any known to civilized society. The fourteen unknown

children represent fourteen lost lives. Their presence can be
neither dismissed nor trivialized by this Court. For it is the
children, the fourteen unknown children, who demand retribution and it is their moral right to present this demand to
this Court.

The defendants traded the lives of the fourteen children
for seventy-five dollars per reel. The life of a child was measured in dollars per reel of film.

Unless individuals who engage in the promotion of child
pornography are made to realize that society will deal
harshly with those who sexually abuse its children, this ab-
horrent motion picture venture will continue. As Scott Hyman
told [Police] Detective Montanino, "If the money's right, you
take the risk."

Judge Galligan gave them two to seven years. It's considered a
harsh sentence in New York.

Neither of these men was a low-level employee. They were rela-
tively important figures in the industry of parnography. Clemente
D'Alessio and Scott Hyman were managers of adult bookstores, sub-
sidiaries of the Show World porn empire. With its major center on
Eighth Avenue and Forty-second Street, and its ties to an organized
crime family in Philadelphia, Show World is the very epitome of the
well-run and well-financed—and enormously profitable—organized-
crime-controlled American sex industry.

As evil, menacing, and corrupting presences in the heart of this
country's largest city, Show World and Show Palace are the first
places—there are dozens of others—seen by homeless, scared runaways when they walk outside New York City's mammoth bus terminal.

"A minimal transaction," says Marvin Kornberg, in defense of his
client. "If the money's right, you take the risk," says Scott Hyman.
Clemente D'Alessio just laughed, and until he went to jail last Monday, continued to manage his porno bookstore.

This case has to be considered a landmark conviction, the first
under the newly upheld New York State child-porn law.

None of the television stations thought it was very important. Not a word was said by CBS, ABC, or NBC or any of the others. The New York *Times,* the *Daily News,* and the New York *Post* ignored the conviction. When Scott Hyman and Clemente D'Alessio were sentenced last week, the *Times* and *Post* and *News* carried minor news stories, the TV networks again didn't bother to mention it.

Fourteen unknown children, little children casually abused and mistreated and defiled so that men like Scott Hyman and Clemente D'Alessio could make money. "When the money's right . . ." says Hyman.

I wonder why the media, both print and electronic, didn't think it was an important story. I wonder why this kind of grotesque child abuse only merits two to seven years. I wonder why the Probation Department recommended only weekends in jail for Scott Hyman.

I wonder when we are going to stop merely wringing our hands about this buying and selling of our children. Children should not be exploited. They should not be bought and sold. And men like Clemente D'Alessio and Scott Hyman should not get away with it.

Are we that indifferent to the moral murder of our children?

"I Hoped You Wouldn't Hurt Me"

"How much do you go for?" I said.
"Eighty dollars," he said,
"but I do everything for that.
I can go for less," he said.

August 1983

The sun came out of the sea off Fort Lauderdale beach and I watched it make a morning begin.

I wasn't exactly crying. It's just that I couldn't stop the tears that kept forming in the corner of my eyes. I couldn't seem to hold them back. Every couple of minutes one would slip loose and start its quick run down my cheeks. I would catch it before it got too far. Nobody was there to see it, but I was still embarrassed.

I had gotten back to my room in the Sand Castle Motel at 4:30 A.M. I was really tired after a long day that began early in the morning in Houston.

The Sand Castle is the motel we would like to purchase for an Under 21 center in Fort Lauderdale, the runaway capital of the United States. Literally thousands of kids come there, hang out, and become part of a street scene that is as bad as any in the country. Many never make it back.

The Sand Castle is a block off the beach and an ideal location for an Under 21 center. A lot of our neighbors—mostly small motel owners and people who live in some nearby condominiums—don't think so. They are violently opposed to locating our program there. Almost everybody without exception likes the idea of a center for homeless kids. It's great work, Father Bruce, but not on *this* block, in *this* neighborhood. . . . We need the program, of course, but not *here.*

It had been a very full day. I had flown direct from our brand-new Houston center to yet another public meeting and series of interviews in Fort Lauderdale. The meeting went well—our supporters were out in force—but it went on for a long time. Afterwards, I came back to the Sand Castle in my dark blue Hertz Mustang. It was about midnight. A Tuesday.

I guess I was too keyed up to sleep, so I decided to check out the Strip, that stretch of beach in Lauderdale beginning around Las Olas on the south to Sunset Boulevard on the north. During spring break, hundreds of thousands of college kids inundate the Strip in Fort Lauderdale. They bring millions of dollars to spend. The beach scene —portrayed in the July issue of *Playboy*—gets pretty wild. Hotels and motels make a lot of money off them. The Holiday Inn on the Strip leases to a bar that sponsors wet T-shirt contests and banana-eating contests. It's definitely not clean, wholesome, family fun.

Over the years, the Strip has developed a national reputation as a "fun" spot for kids. So if you've got to be a runaway and you're cold and hungry and homeless up north, you can always choose to be just hungry and homeless. Anything goes on the Strip. And at least you're not cold anymore. And you can make money.

My blue Mustang was instantly anonymous. So was its balding, fiftyish driver in slacks and T-shirt. Just another john cruising . . .

From midnight to 4:30 A.M. I cruised the Strip—south down to Las Olas, cutting over to Birch Road, driving north to the Sand Castle, and then back down A1A, crisscrossing on each side street, running every block, east to west, inward and then back out to the ocean.

It was a quiet night, but there were still dozens of kids working. Some would just stand provocatively—the hustler's stance. Others would make those minute, secret hand signals. The bolder ones just beckoned or whistled or called. My stopping for red lights gave still other striplings the opportunity to wander over and wonder if I was looking for some action. No thanks, I said.

It was getting on toward 3 A.M., and I was pretty tired and had decided to pack it in. One more trip, I thought. The streets were rapidly emptying and the girls and the boy hustlers stood out now even more obviously.

Heading north, I stopped for a red light on Ocean Boulevard and looked out over the now deserted beach. I didn't see the kid approach my car and was startled when he spoke to me.

"Do you want to give me a ride?" he said.

He was a nice-looking kid, sixteen, maybe seventeen, I thought. Nice eyes, nice hair. A little scared, maybe.

"Sure," I said. The kid opened the door and slid gracefully into the front seat. I took my foot off the brake, and the Mustang moved slowly north up A1A. By now it knew the way.

"Are you a cop?" he said.

"No," I said, and laughed—mostly to put the kid at ease. "Do I look like a cop?" I said.

"You can never tell," he said.

"I guess not," I said. "I'm not. My name is Bruce."

"My name is Dan," he said.

"Where're you from?" I said.

"Minnesota," he said.

"How long have you been in Fort Lauderdale?" I asked and turned off A1A onto Las Olas.

"Three weeks," he said.

"Where are you staying?" I said.

"In a motel," he said, "but I lost my room."

I drove south on Birch Road and made a decision to continue the conversation.

"How are you surviving?" I said. "How are you making it?"

"Hustling," he said.

"Are you hustling now?" I said.

"Yes," he said.

"How much do you go for?" I said.

"Eighty dollars," he said, and hastily added, "but I do everything for that. I can go for less," he said.

And then my eyes began to burn and then they began to glisten and blurred oncoming headlights and I was glad it was dark in the car and he couldn't see the tears forming.

"How old are you?" I asked. It was getting hard for me to talk.

"Eighteen," he said, although there was not much conviction in his voice, as though he didn't really expect me to believe him. (I didn't.)

He was a nice-looking kid. A gentle face.

"How long have you been hustling?" I said.

"I ran away to L.A. when I was fifteen and got into it there," he said. "I've moved around a lot," he said.

The blue Mustang seemed to drive itself up Birch Road, and I pulled it over on a quiet side street a couple of blocks from where the kid jumped into my car.

I turned to face the kid, and I guess he could see the tears in my eyes. He looked at me a little uncertainly.

"Hey," I said, "I enjoyed riding with you. Thanks," I said. I reached into my pocket for a twenty-dollar bill. "This will help you with your motel room," I said.

The kid became very still, his eyes frozen for a moment on nothing I could see. "This is certainly different," he said.

"I know," I said. "Be good to yourself," I said. "Take care of yourself," I said.

The kid hesitated—he didn't want to get out of the car. He opened his mouth to speak and then changed his mind.

I touched him on the shoulder. "Be good to yourself," I said again.

"Thanks," he said. "I hoped you wouldn't hurt me," he said. The boy got out of the car. "Thanks," he said. "Later," he said.

"Later," I said.

I drove back to the Sand Castle. It was almost four-thirty in the morning. I was really tired.

I wasn't crying exactly. I just couldn't stop the tears, so I decided to watch the sun come up.

"I hoped you wouldn't hurt me," he said

September 1983

As I stepped off the elevator, my left knee suddenly buckled beneath me. A two-foot tiny terror had locked my leg in a vise-like grip that would have made any wrestling coach proud. He smiled mischievously and tugged on my trousers. I smiled back. My cry for rescue to Chris, one of our counselors, could scarcely be heard above the laughing and crying babies, banging xylophones, and one very loud toy drum. Little Jesse, my lilliputian captor, was led away, giggling with delight.

Babies? What are babies doing at Covenant House?

Well, you see, many of the children here have children of their own. They come to us with their babies because they have absolutely no place else to go. Young mothers, thrown out of their homes, abandoned by their husbands, have been coming to us for a long time now. In 1981, we decided that they needed a special place of their own, so we set aside a floor for them. That's how our Mother/Child Program (known as "3A" because it's on the third floor of our "A" building) was, er, born. Ever since, 3A has been bulging with kids— from sixteen-, seventeen-, and eighteen-year-old mothers on down to their three-day-old babies.

It's a lot like Bedlam.

I poked my head into the nursery. Babies were everywhere. The only thing I noticed more than the noise was the . . . oh, shall we say aroma of dirty diapers and baby powder.

"Hi, Bruce," said a voice from behind me.

I turned and saw Allison with two-year-old Tommy in tow.

"Hi," I said. "How's it going?"

Allison is sixteen. She's pregnant with her second.

Her mother was a prostitute who spent lots of time getting high, lots of time seeking out the company of some very depraved men— and very little time being a mother to Allison. Through her mother, Allison met thirty- and forty-year-old "boy friends." One of them got her pregnant. She was fourteen. She kept the baby.

Together they were placed in a foster home. But Allison, still yearning for her mother's love and approval, kept running away from her foster home. Once again, her mother introduced her to another "boy friend."

And once again pregnant, Allison arrived as most do—scared, hurting, worried about where to live and whether or not she would be allowed to keep her kids. Things no sixteen-year-old should have to worry about.

"Bruce, Ramona left last night," Allison said. "She moved in with some friends."

Ramona is a sweet, meek kid, mother of six-month-old Hector, a really beautiful baby. Before she wandered in, Ramona had been abandoned by her mother and left to exist with her infant in a squalid apartment with a broken toilet. After three weeks, they fled the bugs and the smell for the relative cleanliness of the streets. In desperate need, scared, almost in shock, Ramona came to us, eighteen and illiterate.

"I have a feeling she'll be back," I said. "She really does want the best for Hector."

There's a lot at stake for the kids on 3A. We look at the mothers and the incredible sadness and pain of their lives. And we look at their innocent babies—and recall all those tired old saws about parents and children . . . the sins of the fathers . . . history repeats itself . . . the apple doesn't fall far from the tree. . . .

These babies don't have to become—*they must not become*—the next victims in an already too long chain. We know their mothers don't want that for them. They are good mothers! They really love their kids, just like you love yours, and they have great dreams for them. We've seen them put their unspeakably ugly childhoods behind and with a little, or a lot of help, blossom into responsible, loving parents.

But first they need to know that they themselves are loved. And they need that practical help, too. Classes in mothering and nutrition. Help in finding adequate housing. Medical care. Guidance in budgeting and housekeeping. Legal help with landlords and battering husbands. Tips on how to find a job, or the skills to get one with vocational training. Family counseling and follow-up when they leave us.

Our young mothers get all these things, as well as the support and comfort of a tremendous staff. They know that these girls are just kids themselves, gingerly walking a tightrope between coping and falling apart.

It's hard for a child to love her own child when her own deposit of love is so shrunken and precarious. So *we* love them a lot. In being loved they learn to love their own children. In many cases, the results are almost miraculous.

Allison is finally beginning to come to terms with her mother's rejection. We hope that her children will never know that same pain. Soon they will be placed together in foster care.

As I left the nursery, I watched a couple of our kids walking toward me down the corridor, pushing strollers that held two of the most peaceful-looking babies I think I've ever seen. I walked over to one young mother.

I didn't have to ask her age. She was no more than seventeen. I didn't have to ask her story. Her eyes told the whole of it. "What's your baby's name?" I asked.

"Aurora," she said.

(Lots of our girls give their babies exotic, wistful, wishful, dreamy names. Somehow that seems to give children a stake in beauty and faraway things that are no part of their mother's lives.)

"Aurora. Beautiful name," I said. "Why did you choose it?"

"I used to work at a day-care center," she said. "One of the other girls, who I really like a lot, had a baby named Aurora. She named her after some town somewhere—in Nebraska, I think."

"Do you like it here?" I asked. "Do you like the staff?"

Her face changed and her forehead relaxed and her eyes got very big and warm all of a sudden. "Oh . . . yes," she said.

The girl standing next to her chimed in her agreement.

"They're real nice," Aurora's mother said. "They remind me of people I met once from California and Colorado. You know, people who are really different and nice, who don't come from around here." She didn't have to explain what she meant.

October 1983

Hello, my friends,

A question I get asked a lot is, "Bruce, how does your staff survive? How do you maintain their morale? Your own, too? When you look at a kid that could be your own kid—that you would *want* to be your own kid—and know that the street is going to kill him?"

I usually try to avoid the honest answer that we can't very well. The hardest thing, the worst thing, is looking at a kid you care a lot about, and his eyes tell you: You know that he knows he's not going to make it.

God is not enough. He's really not. I tell my staff that, when they get overinvested, lose distance and objectivity. God will *not* substitute, I tell them, for their prudence and strength and courage and *detachment.*

I try to explain to my staff what detachment is all about: the prayed-for and learned ability to protect yourself, to let go of everything, most of all your own desire and need to save a particular kid, the need to justify your own existence by helping others. To let go your dependence on your own skills and insight and your need to be successful with a kid.

I try to explain that if your love for a kid and your need to help him cause you a lot of anguish and self-doubt, it's your needs being met, mostly, and not the kid's needs. They don't really understand, my staff, about detachment. That kind of wisdom only comes with too many years of trying and failing and more pain than you ever want to think about.

I tell them that you can only really love someone freely if you're perfectly detached from loving him, that the greatest gift you give someone is not to bind and hold him with your love but to leave him free. Sometimes, even free to die. No strings. My staff doesn't understand that. They understand better when I tell them that it's okay to hurt and it's okay to cry, a little, but not for long.

God is just *not* enough. Grace builds upon and *supports* nature, it doesn't change or substitute for it. So be caring, but careful, I tell my staff. Prudence rules commitment. Distance, objectivity, and ruthless honesty about why you do what you do are always a greater protection and service to kids than self-serving prayers for moral miracles we hope will change them.

And when a kid dies, it wasn't *you* who lost him. Don't blame yourself, or the program, or the world—or God, Who loves him infinitely more than we do. Simply accept it and try, if you can, to forget it.

I tell my staff that if they try very hard, after a while they can grow this little switch in their brain that shuts down the memory banks and disengages the pain so they can go on to the next kid. And the next. Like with these two kids I met yesterday.

"Take it easy, Timmy," I said. "We'll figure something out. It's okay," I said.

"My hands won't stop shaking," he said. "I'm sorry. I'm surprised you put up with me so long," he said. He was a moderately tall, lanky infinitely scruffy kid who really stank bad.

"Can I light that cigarette for you?" I said.

"I'm sorry," he said. "I don't think I can manage it. My hands won't stop shaking. I'm sorry," he said again. "I'm sorry. I guess I do look like hell," he said.

"You smell to high heaven," I said.

"Your staff are real nice," he said. "They keep taking me back," he said.

"They'd better," I said. "We're glad you're here. Stay around," I said. "Don't go away. Where're you from?"

"Ohio," Timmy said. "My mother, she just disappeared, my dad couldn't handle me. I started to drink pretty much when I was fourteen and split when I was fifteen. Been on my own three years."

"The street?" I said.

He bobbed his head up and down. "I'm not pretty anymore. I make party [drinking] money posing for a few pictures. A couple of rich dudes will give me fifty dollars. I deliver porn for them to chicken hawks."

Timmy showed me the contents of his gym bag—a collection of pretty routine child porn. His sad eyes watched me very carefully.

"You know you can't have this stuff here," I said.

"Do you want it?" he said offhandedly, his sad eyes now watchful and calculating.

"No," I said.

"I'm sorry," he said. "I have this heart condition real bad. Your doctors here want me to lay off the parties and stop smoking," he said. "The medication I take for my heart doesn't mix with the booze. Thanks for letting me stay here again. I've got the world's worst hangover . . . but I'm not drinking now. Haven't had a drink all day," he said proudly with a sad crooked grin that made him look sixteen. It was ten o'clock in the morning.

"Your choices are pretty limited," I said. "You're either going to die, go crazy—or give up drinking."

"I know that," he said. He didn't look scared. I guess maybe because he had faced his increasingly bleak future too many times not to recognize the truth in what I said. (It sounds hard when I write it that way, but I said it that way. It's really important to be clear about certain things with kids like Timmy.)

"Let us help you," I said. "We can," I said. "We want to. I know this great program for kids who can't handle their drinking problem. It works; it really does, Timmy."

"I could sure use a shower," he said in reply. "I can smell myself," he said. "I'm sorry to be such a bother."

"You're not," I said. "I'm really glad you're back," I said.

I tried to flip the switch in my head—there was another kid named

Joey that I knew I wasn't going to like very much waiting to see me —but it didn't work too well.

He said he was sorry. I was caring—and careful. But the switch didn't work this time.

It's great theory, Bruce! Right! It's like trying to *tell* a violent toothache to go away at three in the morning. Mind over pain! Right! Why did you cry over that kid in Fort Lauderdale, Bruce? I never said it was easy. And I didn't cry very long. It is *great* theory, and it *does* work, and most of the time, if you don't make it work, you're in real trouble.

It's always the same old story: Practice what you preach, Bruce. And believe, maybe, a little harder, in what you preach. God is not enough, huh? Maybe you should try to understand it better. Does God always have to love and help these kids on *your* terms, Bruce? Maybe you're afraid to get out of the way. Maybe you're not as detached as you thought.

I don't like it when I argue with myself—I wind up losing too often. Look, I said, back to me. I am *not* the truth I teach. I'm just trying to help these kids the best way I know how and to survive doing it. I've seen too many good people go down the tubes trying to help kids like Timmy because they thought God told them to and *they couldn't handle it.* I teach my staff *how* to handle it, not to rush in where there ain't any angels, not to presume. . . . There *are* some devils that are cast out, but only after much prayer and fasting. So, I tell my staff, until you're an accomplished pray-er and fast-er, I'll talk to you about prudence and distance and objectivity and detachment.

I don't know who won that argument.

I wish I understood it better.

Pray for Timmy, and that other kid—Joey. (I *didn't* like him very much.) Pray for me, too. We pray for you every day.

One Pair of Pants

For just a moment the pain was gone from his eyes,
and I understood that innocence destroys pain.

Sometimes God is an abstraction. Sometimes He's not. Sometimes we like God to keep His distance. Sometimes, when we're lonely or scared, we like Him up close.

Sometimes God makes great theory, especially when He is good enough not to get in our way. I mean, sometimes God is good enough to lead us the way *we* want to go.

God is absolutely the best—from our point of view—when He lets us define who He is and what He means to us. But when God gets arms and legs and gets up close and defines Himself as our meaning and purpose and gets into our shape and into our skin and into our clothing, it's a different story.

Babies born in hillside stables to teenage mothers are not an abstraction.

Babies nurse, cry, soil diapers, cry, get hungry, laugh, sleep, get cuddled, soil more diapers, cry, get hungry. . . .

(God does not cry, get hungry, sleep, soil diapers. Don't say dumb things like that!)

Babies are dependent and vulnerable and cute; they grow up to be toddlers and children and gawky, big-footed teenagers, grow beards and breasts and fall in love.

God was never a toddler and certainly not a rambunctious teenager with zits.

I mean, the Father and the Son and the Holy Spirit couldn't really
have had such a crazy idea! Really! God with toenails? And armpits?
And you know what else . . . I mean, really! God is great and all
that and He, I mean They love us a lot, but not that much and not in
that way! Not the way we love each other.

What do you mean, we are what God is? That's crazy! Well, yes,
He did, I mean *They* did create us in Their image and likeness. So I
guess, if He, I mean They, made us like Them, in some sense They
must be like us. Only in some sense, though.

Babies, on hillsides, with stars, a teenage mother and animals . . .
It's a great idea and Christmas trees with balls and tinsel and all. It's
a really *sweet* story. . . . And it reminds us to be nicer to people
and to show that we care more and to give gifts to each other. We
need that. I mean, if we didn't do it at Christmas, when would we do
it?

I really need, sometimes, an excuse to give you a gift. You know,
some kind of ritual, expected time when it's okay to give you a gift.
So you know I care but you don't have to make a big deal about it
and I won't be embarrassed.

Yeah, I know, babies are no big deal, but *God* as a baby—that's a
big deal, to become that much like me. So I can love Him the way I
love you. So that He can love me the way I love you. You've got to be
kidding!

It's just plain undignified! Can't we just say that Jesus was a man
who was godly, even god-like, if you want? Nope? You say the
Church gets really upset when people talk like that, huh?

Well, can't we say that Jesus *was* God all right but that He only
looked like a man? Maybe we just imagined that He had a body, or
maybe He had one made of ectoplasm or some other kind of immate-
rial stuff? Stardust, maybe? The Church still gets upset, right?

C'mon. God with toenails and armpits and you know what else.
Archie Bunker must be twirling in his grave!

You mean the Father and the Son and the Holy Spirit, They just
couldn't stand it up there all by Themselves with a million angels
and wanted to get together with us?

So the Son became who Jesus was, or is, or whatever? Because He
loved us? I mean, They loved us that much? Well yes, I guess it is

easier for me to believe that you love me if you're like me and touch me, and I can touch you.

Is it really *that* simple? The Church says yes, huh?

Why did They do it? I mean, why did one of Them become a man like we are? I know we had problems, but . . . To make us more like Them? That's weird. Well yes, at Christmas we love each other more—it's easier. And They love each other all the time? That's *all* They do? Nothing else?

So if I love you all the time and you love me all the time we're doing what They're doing? We're like Them! That's what being made in Their image and likeness means! If we love each other. Wow!

God with toenails and armpits and . . . He's, I mean *They're* a little bit easier to understand now. It's pretty practical and, er, down to earth now.

Bruce's kids? They're not an abstraction either, and they are certainly down to earth. They're through the damp-diaper stage—much more the pimply, big-footed, rambunctious teenager now. They still cry, and boy, do they get hungry!

Mostly hungry for what you'll give *your* kids a lot of this Christmas. Love, security, hugs, warmth, family rituals, a place in your heart.

If we love them—and give them a chance to love us back—we make them like God. Us, too! Toenails and armpits and all.

January 1984

I saw an innocent kid today. His face wasn't, but I think he was. There was too much pain and longing in his eyes for him, at least at that moment, not to have been innocent.

It got me thinking: Did I want to be innocent again? I'm not really sure. Could I even stand it? What would happen to all my hard and painfully won knowledge—about myself, my kids, the world in general, the healthy ingrained suspicion of my motives? If I became innocent again? Would I lose it all? Would I have to go through it all over again?

This kid had definitely been around the horn. I mean, to use an earlier metaphor, he had definitely "seen the elephant"—and had been trampled. . . . He wouldn't take his eyes off me, but I didn't mind. I mean, I wasn't uncomfortable. Even though he was crying.

I was in one of our centers after being away too long, for a visit, a board of directors and an all-staff meeting—and also to celebrate a pre-Christmas Mass for our staff and kids.

I was surprised at how many kids came to the Mass. I didn't expect so many. Almost fifty. I was surprised at how attentive they were (and how well they sang).

I watched the kid watching me and decided to throw out my prepared sermon—it was directed more to an adult audience, and I knew the kids would not "hear" it. I knew *he* wouldn't.

"Hey," I said, to all the kids, to everybody, but really, only to him. "I'm really glad you're here. I hope you stay around. I missed not coming here for a long time. I never see my kids enough.

"Most people don't know this," I said, "but most of the really important things I've learned about myself I learned from you. It took me a while to understand what," I said.

This kid wouldn't take his eyes off me. His face got stiller and stiller, his eyes more watchful. He was skinny and seventeen.

"In the beginning," I said, "when you kids were crowding into my apartment, I listened to your needs. That's all I could really hear then. It took me a long time to learn to listen to *you*. That's when I began to learn about myself," I said.

"That's when I began to understand how good you are and how brave you are and what a gift God gave me when he gave me you. Thank you," I said, "for being here so we can love you." (I wanted to say "*I* love you" but I chickened out in midsentence.) "That's what Christmas is all about," I said. "That's why God came as Jesus. So we can love God the way I love you. So we can touch him the way I touch you.

"Thank you for changing me," I said. "More than anyone else, when I needed changing, you did it. Thank you for making me grow," I said. "It was really painful, and I didn't want to, but I did. You really changed my life," I said. "I owe you. I really care a lot about you," I said.

It wasn't a sermon really. I just wanted to thank the kids for being my Christmas present.

After Mass was over I moved around to meet the kids. It was really great. I loved being there. It was no accident that we met in the middle of a crowd of kids, but nobody else was there.

"Where are you from?" I said.

"It doesn't matter," he said. "I just came back. I've been here before," he said, "but I've got a drinking problem. . . ."

"I can see it in your face," I said.

"I've tried really hard," he said. "I'm afraid," he said.

He was a skinny seventeen-year-old kid with a shopworn face and haunted eyes and a battered, smashed-out-flat ego. There were no barriers between us. The pain was there, and the fear. He wanted to give them to me, but there was no way I could take them. Our pain is our pain.

The innocence was there, too. I think if you hurt enough and are afraid enough and alone enough, the pain, for a time, pushes back the bad and corrupt part of us, the evil habits, and lets the innocence show through. Maybe pain creates innocence. Maybe pain pushes us back through all the garbage and dirt to the time when we were clean. When we were children. And innocent.

Unless you become as little children you shall not enter the Kingdom of Heaven. Did Jesus mean *that?* Did Jesus mean that our good and evil are measured by love and pain? And that becoming innocent again means reliving the *pain?* I understood better then what purgatory must be like. And I was very afraid.

"Look," I said. "You've got to get it together."

"I know," he said.

"Stay with it," I said. "Let us help you," I said. "Don't go away," I said. "Stay around," I said. "I'm glad you're here," I said.

"I know," he said. And he smiled an innocent smile. And for just a moment the pain was gone from his eyes, and I understood that innocence destroys the pain that restored it.

"See you around," I said.

"Later," he said.

"What's your name?" I said.

"Michael," he said.

Lent 1984

"You were always like a father to me," he said. He was just one of the thirty or more overflow kids we had bedded down on the floor that night.

I didn't know his name. I didn't remember his face.

"Thanks," I said. "I'm glad I was." I said. It was six forty-five on Ash Wednesday morning.

I had just come downstairs from my room on the fifth floor and was passing through the ground floor of our center on my way to morning prayer in our community chapel.

"You really were," he said.

"Thanks," I said.

Another kid noticed my prayer book under my arm. "You've got your Bible," he announced.

"Yes," I said. "Morning prayer begins at seven o'clock."

"You wouldn't catch me praying at seven o'clock," another kid said.

He was one of half a dozen kids standing around in their jockey shorts waiting to iron their pants.

This was a pretty tough bunch of kids. The older ones. The ones who have been on the street too long. The used-up ones. Most don't really expect to make it: their short, final journey already begun.

Every night, when the kids are sleeping, our staff gathers their meager belongings—the inevitable pair of jeans and a shirt—and takes the soiled clothing downstairs to our laundry. When the kids wake up they can put on clean clothes. It's really important that they dress clean.

Every day half a dozen kids insist on lining up to iron their only pair of pants. They wait patiently, standing around in their jockey shorts, or with a towel wrapped around their waist, for their turn at the ironing board.

They want to look good, even if they do have only one pair of pants.

They have a hard time understanding why they are not going to make it, and why their dying has to be so hard.

Jesus' friends, who accompanied Him on His short, final journey to Jerusalem, had a hard time understanding it, too.

Jesus wasn't going to make it either. He was going to be legally murdered in an impossibly painful way, the manner of His dying protracted, ugly, cruel.

Jesus knew that. He was under no illusions. Mercifully, He permitted His friends not to understand.

How can any man—or any kid—get up in the morning one day closer to a certain no tomorrow? How does a man—or a street kid—

face his personal Ash Wednesday, the beginning of that short, final journey? I mean, there are a definite number of days left now. We can count them down, one by one.

You see, it's almost as though by that act of counting, that reckoning, that we can share—if we want to—Jesus' growing isolation from His friends, His deepening loneliness, the anxiety becoming fear turning to terror—and, finally, the unspeakable aloneness: My Father, why have You abandoned Me? (Don't *You* know My name anymore? Don't *You* recognize My face?)

And is it really fair, Jesus, as we count down the days of Your dying, for You to turn to us and say, Unless you take up your cross and follow Me you are not worthy of Me . . . that no disciple is greater than his Master . . . that if I wished to be saved I must take up Your cross . . . ?

Can't I choose? Are You saying I don't have a choice? Do You really mean me, Lord? You were only making symbolic statements, Jesus. Aren't You?

I know You want me to try harder to be good, to be nice, to be kind, to be helpful, to be polite, to be patient—in short, to be a good, upstanding citizen with nice, kind, polite, helpful kids.

A street kid? The used-up ones? With one pair of pants? I wonder if they are maybe closer to You than I am? I mean, there's their aloneness and fear and terror and abandonment. . . . They shared that with You. I never did.

A street kid hoping for a father who won't forget his name and face, who doesn't know how to say prayers but wants to look good in his only pair of pants . . .

Do You love him more than You love me?

I guess if I were You, God, I would.

Thank God, I'm not You, and maybe because You are, You at least won't love me any less.

Please don't love me any less. Maybe if I love these kids the way You do—because You walked the same journey together—I can learn to begin to have the courage to at least follow where You and these kids have been before me.

I know it's supposed to come out all right in the end. Maybe I just believe that and don't know it. Maybe I just hope that and don't believe it.

At the end of the countdown, at the end of Lent, please let me know that it will come out all right for me. That Easter will happen to me, too.

Easter 1984

It was fourteen years ago when I met this nine-year-old kid. That September Sunday morning he was sitting three rows back from the pulpit in a small mountain parish in upstate New York, safely scrunched in between his five sisters—and all of them carefully bookended by a vigilant father and mother.

I was there for the weekend, preaching at all the Masses—nine times—trying to raise money to take care of my kids back in New York. His name was Billy.

His mouth was halfway open and he was listening hard. Some of the things I had to say weren't easy to hear.

Covenant House was just a half dozen ramshackle roach- and rat-infested apartments on the Lower East Side then, about thirty randy street kids living with this perpetually tired priest.

I had more hair then, and my voice hadn't yet darkened to its present soft rasp.

I was broke, as usual, and couldn't pay the rent, and, as usual, couldn't afford the food, couldn't buy the clothes my kids needed. And so I begged.

The mountains framing the little church were absolutely beautiful. An early fall had splashed the ravines and hillsides with color, and the air was crisp and clean. I spoke of my own hot, dirty streets and my own beautiful kids and how good they were.

This little kid never stopped listening. He closed his mouth every now and then to swallow.

I got to know him and his family very well over the years, returning often as to a second home to that village in the mountains and that beautiful family.

I'm going to come down and help you someday, Billy would say to me. When I'm old enough, he said. When my mom and dad will let me, he said. When I finish school, he said. When I finish college, he said. Year after year he said it. Because I loved him very much I wanted to believe him.

In his last year of college he wrote, "I'm coming. Tell me when." I loved him too much to say come, so I didn't answer his letter.

He came anyway, to join our faith community—the exactly one hundred volunteers: teachers, doctors, lawyers, a journalist, retired businessmen, grandmothers, engineers, nurses, recent college graduates, a farmer—who live with me on Eighth Avenue (or in one of our other centers) and help me, full-time, with our kids.

They each promise to commit at least a full year to God and my kids.

In exchange I provide room and board and ten dollars a week (twelve, if they insist; salary is negotiable up to twelve dollars a week). I also provide an opportunity to practice the corporal and spiritual works of mercy: to feed the hungry, to clothe the naked, to shelter the homeless, to comfort my kids.

I ask them to pray together three hours a day and to fast once a week.

I am inordinately proud of them, and I love them very much.

They are the Resurrection happening all over again. Christ alive in them, living through them. Causing grace and goodness and love and life to occur once more in the murdered lives of our kids at Covenant House.

How else can the Resurrection occur in the life of a dying child? If not through love?

"It must have been that God led me down here," said Billy. "I couldn't seem not to come."

He starts tomorrow, working on our third floor, the one we reserve for the hundreds and hundreds of desperate young teenage mothers who will come to us this year. Who will walk in off the streets with their week- and month-old babies they didn't want to abort. They had no place to live, and you can't raise a brand-new baby in a phone booth or a doorway of an abandoned building.

In this enormous country, filled with compassionate people, the wealthiest country in the world, that just shouldn't happen to a brand-new baby.

Billy is a lover. It pours out of him. He would burst wide open if he tried to contain it.

Billy will be a resurrection for these kids with their babies. He will be Easter for them.

He is an Easter for me.

It's almost fifteen years since I saw him in that little mountain church. I had thirty kids then and knew and loved them all, and I was their Easter.

More than fifteen thousand kids will come to Covenant House this year.

I need more Billys. To be resurrections. Please, come.

Write first. *You've got to write first.* Mark the envelope "Faith Community" so it gets right to my desk.

SOMETIMES GOD HAS A KID'S FACE

1984–87

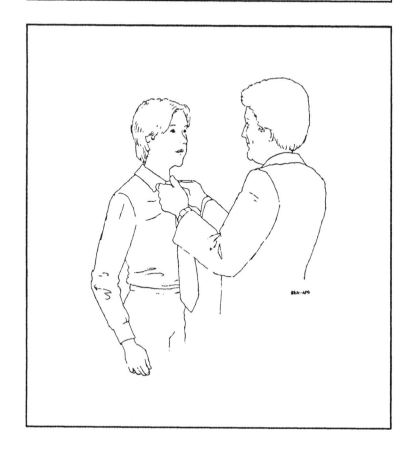

What our kids have in common
is how good they are
and how brave they are.
It's hard not to love them.

It's not the same now, as it once was. Covenant House has changed a whole lot over these past fifteen years.

I mean, fifteen years ago I cooked the meals and changed the beds and did my kids' laundry and cleaned their toilets. I had a thing about clean bathrooms. (I still do.)

I knew them all by name, and since they didn't have any fathers, I was always glad to oblige.

They lived in my apartment on the Lower East Side on East Seventh Street. Our neighbors were junkies and pimps and derelicts and lots of good and very poor families.

It wasn't exactly a garden spot, but there were some great people living in my neighborhood. There was never a dull moment on East Seventh Street.

Now more than a thousand kids a month come into Covenant House, and I don't know any of them very well. I know a little about a lot of them, of course. I don't know any of them as well as I would like.

I'm not complaining. It's just not the same now. It can't be.

One thing is the same, though.

*It's called "open intake." That's a phrase I invented fifteen years
ago because of my anger and frustration at the New York City child-
care system when I couldn't find a single agency that would take ten
homeless, abused, and sexually exploited youngsters who fled a group
of junkies who were pimping them, who fled some pornographers who
defiled them.*

*My first ten kids were either too old or too young. Too sick or not
sick enough. They were from out of state. They were not eligible for
care. They were not, er, "reimbursable," which means nobody would
pay for them.*

*I promised myself that I would never turn a kid away—that if other
agencies closed out kids, Covenant House would always be open to any
kid who came wanting help. I broke this promise once and I bitterly
regret it. I turned two kids away one night. I can still see their
faces. . . .*

*"Open intake" has become the cornerstone, the hallmark, the only
absolute of our program.*

I became disgustingly self-righteous about it.

*Yesterday, more than sixty new kids came to our centers and asked
for help. Not one was refused shelter.*

*It's a condition of employment for our staff that they never turn a
kid away. I won't let them make the same mistake I made.*

*Open intake (twenty-four hours a day, seven days a week, no ques-
tions asked) is brutally hard on my staff.*

*They never know what kind of hurting kids will come through our
doors, or when, or how many.*

*Some are young innocents experiencing their first brush with de-
pravity.*

*Some are cool, wary streets kids who have seen it all and whom,
seemingly, nothing bothers.*

*Still others are running for their lives—victims of the American sex
industry. They are the used-up commodities, the bartered merchandise, the bought-and-sold objects of a commercial traffic in young
lives.*

*Some are burned-out, hopeless drifters before they are eighteen.
Only the Resurrection on the Last Day could restore life to them.*

*Some, many—most—are desperately good kids, wanting to make it,
wanting to survive, wanting to be loved.*

*Whatever they are, whoever they are, they have some fundamental
rights at Covenant House.*

The most important thing is to get in.

*And then to hear, Hey, we are glad you're here. Stay around. Don't
go away. Let us help you; we can.*

*Open intake in Times Square may sound romantic, even sentimen-
tal. It is, in fact, brutally hard, impossibly difficult to achieve. And yet
we do it.*

*Because we really do have a great, hardworking, risk-taking, com-
passionate staff who never count the cost. They are smart, tough-
minded professionals who are really good at letting the kids know they
love them.*

It's not hard.

*You see, what our kids have in common is how good they are and
how brave they are. It's not hard to love them. It's almost impossible
not to.*

If I'm proud about anything, it's open intake.

*Sometimes I get letters telling me what a great person I am for
doing this work. I know they mean well, but the truth is, of course,
that Covenant House owes more to my vices than to my virtues. I wish
I could tell you that my motives were honorable, that I was motivated
by zeal and charity and compassion.*

*But the truth is, my motives were not that noble. I had just been
driven off campus by my students who had told me to practice what I
preached. My assignment from my superiors was to be useful to the
poor. I didn't have the guts to kick these great kids out in the snow, so
I kept them.*

*My motives, for the record, were anger, stubbornness, pride, vanity.
I am a very competitive person. I hate to lose—and I didn't want to
lose a second encounter with a bunch of kids!*

I have to admit that I had also begun to love them.

*That bothered me even more. I knew I was going to get trapped, and
I kept right on walking into the quicksand. I was the moth flying into
the flame, and I knew it.*

*For the record, I am not all those extravagant things people some-
times say about me. I am a very ordinary person who is still arrogant
and stubborn and vain and competitive and given to self-righteous
assessments of other people's faults.*

I think that's why I find it so easy to like my kids. We have lot of faults and vices in common.

And maybe, when I praise and excuse them, maybe I'm hoping God won't be inclined to distinguish one sinner from another. Sometimes, when I'm writing these letters, it gets very personal for me. I want you to understand why I do things. If you really asked me why I do what I do, the answer I would give is that I do what I do for God. I think that's a true answer. I hope it is.

But sometimes God has a kid's face. . . .

"I Ain't a Bad Kid"

*"There's not much about me you'd want to know.
God either."*

How old were you?

How old were you when you learned insight? When you learned what your experience meant? When you really learned—in your heart and in your gut—that choices have consequence?

How old were you when you realized that bad things don't only happen to other people? They can happen to you, too. When you learned about evil?

Kathy learned it before her fifteenth birthday. She almost didn't.

Kathy is tall and quite beautiful and looks much older than any brand-new fifteen-year-old should. Her warm, engaging personality endeared her to just about everybody at Covenant House. Last Friday, when she turned fifteen, a few of my staff brought a birthday cake to her hospital bedside.

She couldn't see the cake very well. Both eyes had been beaten shut, and only one worked a little. Her body was covered with severe welts and cuts and bruises, and most of the skin on her back and chest and legs had been burned off by the scalding water Bonnie had poured on her—to punish Kathy because she couldn't stop screaming after Bonnie and Carol tied her naked to a chair, burned her with cigarettes, and beat her savagely with fists and a studded belt.

The beating and scalding lasted four days. Kathy's torture provided the entertainment for guests at a cocaine party Bonnie threw for her friends. They stood around at this party and laughed.

Kathy is tall for her age, younger than she looks. She ran away from Georgia at fourteen, looking for the excitement and money and designer jeans and beautiful clothes that life in a small town and her solid, hardworking mother couldn't provide. She was no stranger to sexual abuse. As a preteen she had been sexually assaulted by her brother-in-law.

For a while, working the streets, the money was good, the life free. Until one night. Kathy got beaten up by her pimp and ran to Covenant House for help. We immediately returned Kathy to her mother in Georgia. Not for long.

Back home and bored, the bad memories of New York faded quickly. They have a way of doing that for a kid. The memories of the excitement and parties and good times and money and clothes enticed her back to New York.

The moth flew back into the flame.

Her pimp, James, forgave her and put her to work in a brothel on the 200 block of West Fifty-sixth Street, between Broadway and Seventh. A woman named Danielle was the madam. Danielle saw a chance to make a lot of money.

Kathy was forced to work a double shift in the brothel—sixteen hours a day of assembly-line sex, servicing as many as thirty to forty clients a day. Her clients were almost always respectable businessmen.

They didn't want to know that Kathy was only fourteen and three quarters. They just wanted Kathy.

It's okay in our sex-for-sale society to buy a kid thirty to forty times a day in a brothel on the 200 block of West Fifty-sixth Street. All those dozens of respectable business customers—the johns— never attracted any attention, of course.

Kathy escaped the brothel, intending to return to Covenant House and once more seek help. She went to the apartment of Bonnie and Carol—two older prostitutes who had worked the streets with Kathy —to pick up some clothes she had stored there.

Bonnie saw the chance to make some big money. You're gonna work for us now, she said. Kathy refused. Bonnie and Carol attacked Kathy, ripped off her clothing, and tied her naked to a chair. Her four-day ordeal of torture began.

How old were you? When you understood what evil is? When you looked on the face of malevolence? Were you almost fifteen? Was the knowledge burned into your flesh with cigarettes and scalding water? Kathy escaped by chewing through the cords that bound her. Pretending she was unconscious, she waited until Bonnie left the apartment for a pack of cigarettes, quickly dialed 911, grabbed a sheet to cover her nakedness, and fled the apartment. She hid in the stairwell until she heard the sirens of the police ambulance.

Horrified, hospital security guards keep a close watch on Kathy. They keep changing her from room to room so that the friends of James and Bonnie and Carol and Danielle can't get to her. They've tried three times and will probably try again. Nobody wants her to testify. You see, Bonnie and Carol are in jail, indicted by a grand jury on charges of kidnapping and first-degree assault.

Bail for these animals had been set at twenty-five hundred dollars —until Kathy, swathed in bandages from head to foot, was carried into court. The outraged judge, at the urging of the district attorney, raised the bail to ten thousand dollars.

Kathy will be flown home soon by air ambulance. She will need extensive skin grafts and a lifetime of good memories to at least partially erase the horror that will always remain just behind her eyes.

I think Kathy has learned about our adult world. I think she has gained insight. I think she has looked upon the face of evil.

She's paid a terrible price for her knowledge—and I don't think she'll make the same mistake again. But it will *happen* again—to other kids.

You see, we adults have taught millions of kids like Kathy the same kind of lies that deceived and almost destroyed her: that it's okay to be seductive, to be erotic, to be a sex object.

Just watch the jeans commercials. Just watch "Dynasty" and "Dallas" and "General Hospital." Just go see the movies *Police Academy* and the new *Where the Boys Are.*

We've taught millions of kids who grow up to be respectable business types that it's okay to desire children.

They've watched the same commercials and TV shows and films. They've learned that it's okay to pay for sex and to be paid for it. Even when the merchandise offered for sale is a teenager.

The well-patronized and -protected sex industry trumpets the freedom of the American consumer to pick and choose from a veritable smorgasbord of commercially available sex. You name it, you can buy it. Free from guilt, free from acountability.

Things will change when *we* do. Not before.

Pray for us here at Covenant House. It's not easy to deal with the pain of these children—and the anger. I guess I shouldn't have called James and Danielle and Carol and Bonnie animals. I didn't do that to the hundreds of businessmen who patronize that brothel in the 200 block of West Fifty-sixth Street.

It sticks in my craw, and I guess it's a measure of my own lack of compassion and understanding, but I find it hard to ask you to pray for James and Danielle and Bonnie and Carol.

But we'd better. If only because we need forgiveness ourselves.

If I were a better person, more compassionate, I wouldn't find it so hard to say, "Father, forgive them, they know not what they do." I think you'd better pray for me, too. Please. And the businessmen, too, I guess.

Thanks for helping our kids. Because of you, kids like Kathy have a place to run and get help when evil reaches out to destroy them.

Beyond any possible way of saying it, we are grateful to you and for you for loving them. Without you and your constant help, we simply would have to close our doors.

September 1984

"You'll have goose bumps on goose bumps," my friend said as he handed me a ticket for the opening ceremonies of the Los Angeles Olympics.

It was one of those once-in-a-lifetime opportunities. I was out in Los Angeles anyway, speaking before a group of Franciscan superiors about the work of Covenant House, so I gleefully grabbed the ticket.

I had a couple of days before the games began, and had already decided to check out the local street scene once more. Five years ago, on a previous visit, I was exposed for the first time to the malignant evil in the City of Angels that corrupts and destroys thousands of homeless kids on the streets of Hollywood.

It was no better now. Maybe even worse. I drove up and down Santa Monica Boulevard—the most *notorious* meat rack in the country—half a dozen times. It was as I had remembered it. I could have picked up at least fifty kids. They seemed younger, more hopeless than before.

I stopped for a red light on the corner of La Brea and Santa Monica. A kid was sprawled on a bench there, facing the oncoming traffic. His left leg was thrown casually over the back of the bench, the other stretched straight out along the seat. His right thumb pointed somewhere in the direction of the Pacific Ocean, in the Hollywood hitchhiker's gesture. It meant he was available.

He seemed to be about sixteen. An average, everyday kind of kid. A nice kid.

The light took a long time. We looked at each other. I didn't say anything. He didn't either.

The light turned green, and I took my foot off the brake and my eyes off the boy.

"I ain't a bad kid," he said suddenly, softly.

The car was already moving, and I was afraid to look back—the traffic was very heavy. I didn't stop. There was not much I could have said to him. At that time of night—it was about one o'clock in the morning—there was no place I could have taken him.

I wondered what he saw in my face. Did he see the dismay and sadness and misunderstand? Did he think I was condemning him for trying to pick me up? Or maybe something else? Did he see concern? Did he suspect that I cared? Did he know that I liked him?

I thought about driving around the block and trying to talk to the kid, but I didn't.

Los Angeles has *thousands* of kids like that. I mean thousands. There is really no place for them to go where they can get the kind of very special help they need. (According to a recent article in *USA Today,* there are only fifty beds available in the entire area, and most of these are not set up to help girls and boys like these.)

Dionne Warwick sang a song about Hollywood and lost kids like that: "All the stars that never were, are parking cars and pumping gas." And displaying their wares on the Santa Monica meat rack.

I went to bed that night depressed and angry.

My dark mood was quickly dispelled the next day, Saturday. The weather for the opening ceremonies was flawless. Anxious to avoid the expected traffic jams, I arrived early at the Los Angeles Coli-

seum. For the next hour I watched enthralled, as tens of thousands
of people quickly filled almost one hundred thousand seats.

I couldn't get that kid out of my mind! Despite the magnificent
pageantry. I wished, too late, that I had stopped and at least talked
to him. I wished I hadn't blown the chance to tell him I thought he
was a good kid.

The final event, the Parade of the Athletes, was absolutely inspir-
ing as the best and finest, the most disciplined and superbly condi-
tioned and gifted young people in the world marched into the sta-
dium. The welcoming ovation for the American athletes was mind-
blowing: "USA! USA! USA!"—the chant was *thunderous*.

I had this big lump in my throat. I mean, here I am, almost fifty-
eight—I've been around the horn a few times—and I had this big
patriotic red-white-and-blue lump in my throat!

I will never forget those three glorious hours in the L.A. Coliseum.
The best and finest young people in the world, from every nation in
the world. And just a few miles away, a young kid hanging out on a
street-corner bench . . .

I don't think I will ever forget the face of that kid. It's tucked
away in an unquiet corner of my mind that I reserve for sad, unfin-
ished memories.

I wish I could have helped him. No, that's a cop-out. I wish I *had*
helped him. I hope he knew I thought he was a good kid. I hope
that's what he saw in my face.

I would really love the opportunity to open a Covenant House for
kids like him in Los Angeles.

I'm writing this letter back at my desk in New York. The Olympics are winding down, and I keep glancing up from this page to
watch the last thrilling moments of the men's marathon.

Thank God, we'll soon be able to help the kids on the Fort Lauderdale Strip—we're scheduled to open in December—and our architects are working on a beautiful new Covenant House in New
Orleans. The kids will love it. I try to make each new center for our
kids more beautiful than any of the others. For the kids' sake.

Last year almost eighteen thousand kids came into all of our residences. Next year close to twenty-five thousand will come.

We really do need your prayers. Me, my staff, my kids. Pray,
mostly, please for that kid sprawled on a bench along Santa Monica
Boulevard.

He will never be counted among the best and bravest and finest. . . .

October 1984

I had seen this kid around the center a few times. We had nodded
at each other, said hello. He was easy to remember. Dark, quiet eyes,
quiet face—no longer a boy's face. Too watchful. Too careful.
Each time we had passed in the corridors or in the lounge he
would look at me intently, longer than necessary, as though he
wanted me to know something about him. Or maybe, it was the
other way around.

I saw him again—the second time that day—outside our center,
where a documentary was being filmed about street kids and Covenant House.

"I'm Rick," he said. "I volunteered to be one of the technical
consultants for the documentary."

"Oh?" I said.

"Yeah," he said. "The director didn't really know how the street
works, or how the kids really are."

"Not many people do," I said.

"*I* do," he said.

"You've been around?" I said. It was more a statement of fact than
a question, but he answered anyway.

"I've been in San Francisco and Los Angeles and New Orleans
and Fort Lauderdale. In Houston, too. I looked for you when I was
in L.A.," he said, "but you weren't there."

"I know," I said. "We don't have a Covenant House there."

"So then I ended up at your center," he said.

"I'm glad you did," I said. "I'm really glad you're here."

"Thanks," he said. "Thanks for starting Covenant House."

"Thank *God,*" I said.

"No," he said. "Thank *you.*"

"Don't you believe in God?" I said.

Rick shrugged slightly. "Why should I?" he said. "God *never* did
anything for me." He paused for a moment and gave me another one
of those curious, intent looks. "It's been pretty bad for me, Bruce.
I'm a drifter—four years." He spaced out the words slowly, with a
quiet exactitude that tore my heart. "Have been since I was fourteen.

There's not much about me you would want to know. God either."
He gave a grim little hurting smile.

"You're *here,*" I said, "and that's enough. We don't have to start anywhere else. I think God sent you here."

"No he didn't," Rick said. "I needed a place to stay. That's all. A john dropped me off. Not God. Why should God care about what happens to me?" he said suddenly. "Why should I care about God?"

"Did you ever fall in love with somebody?" I said. "Really in love?"

He nodded slightly.

"Did they ever ask you why you loved them? Did you have a reason? Did you need a reason?"

"No," he said.

"Neither does God," I said. "He doesn't need to have you love him back."

"That's good," he said, "because I don't."

"Your big scene is coming up, Bruce. You know, the one where you talk about those six kids who knocked on your door after they made the porno film. The ones who started Covenant House."

"I'm no actor," I said. "I hate this part of it. How can I act the part of being me? Besides, the director wants me to look old and haggard and worn out after worrying about my kids for fifteen years. I'd rather look young and skinny and handsome," I said.

"Like Robert Redford?" he said. And we grinned at each other.

"You'll do just great," he said. And then he gave me a rib-crunching hug. I hugged him back.

"Thanks," he said.

"Thank God," I said.

"No," he said. "Thank you."

"Maybe thank God?" I said.

"Maybe," he said. "It's easier to trust you, Bruce. You're here. I never saw God and I never will."

"Don't be so sure," I said. "You will," I said. "If *I* will you will," I said.

At the end, the reporter asked me why I do what I do. "I do what I do because of God," I answered. "And sometimes God has a kid's face."

It wasn't hard to play that scene. I just kept thinking of God and seeing Rick's face.

Not Ready
for God Yet

He will surely die.
Barring several massive convergent miracles
that won't happen,
Jeff will surely stop breathing soon.

January 1985

I wish I could get bored. For just one day. I would love to get bored, with nothing more exciting to do than watch grass grow. There would be no phones around, of course. So my 3 A.M. friend couldn't call. She never calls before then, and she is always drunk out of her mind—and crying—when she does. She doesn't understand anything I say, and when I tell her that I've got to get some sleep and would she please call back in the morning—sober—my 3 A.M. friend goes bonkers and screams and yells until I simply have to hang up. I've never met her, of course, and I don't know her name.

If there were no phones around I wouldn't have answered that excited voice out of my past with "Is that really you, Shirley? After fourteen years?"

"Yes," she yelled, "and it's good to talk to you, too, Bruce, but I've got this nice little girl over here and her pimp says he's going to kill her if she goes back to her two kids in Connecticut and I can't keep her here anymore because I have nine of my own. . . ."

"Bring her over, Shirl," I said.

"Thanks, Bruce, I will. How're you doing? They shot my husband four years ago. Real nice talking to you, Bruce."

But then again, if Mr. A. G. Bell hadn't invented the phone I wouldn't have picked it up today to hear that beloved soft, uncertain voice that pulled me back instantly into a relationship so profound, so much deeper than words or feelings that it defies description.

"Brian," I fairly yelled. "Where are you? How are you? What are you doing? It's been five years! Tell me, how are you?"

"I'm doing great, Bruce. My wife is great. I got a great job selling software. Let's have dinner."

"Sure," I said. "The first night I'm free, Brian, is twenty-three days from now."

"Great," he said, and I said good-bye to a boy who I had made stop dying because I wouldn't let him, because I willed my life and breath and blood into him. And it didn't matter that we hadn't spoken in five years. There is no time between us.

I wouldn't have heard the phone ring today if it hadn't rung. If Jeff hadn't called. "Bruce, remember me? The first kid to ever come into your Eighth Avenue Center? I was sixteen. I'm twenty-four, I need a job, and I been sleeping around, and, good ol' Bruce, you never ask any questions, we understand each other, okay? And, Bruce?" The husky, raspy voice, the uneven breathing, faded to an uncertain silence.

This is crazy, I said to myself. Is today another kind of nutty time warp? How can a phone wire transmit total awareness? What is that mysterious power that pours pain like water out of a pitcher into the mouthpiece of a pay phone on Forty-second Street, and makes it come out a bloody truth into the side of my head?

"Sure, Jeff, I remember. You really were the first kid. We sure did like each other, Jeff. C'mon over. Let's talk. C'mon over, Jeff."

I hung up. (There's not much else you can do with a phone except throw it against the wall.) I mean, I broke the connection.

He will surely die. Barring several massive convergent miracles that won't happen, Jeff will surely stop breathing soon. It's hard not to think that he won't mind. Maybe Jeff was just saying good-bye before the final one?

If I didn't have a phone it would be a lot easier. For just that one day . . .

If I were God I'd go bonkers. At least *I* can hang up.

God can't ever break the connection. Pain always comes out truth in God's head, forever and ever. God can never hang up—on a babbling drunk, on a dying kid living on bits and pieces of hope because he's afraid to just let go. . . .

If I didn't have a memory, it would be easier to get bored—after I didn't have a phone.

April 1985

"No girls, Bruce. There can't be any girls!" The kid was deadly serious. He was an almost-eighteen-year-old kid, one of ten sitting around my office. They were painfully alert. A studied nonchalance was their disguise.

Taken altogether they were a mean-looking bunch of street kids.

My other guests were three prominent businessmen whom I had invited to meet some of my kids and to discuss the possibility of a new job-training program.

"Girls would wreck the program, Bruce. We couldn't concentrate." The other kids laughed. "Put them in another building, Bruce."

We're only able to help about one third of our kids make it back off the street. We lose the rest. They start from too far back, many already damaged by what happens to a kid on the street.

The kids in my office were in the last two thirds. They knew it. I think that explained their curiously watchful intensity.

They weren't anything special. You see, I had sent word to my staff that any seventeen-, eighteen-, or nineteen-year-old kids who wanted to talk to me and some of my friends about their future could come to my office. This raggle-taggle, bobtailed bunch of mavericks showed up. I didn't know any of them.

What they needed, of course, more than anything else in the world, was a place to live for twelve to eighteen months until they could graduate from a first-class job-training program with a marketable skill, a job—and a chance to get married and have kids, and even to pay taxes!

(Their other options are too painful to think about: a mind-warping loneliness, the endless tiny swallows of daily terror, the habitual Forty-second Street diet, and, almost certainly, either prison or an early death—or worse, a slow, dragged-out one.)

So they watched me. Their hard, careful eyes rarely leaving my face.

"I can give you a place to live," I said, "for a year, even longer.
And the job training. But I have to know a few things. Can you
handle it? Really? Do you want to, really?" The kids knew what I
meant. I didn't have to spell it out.

"Try me," one kid said. "I need it, Bruce. I can go downstairs and
find ten more kids like me who need it, too."

"And each of us could find ten more," another kid said.

"Bruce, I'd do anything, Bruce. . . ."

"Could you let me inside your head?" I said. "Would you let me
inside your head and walk around there? Would you let me tell you
how to walk and talk and act? Could you accept discipline and structure from me?"

"We could do that," a kid said. He had an old-young face. The
intelligence burst out at me. (I have a weakness for really smart
kids.) You could tell he was still a boy, but you knew what he would
look like at thirty.

"The counselors here say I have an alcohol problem, Bruce, but I
could handle that if I had a chance. I mean, if I had a reason to."

And, quite suddenly, his face didn't care anymore that it stood
naked in its pain and loneliness before me. . . . He wanted me to
see.

I spoke directly to him. "Where do you want to live?" I said. "You
can either live in an inexpensive hotel nearby—I can get you a room
—and go to classes every day. You'd be pretty much on your own,
though," I said. "Or you can live here, on the fourth floor. I could
give you and twenty-five other kids the fourth floor. But there would
be plenty of structure, a curfew—and I'd be inside your head. All the
time," I said.

"I wouldn't make it in the hotel, Bruce. I wish I could say I could.
I can't make it on my own, Bruce." He didn't care that the other
kids were listening.

"None of us can, Bruce," another kid said. "We know that—we
won't mind the rules. We know we need them."

We talked for almost two hours, the kids and I. My three friends,
the businessmen who wanted to help, just listened and didn't say
much.

After a while it got a little scary, and I had to be careful.

I mean, one by one the kids began to understand what was happening. It didn't start out that way, but it became clear what was

really happening. They had been afraid to hope, and now they were
beginning to. They hadn't wanted to. They didn't want to, but they
couldn't help it.

(You can't play around with hope. You can't play games with
hope. It's a live grenade in the heart of a street kid.)

I got this stupid lump in my throat that wouldn't go away, and my
eyes began to sting and only long practice at being functional and
long grinding down hard on my teeth saved me.

I almost lost it again when the words from a haunting song by a
group called Foreigner drifted up to the top of my mind and flicked
across the back of my eyes:

> "I want to know what love is.
> I want you to show me.
> I want to feel where love is.
> I know you can show me."

The kid with the old-young face, the ravaged face, looked at me.
"Keep me in mind if you start this program, Bruce. I'll let you in my
mind," he said. I wanted to say that I was already there, but I think
he knew that and I was embarrassed. . . .

The meeting ended at that point. I didn't make any effort to hide
what I felt. They didn't either.

One by one as they left, the kids reached out to shake my hand,
but it was really just so we could touch each other.

The three businessmen and and I looked at each other. "That was
very moving," one of them said finally.

"Yes," I said.

This conversation took place a little over a week ago. At first I
didn't want to write about it, or even talk about it. It was very
personal, and there was something very special about it. I learned all
over again, for the thousandth time, how good these kids are and
how easy it is to love them.

I need your help. I really do. It will take a lot of money to do this
program and we're already hurting financially, but I do have to do it.
(There are ten more like me, Bruce, and each of us can find ten
more. . . .)

It seems like I'm always asking you for money, and I guess I am.
I'm a rotten beggar and I really hate it even though St. Francis told

us friars that we should never be ashamed to beg. In fact, he said we had to.

But he said we could only beg for the love of God, and for the poor.

P.S. You know if this program is really going to work, our kids are going to need jobs that will let them grow, learn, and develop. Jobs with a future. They've run into far too many dead ends already. If you are able to offer my kids some entry-level kinds of jobs, I'd really like to hear from you.

June 1985

"If you're going to make it, Tony, you'll need a mentor. I'd like to be that for you," I said.

"What's a mentor, Bruce?" The kid in my office twisted uneasily in his chair, crossing and uncrossing his Adidas. He had big hands and feet—the rest of him hadn't caught up yet. His eyes were very dark and very guarded.

"It's like being a teacher, Tony," I said, "but like being more of a friend than a teacher, an adult friend."

"I'll never let you be my friend, Bruce," the boy said quickly. "You can be my father or mother, you can be my brother, my uncle but never my friend. You get over on friends, Bruce, you con them."

He was very emphatic, even vehement, about it. Trusting people was not Tony's style. Not much happens on the street that makes you want to trust anybody. You just get hurt that way; people will get over every time. Friends are just dudes on the street who haven't hurt you yet.

The kid had a lot of fire in him. I liked that. It's the quiet, passive ones, the kids who have already given up, who are the most difficult to reach. The street squeezes all the juice out of a kid. The best way to handle the pain, the despair, the knowing how it's all going to end, is not to care anymore, not to let it get to you.

The "best" way to handle the street is with a bottle of beer or cheap wine in your hand and a pocketful of 'ludes or big reds. The "best" way to handle the loneliness and the fear is some grass with some friends.

So they get over on you. You get over on them. Nobody trusts nobody. . . .

The kids with the fire still in them, the kids still capable of passion and caring, the kids still capable of anger and hate—these are the ones who can make it back. If you can turn the anger and hate around, back into positive energy.

Without a mentor, somebody who can kick around inside a kid's head, talk to him about his attitudes, about why he does what he does, about how important it is to meet other people halfway . . . a kid won't make it.

(Only God can help the burned-out, used-up kids. And after a year on the street there aren't any other kind. What He usually does is help them die.)

How can you teach a kid to trust again, to take a chance on another person, to believe in another person? Especially when he can't trust himself or believe in himself anymore?

You love him. And if you really do that, and if you don't stop—and you survive his testing, and if you do love him—then a kid can begin to believe that he really is okay, really good, really worth it, because nobody would love a piece of garbage.

"Tony," I said, "I can't be your father or mother. I don't want to be your sister or brother or uncle. I want to be your friend, and I won't get over on you. Trust me," I said. "At least begin to believe that you want to," I said.

"Let me teach you about passion," I said, "and about compromise. Let me teach you about good anger and good hate and how to conform," I said.

"I don't know what you're talking about," he said.

"I know," I said. "But you really do," I said. "It's just that you haven't put the words together in your head yet. That's what a mentor is for," I said. "And to be a friend."

"Why is it so important for you to be my friend?" he said.

"Because I can't be anything else," I said. "If I can't be your friend, I can't be anybody who you can care about."

"Oh," he said. "I understand," he said. "I understand," he said again. He smiled at me and relaxed totally, slouching down so far in his chair that he hung his head on the back of it.

"That's lesson number one in trust," I said.

"I know," he said.

I didn't talk to Tony about God. Tony is not ready for God yet. A mentor has to be up close and personal. God's not there yet. God can be his mentor after I get Tony ready.

Before He Got Mad, God Would Laugh

"It's harder to hear that you have to love them,"
the cameraman said.
"I'd rather feel guilty or afraid."

August 1985

"Look at me and not at the camera," she said. There was a grim undercurrent to her voice, although she smiled as she spoke.

"I'm having a really tough time putting this documentary together," she said. "A dreadful time! My boss likes the idea of a show on throwaway kids, but he says nobody will watch it."

"That's the name of the game," I said. "Rating points. You can't put a show on throwaway kids up against the sex and violence of 'Dallas' or 'Dynasty' or 'Miami Vice' and expect people to tune in."

"It's more than that," she said forlornly. "My producer says that nobody likes these kids. They don't care about them. He says I need some hard data, like how many kids are there on the street and how much tax money this country would save if we helped these kids."

"You mean how much in taxes these kids would pay if they had jobs and a place to live?" I asked. "You mean how much wouldn't we have to spend on our prisons and mental hospitals and our police departments and our court systems, if these kids weren't on the street hustling and committing crimes?" I said.

"Yes," she said eagerly, hope flaring in her voice and eyes.

"I don't have very much hard data," I said. "That kind of information is almost impossible to come by.

"I can tell you that over twenty thousand of these kids come into residence at Covenant House alone, each year, every year. To speak of hundreds of thousands of runaway and throwaway kids on the streets around this country would not be an exaggeration.

"I can't tell you how many crimes are not committed in Fort Lauderdale because these kids are with us, off the streets and safe. I can't tell you how many millions of dollars are saved or how many thousands of hours of police work, or how many hundreds of jail cells go unfilled.

"It's hard to prove that something didn't happen," I said. "But we make a difference in the lives of thousands of kids."

Her face fell, and the hope died away in her eyes. She was young and eager and wanted to make this a really important documentary.

"My producer tells me that I have to motivate people to watch this show," she said. "He thinks I should make people afraid of these kids. Maybe people will help if they are afraid."

"Don't do that," I said.

"Maybe I could use the guilt approach," she said. "You know: We all have so much and they have so little and we're to blame that they turned out the way they did. . . ."

"Don't do that," I said.

"What can I do, then?" she said. There was a note of desperation in her voice. "If I can't talk about how much money will be saved if we help these kids, or if people are not afraid of them, or don't feel guilty . . . Why should anybody help?"

"Because they love them," I said.

"Nobody loves them," she said angrily. "I can't find anybody who loves them. My producer says to make people feel angry or guilty or afraid. That's the best way to get their attention."

"Don't tell the people who help my kids that," I said. "Don't tell the people on my mailing list that," I said. "They help my kids because they care about them, because they love them."

She looked at me in real disbelief, and then her face cleared a little. "That's what the cop said who sent me over here to talk to you," she said. "He said that Covenant House works because the people here really care about the kids."

"Not just my staff," I said. "Almost everybody does. Believe it," I said.

She didn't even try to hide her skepticism. "Why should I?" she said. "Why should anybody?" she said. "We have our lives, our families, our careers a million miles away from these street kids."

"Because they're good kids," I said. "What my kids have in common is how good they are and how brave they are—and their homelessness, and their despair, and their pain, and their loneliness. They have their tears in common," I said.

"And that God loves them. More than us, I think.

"What they also have in common is how many people really love them and are trying to help them."

She looked really exasperated. "What can you do for them? I can only give you ninety seconds at the most on my program. Can you give me four points, bing, bing, bing, bing, that will give me answers? My producer says I need concrete answers or nobody will be interested. He says that people always want simple answers."

"In ninety seconds?" I said. I laughed. I couldn't help it. By this time I was bouncing up and down in my chair. I was getting pretty excited, and the cameraman had a hard time keeping me in focus.

"That's a dumb question," I said. "Pardon me for saying that. I don't mean to be offensive, but that's a really dumb question.

"There are hundreds of thousands of kids on the streets being bought and sold and abused and killed and flushed away in our social sewers because millions of families are breaking apart . . . because millions of American families are undergoing a kind of moral and physical disintegration for a dozen complex reasons.

"There are no simple answers, but there are answers. The answers have a lot to do with human dignity and poverty and our inability to think about sex and love and marriage and children within a context that is sacred and holy.

"The answers have a lot to do with a society that has become so materialistic and hedonistic that it frequently values property over people."

The tape came to an abrupt end, and the cameraman interrupted our discussion. "I'll have to put in a new tape," he said.

"I think I've got enough," she said. "I hope the producer likes it."

"I hope so, too," I said. "We help thousands and thousands of kids make it back to useful, productive lives each year. I wish I could say that all of my kids make it . . . but they don't," I said.

"What happens to your kids if you can't help them?" she said.

"They die," I said. "Quite young. Or they're killed. Or they go to jail. We can identify over a thousand kids that Covenant House couldn't help who are now somewhere in the New York State prison system."

"Why do they go to jail?" she said.

"What else can you do?" I said. "When you're too old to make it on the street? When you can't find a job and a place to live? After you grow a beard and nobody will buy you? What else can you do except steal and deal drugs and snatch chains and mug somebody? What else can you do?"

"You should have said that on camera," the cameraman said. "You should have said that on camera."

"It's strong medicine," I said. "It's hard to hear," I said.

"It's harder to hear that you have to love them," the cameraman said. "I'd rather feel guilty or afraid."

"I know," I said. "Look. Nobody should help my kids if they don't love them. There isn't any other good reason to help them."

"Is that why people send you money for your kids?" she said.

"Yes," I said, "but it's getting harder and harder for us to make it financially. There are thousands of good causes that need help. My kids are only one of them," I said. "If people love my kids they've got to love other kids, too."

"I'll pray for your kids," she said.

"Pray for all of them," I said.

"I will," she said.

"Pray for me, too," I said.

"I will," she said.

August 1985

I really envy people whom God talks to all the time. Who seem to get these direct messages from God telling them what to do with their lives.

Me? I never got any messages like that myself, and I'm a little embarrassed about it. Sometimes people seem to think that because I'm a priest I must have lunch with God every day.

God does do some pretty weird things in my life, though. I mean, God pushes me around a lot—making some choices so inevitable, so necessary, so unavoidable that I figure it's got to be God.

Take, for example, those two kids I met in Guatemala. . . .

I had absolutely no intention of ever opening a home for kids in Guatemala. I didn't want to either. You might say that God seduced me into it.

Back in the summer of 1980, I was invited to talk about my kids at an International Conference on the Family being held in Guatemala City. The speaker who preceded me was none other than Mother Teresa of Calcutta. She held this huge audience in rapt silence for over an hour and left most of us in tears. This tiny little woman is a giant among men!

And then I got up to speak. Can you imagine following Mother Teresa? I felt like Mortimer Snerd! It was a ghastly experience.

So I was a little surprised when, after my talk, people from a dozen Latin American countries came up to me and talked, with great feeling, about their own street kids—and asked me to open a Covenant House in their countries: Bolivia, Costa Rica, Colombia, Venezuela, Mexico, Honduras, and Guatemala.

Not a chance, I said. I'm on my way to Rio de Janeiro tomorrow to visit my Franciscan friars there, and then back to my kids in New York.

God must have laughed out loud.

Tomorrow came, of course, and with it also came the 446th revolution in Peru. Really! Naturally they closed the airport in Lima, and naturally they canceled my Pan Am flight to Rio, which, naturally, connected through Lima.

I was stuck in Guatemala for an extra day. So that night, having nothing special to do, I wandered around Guatemala City. It was close to midnight. And . . . I stepped over a couple of kids sleeping under a pile of newspapers. They were about six and seven. Cute kids. Nice kids. Gorgeous kids.

No fair, I said to God. (Even though he doesn't talk to me, I talk to him a lot.) No fair. You don't have to hit me over the head, I said. You played this game on me once before in New York when those first six kids knocked on my door and you knew I wouldn't have the guts to kick them out in the snow!

So I started looking for a home for these kids. What else could I do? And I found the most perfect spot in the most beautiful place at the foot of this fantastic (now defunct) volcano, and I bought it— with some help from my friends—for those kids who would soon be my kids. It was called the Inn of the Flowers. What a great name!

The Inn of the Flowers is now filled with the most beautiful, the most gorgeous, the most lovable children in the world. I mean it—230 boys and girls ranging from five to fourteen.

About half of them are war orphans. The conflict in Guatemala is bitter and savage. Tens of thousands of children have been orphaned or made homeless. Some of our five- and six-year-olds come in with bullet wounds and burns. Others are found wandering around in the jungles.

The other half of our kids in Guatemala are victims of another kind of disaster: the most dire poverty I've ever seen. Hundreds of thousands of people live in wretched slums that ring modern Guatemala City.

Their poverty is so great that when the sixth child comes along the mother will simply tell the oldest child—a six- or seven-year-old, Look, I'm sorry. I love you. I can't feed you anymore. You've got to leave.

And they do: to live on the street, begging, stealing to survive, diseased and dying young.

I had stepped over two of them that night. . . .

We have an absolutely great program for them now, and a great school, and pigs and chickens and rabbits and sheep and goats and orange trees and a soccer field and basketball courts, and a staff that loves them to death. It's a long-term program: The kids will stay with us until they grow up and finish school.

I just came back from Guatemala last night. Before I left I collected at least a thousand hugs. You wouldn't believe how beautiful these kids are.

My kids in New York and Houston and Toronto and Fort Lauderdale are really great and beautiful, too. I mean, really! Some people believe that I should worry most about our kids here in the United States. I can understand that. And in fact, we will, because of your help, care for about twenty thousand kids in the States this year.

But if you could see these 230 kids in Guatemala. . . . If you had stepped over those two kids under a pile of newspapers, late at night, what would you have done?

October 1985
Driving back into New York City from Newark Airport late last
Sunday I punched on my car radio, pushing randomly at the but-
tons. I was looking for a few soothing ballads to while away the end
of a long day.
What I got was FM 97 WYNY and Dr. Ruth Westheimer holding
forth on her weekly NBC radio show, "Sexually Speaking." The
high-pitched nervous laugh was instantly recognizable.
I listened in fascinated horror while she delightedly praised Pete, a
seventeen-year-old boy because he could bring his girl friend to multiple orgasms.
"You're so lucky to have such a girl friend," she chortled to this
seventeen-year-old kid. (He had a nice clean-cut voice.) "Don't share
her with anybody," she advised.
Pete was overjoyed. (His voice had an appealing golly-gee-whiz
quality.) "You're really great, Dr. Ruth, but I need some more ad-
vice," the young voice said. "I think I have multiple orgasms, too,
when my girl friend performs oral sex on me," he said. "Is that
possible?"
Dr. Ruth's voice positively beamed with pleasure. I mean, she was
ecstatic. "Of course," she said, but added a cautionary note. "As you
get older you won't be able to have as many orgasms as you do now!"
In her final benediction to this young Lothario, Dr. Ruth urged
him to wear a T-shirt saying, "I'm the greatest lover in Washington,
D.C."
Now, maybe you think I should have turned off Dr. Ruth,
splashed some holy water on the car radio, and pulled out my rosary.
I did no such thing. I listened unbelievingly through a short station
break to find out what she would say to the next caller.
He turned out to be—his description—a respected, happily mar-
ried man of some prominence in the community. He loved his wife.
She loved him. They had nice kids.
There was only one small problem: His wife wanted him to watch
her having sex with another woman. It would liven up their marriage.
Dr. Ruth was wary. Dr. Ruth felt that he might be sexually attracted to this other woman and that the green-eyed monster of
jealousy could wreck the marriage!
Dr. Ruth hit on the perfect solution immediately. "Why don't you

go down to your friendly neighborhood video store," she said, "and rent a porno film of two women making love. You could both watch it together. Maybe that will satisfy her fantasy."

The respected, happily married man of some prominence coughed apologetically. "I think that's the problem," he said. "We've already done that. I think that's where she got the idea," he said.

What are we to think of the enormously popular—and influential —Dr. Ruth? Leave her to heaven? Laugh at her?

What are we to think of NBC radio that brings this insane drivel to tens of millions of homes every week?

What, more importantly, are we to think about ourselves and the part we all play in the creation of our totally eroticized society?

And, most of all, what are we going to say to that seventeen-year-old boy and his teenage girl friend and their millions of brothers and sisters in the United States? Dr. Ruth has just given them all permission to have practically unlimited sex anytime they want, as long as they're "protected," of course. That means it's perfectly okay as long as they use contraceptives!

This high priestess of hedonism has blessed premarital sex—and just about every other kind.

Maybe the real question for all of us is what have we already taught our kids about the beauty and goodness of sex within a wholesome, loving marriage? That can help them put into perspective the nonsense taught by Dr. Ruth?

Maybe the real question is, When did we teach them? Did we ever teach them?

Or did we leave that sacred duty of education in responsible sexuality to the Dr. Ruths of this world? And to the purveyors of the hard-core pornography that has become a cultural universal in our society and that has become the chief source of information on sex for our children.

We cannot hide any longer from the bitter truth that our kids are turning to the Dr. Ruths for the information about sex that we have denied them—or, at the very least, have made little effort to provide.

Not everything that Dr. Ruth says is errant nonsense. She deals explicitly, directly, and simply with a great deal of factual material about human sexuality that our young people—and old people, too —find informative and interesting.

It is Dr. Ruth's almost totally secular and incredibly hedonistic value system that offends and distresses—and tragically misleads—millions of people who see human sexuality as sacred and wholesome.

For men and women of faith, however, fidelity, sacrifice, commitment, and dignity nurture the almost divine creativity found in the fullness of love between a man and a woman. And, more importantly, safeguard the strong, wholesome families that are the bedrock of any society that hopes to survive.

Look, the more our families and our society are flooded with the kinds of intellectual and moral garbage now poisoning our social environment, the more our kids need age-appropriate, value-laden education in affective sexuality.

And if we do not personally feel up to the task of providing this education ourselves, we must insist that our schools—both public and private—take the obligation seriously.

I am not naïve about the difficulty involved. We live in a religiously pluralistic society. We must all work together to provide the basic common teaching materials that will illuminate instead of distort the beauty and intimacy of human sexuality.

It will not be easy, but it can be done because it must be done. Until we do, Dr. Ruth will happily fill in for us.

That seventeen-year-old kid—the one with the nice clean-cut golly-gee-whiz voice—might be your kid or my kid. He has a right to be protected from the high priests and priesteses of sexual license who make millions of dollars celebrating lust while they warp the attitudes and morals of our children.

Christmas 1985

Merry Christmas, mister. Hey, mister, do you wanna party? Are you looking for a good time . . . on Christmas Eve?

It's ten bucks for the Globe Hotel and twenty bucks for me, mister. . . . Give yourself a Christmas present, mister.

Jeez, I've got to stop crying. Nobody is going to buy me if I'm crying. It's bad for the john's head. It wrecks his fantasy when a kid he wants to buy has tears in her eyes.

I feel like such a jerk. Working the Cameo on Christmas Eve. People look at me real quick and then look away. Except the johns.

Bruce wants me to come to church on Christmas. He says God won't mind at all. In fact, He'd like to see me there, Bruce says.

I'd be afraid. With these clothes on! Midnight Mass would never be the same! Besides, if I ever tried to sing "Silent Night" I'd start to cry. Can you imagine me in church singing "Silent Night"? God would laugh.

Before He got mad, God would laugh.

I wish I could call my mother. It would be nice to know if she's okay. It being Christmas and all. She'd want to know what I was doing and where, but she already knows, and it would spoil her Christmas to know I was alive.

I wonder if she'd rather think I was dead. Maybe it wouldn't hurt her so much then. She could go back to thinking how it used to be on Christmas. When I was little. Before I left. Before I ruined things. Before Dad died . . .

Jeez, I've got to stop crying. Blue Fly will get real mad if he sees me crying.

Bruce says I should come to Covenant House for Christmas. The place looks great, he says. Christmas trees and presents for the kids and a big turkey dinner.

It's hard when it's somebody else's Christmas tree. You walk around all day long thinking of the time when you had one all your own.

When you had a family, and you got presents, and you were with people who loved you and who wanted to have you around.

It's hard to get presents from somebody you barely know. Who you never saw before yesterday. Who is just trying to make you feel good and be happy.

Sometimes it just makes it worse.

It's Christmas and everybody wants me to be happy.

Except Blue Fly! He wants me to work the Cameo porno theater and pick up ten johns. Maybe they'll be sorry for me and give me some big tips—before they go home to their own wives and kids and decorate their own Christmas trees!

I wonder what kind of presents they're going to give the kids at Covenant House this year. I wonder if they'd let me in again, one more time. Bruce says he will.

My pimp, Blue Fly, sure won't like it. He really hassled me the last time I went to Covenant House. He beat me real bad. I don't want to go through that again!

I sure don't want to keep doing this either.

Maybe Bruce is right and God won't get mad at me on Christmas.

"Rules" Is a Dirty Word

"There's no other place I can go, Bruce,
where I want to go.
Where they want me to come."

January 1986

"**B**ruce, I've been here twenty-four times! Since I was four-teen, Bruce. I'm twenty now. I'm really scared to turn twenty-one.

"I won't be able to come back anymore, when I'm twenty-one.

"Covenant House is my home, Bruce. I don't have anybody else," Timmy said. "What do I do, Bruce?"

The issue between us was a deadly serious one. For Timmy and for me. For Covenant House and for thousands of other kids like Timmy.

You see, sixteen thousand different kids will come into Covenant House residences around the country this year. About four thousand of them are repeaters—we've seen them before.

Of that four thousand about half return two or three times before they make it. Or before they don't.

The others, like Timmy, are constant visitors. Unable to make it at Covenant House, unable to make it on their own, or on the street, they move in and out of our program or other shelters around the country.

There are easily tens of thousands of these kids in the United States. They are America's street kids.

Timmy has the record at Covenant House for returning. Twenty-four times he has come back to us! (Timmy knows the rules better than half our staff.)

What do you do with the Timmys? The repeater kids?

I sighed for the thousandth time, as I pondered that question once more. Are we helping these kids at all, by being good to them? Are we, maybe, making them dependent on us?

Should we be more hard-nosed and put a limit on the number of times a kid can come back? For the sake of the other kids? For the sake of our staff? To save money? To make more beds readily available for kids we can help?

Please, God, can I—should I—write off the Timmys and leave them to Your mercy?

As professionals, we know they're not going to make it. We all know that. Including the kids. Everybody knows that they are permanently disconnected from society.

Can I, should I, disconnect them from Covenant House after, say, five or maybe even ten tries here?

Can I pull the plug? Should I? As a humane, caring professional, mustn't I? For the sake of the other kids . . . ?

I sighed again and looked at Timmy, and decided that one of his most irresistible qualities was that slow, sad smile on an incongruously cheerful face. I have a weakness for lost skinny kids with sad smiles.

Timmy's six-inch-thick file lay on my desk. In clinical, detached, professional language it spelled out the biography of an American street kid:

When, at age fourteen, he couldn't take the beatings and the fights and the not being wanted anymore, Timmy ran away. Our case records methodically list the bruises and scars on his body.

At age fourteen, on the run, nothing or nobody at Covenant House could hold him down. Foster homes didn't do it either. Or hospitals.

Timmy was a nice kid. I mean really nice, when we first met him six years ago. He just couldn't connect with anybody long enough to take a chance and settle down to loving someone, or letting someone love him.

He drifted in and out of dozens of programs and cities and relationships, always coming back to us. Glad to see us. Glad to be back home for a few days. For a couple of weeks. For a whole month!

Timmy stopped being a runaway at sixteen. The law in New York says you can no longer be a runaway once you blow the candles out on your sixteenth birthday cake. The law says you're just a homeless kid who can't go home and can't get into foster care without a battle. You have to make it any way you can.

At age sixteen you've got problems you never dreamed about when you couldn't stand the beatings and the not being loved by anybody and ran to the street.

You didn't think about the fact that at age sixteen, without a high-school diploma, you wouldn't be able to get a job.

You didn't know that at age sixteen you couldn't legally register in a hotel.

You find out that welfare workers and Family Court officials will tell you to go back home, even though you can't.

You did know that the law says you're too young to drink or vote.

You didn't know that you had practically no rights at all.

You found out real quick at the age of sixteen that to make it on the street you had to get into some pretty rotten things.

You found out that in New York State in the United States of America, at age sixteen the law says you can legally make a porn film. Legally!

New York State says that you're too young and immature to drink, vote, find housing, work, get medical help—but that you're old enough to take off your clothes and stand in front of a camera and become a porn star. It's legal to do that, if you're cold and hungry and homeless and need money.

If you're lucky, before you have to do this stuff, you'll find out about Covenant House and our open-door policy, that Covenant House is easy to get into twenty-four hours a day, no questions asked.

But twenty-four times! Twenty-four times in six years?

"Timmy," I said, "are we any good for you at all? Is our being good to you good for you? Isn't there any end to it?" I said. "Twenty-four times! That's a record, Timmy. That's the most times any kid has ever come back to Covenant House."

"I like it here, Bruce. I like the staff. They like it when I come back. They're glad to see me.

"There's no other place I can go, Bruce, where I want to go. Where they want me to come."

He didn't look desperate. He just looked sad. Even when he smiled.

There isn't anything really wrong with Timmy. He just doesn't know how to stay alive. Or what to do, or where to go, or what to say, or what to think about anything.

Professionals devised a treatment plan for Timmy: a foster home, a drug program, a good job-training facility, medical and educational and psychological services, etc., etc., etc.

Twenty-four times we and he failed. That is, Timmy couldn't make it. He didn't make it.

We don't know what to do about Timmy and we love him.

I can't pull the plug on Timmy. I just can't. Even if I should, I won't. I don't care if that makes me unprofessional.

Timmy clutters up my life. I'm glad he does. I guess I'd rather have him around than out on the street knowing he couldn't come back.

I couldn't stand knowing that he knew that he couldn't come back. Besides, I'd miss him.

Until he turns twenty-one. Then I won't let myself miss him anymore.

Holy Week 1986

For most people, Holy Week and Easter simply aren't in the same league as Christmas.

Americans come home for Thanksgiving and Christmas. They send flowers to their mother on Easter.

A couple of months ago winter was hardly upon us and it was Christmas and trees and lights and gifts and babies born in stables— and angels singing.

It was peace on earth and parties and Midnight Mass. And families home together.

Now it's Lenten fasts and penance and more somber symbols: statues covered with purple, sad hymns, and a row of empty crosses outlined against a bleak sky.

I don't know which is more important: the birth of God as a man or the death of a man who was God?

My kids don't know either. I mean, if you put that question to my kids you'd get some dumb stares and some impatient ("Are you trying to put me down, Bruce?") looks.

If you asked my kids an even more impertinent question—Are you like Jesus in any way?—they'd be sure it was a put-down, a prelude to another question with a real hook in it: Well, why not? Shouldn't you be?

If my kids understood very much about what really happened to Jesus and why He let it happen to Him, they wouldn't have too much trouble answering the questions.

I didn't think I'd like the answers, but I whomped up, in my mind, a couple of real street kids, a boy and a girl, and had this imaginary conversation with them:

"Bruce," the boy spoke first, "Jesus was beaten up and so was I. He was stabbed and I was, too. He was hungry and I'm always hungry. He had no place to live and neither do I. He didn't make it and I won't either. Does that make me like Jesus?"

"Yes," I said.

The girl laughed, a little self-consciously, and murmured that she had been tied up and held prisoner and that her pimp beat her a lot and spit on her.

"Bruce, I'm alone—I have nobody, Bruce—and all my friends took off. I'm afraid all the time, Bruce, and I have to act strong, as though I know what I'm doing.

"The system doesn't work for me, Bruce. It just needs me for a while, before it gets rid of me. People like me around when it's parties and fun and games and Christmas trees? Who wants a kid in a shroud with ashes? Does that make me like Jesus?"

"Yes," I said.

"But I'm not holy, Bruce," the boy said, "like Jesus was holy, and it would be a real hassle for me."

"I'm not either," I said, "and it's a real hassle."

"I don't even know what it means, Bruce . . . being holy."

"Neither do I," I said. "It has something to do with how much you love God and how close you model your life on Jesus—and how hard you try to do what you do because of God.

"I think you and I have a lot in common," I said, "and I think you have a head start on modeling. Maybe the other things, too," I said.

"You know a lot more about being hungry and alone and being

beaten up and stabbed and stripped and having people spit on you and run away from you than I ever will," I said.

"Are you saying I'm lucky, Bruce?" the kid said doubtfully.

"It would take me too long to explain why I would say yes, so I'll say no," I said.

"Oh," the kid said. "Maybe I understand."

"Maybe you do," I said.

"Why did He do it, Bruce? Jesus, I mean?"

"Because He loved us," I said. "You more than me," I said. "You more than almost anybody," I said.

"But I'm no good, Bruce."

"Yes you are," I said. "And it doesn't matter that you don't even know that," I said. "God doesn't love us because we're good."

"I know I don't understand that, Bruce."

"Nobody does," I said. "That's our problem. We don't understand it. We're afraid to. We'd almost rather it wasn't true. We'd rather deserve things. We're used to running our lives that way. It scares us to death to know that we're good because God loves us, not the other way around."

"Am I going to make it, Bruce?" the kid said.

"Of course you are," I said. "Jesus did. That's what Easter means," I said.

"When you do, pray for me," I said.

March 1986

He came into my office very quietly, erect, self-possessed, I thought. A solid kid. Not fat or sloppy, but the kind of boy who would become a big man with too much weight on him if he let himself go.

His face was—I struggled to understand it—patient. Carefully, courteously watchful . . .

I waved him to a comfortable chair near my desk and flopped down in another angled nearby.

The boy sat down slowly, methodically, placing his hands rather precisely on his knees and leaning back carefully until his body touched the back of the chair. He waited for me to begin the conversation.

"Hi," I said. "My name is Bruce. Your name is . . . ?"

"Mike," he said. He had a pleasant, controlled, modulated voice. A nice-looking kid.

"I'm interviewing kids for our Rights of Passage Program," I said. "That's our job-training program that we're going to begin next month. We have room for twenty-five kids to start with," I said. "The floor is almost ready, and it's going to be really beautiful. Kids who need about twelve months or eighteen months to complete school and a job-training program, winding up with a good-paying job, with a career attached . . .

"Will you tell me something about yourself," I said. "Nothing terribly personal. How old are you? Where are you from? Tell me something about your family. How did you find Covenant House?" I said.

"I'm eighteen," he said, "from New York. I got messed up with the police. They thought I committed a robbery. I spent four months in jail. I finished my high school there," he said.

"I can't go home," he said. "My stepfather and I don't get along. I guess he likes his other kids better," he said. "My mother"—he hesitated a moment—"My mother doesn't seem to"—his composure cracked for a moment, but he quickly recovered—"think it's a good idea for me to stay home. . . .

"So I went to live with my aunt. She loves me, and I really love her. But I couldn't get it together. Ever since we moved and I changed schools and couldn't make any friends."

"How smart are you?" I said.

"Just average," he said. "Just like any other kid. Nothing special," he said.

"What are you good at in school?" I said.

"Math. I'm really good at math," he said.

"Why are you here?" I said. "Why did you come to Covenant House?"

"I couldn't stay home," he said. "I couldn't stay at my aunt's. I went to the men's shelter, but it was really bad. I asked a cop if there was another place for kids like me and he told me about Covenant House."

"I'm glad you're here," I said. "Why couldn't you stay at your aunt's?" I said.

"I really love her," he said slowly. "But I couldn't stay. She tried to get me moving. She said that I should go out and work harder.

She said I was being a bad example for my brothers and sisters and her own children.

"It really hurt," he said. "I really love her. I was really hurt. I had no place to go. So I went into the bathroom and swallowed a bottle of pills."

He stopped and looked at me mutely. He kept his hands carefully placed on his knees, and I realized that he had not moved an inch since he sat down fifteen minutes ago. I almost told him to cross his legs or something.

Instead I made a bunch of sympathetic noises with my mouth and began a careful rearrangement of my face.

"Did you see a psychiatrist after that?" I said.

"Yes," he said, "for a couple of months or so, but it didn't do any good. He would always ask how things were going and I'd say great, but they weren't," he said. "They weren't great at all. So I stopped going."

"Do you have any friends?" I said.

"No," he said quietly.

"Do you have a girl friend?" I said.

"No," he said. "I don't have anybody," he said. "I'm alone," he said.

"Do you love your aunt more than your mother?" I said.

The boy opened his mouth to say yes, but then stopped for a moment as though that simple act of betrayal was more than he could bear.

He looked at me very hard. "Yes," he said. "I guess I do," he said. "But I still love Mother. And she loves me," he said.

For the first time the boy relaxed, exhaling gently, and settled back into the chair, placing his elbows on the arms of the chair.

We went on talking for another fifteen minutes. Mostly I just described the program we had in mind. The boy listened intently, but he didn't ask too many questions.

"Is there anything else you would like me to know about you?" I said. "Something that hasn't come up between us and that you think you want me to know?"

Mike looked at me for a moment. His face didn't change very much, and nothing much happened in his eyes, and he didn't move his arms or legs, but his face was different, his eyes were different. There was a suppressed vitality, a suppressed eagerness about him, almost as though he was trying to open a window to see out of—or maybe to let me see in.

"I guess you should know that I have a hard time expressing my feelings," he said quietly.

"I know," I said. "So do I," I said.

"I can't promise you a place in the program," I said. "We haven't made our final selections yet. We only have twenty-five openings. There are a lot of kids who want in, I said, so let's stay in touch. I hope you make it in," I said.

I had to stop there, knowing that I would say that to every sad, feckless kid poised on the brink of his own personal precipice, looking down over the edge. . . .

We got up and walked to the door of my office. The patient look was back on his face.

"You've had a really long Lent," I said. He didn't ask me what I meant.

I guess my face must have gotten unarranged again, because he looked at me and tried to comfort me.

"It's okay," he said. "Don't worry, Bruce."

April 1986

"There ain't any," I said. "There just ain't." I bore down hard on the "ain't"—it seemed to add emphasis to the very important point I was trying to make to my staff.

"Bruce, there's got to be. There just has to. You can't run Covenant House without any rules. It's impossible." There was a desperate note in his voice and a look of total disbelief on his face. Most of the staff assembled in the lounge for a training session obviously shared his shock and dismay.

" 'Rules' is a dirty word," I said. "We don't have any. We don't need them. The word should never pass your lips," I said. "It should never be heard in Covenant House."

"Bruce, how can we control the kids if there aren't any rules? They'll run wild. The place will fall apart."

"Nope," I said. "Just the opposite! Look around you," I said. "Do you see any kicked-in doors or walls? Do you see any broken windows or slashed furniture? Do you see any graffiti?" I said.

"There ain't any of those either," I said, "and we have the

toughest kids in the world come in here—and nobody gets turned
away!

"Rules would kill this place," I said. "Rules would make it impossible to run a program for our kids.

"We have a covenant," I said, "that's a thousand times stronger
than any set of rules. You explain that to our kids. You say it very
simply. You say it in your own words.

"Look, you say to a kid, I'm really glad you're here. Don't go
away. Please stay around. If you stay I'm going to do my best to love
you and to treat you with absolute respect, to care about you. If you
can, care about me, treat me the same way. That's what a covenant
means.

"Kids understand that right away. There's nothing mysterious
about it. It's normal and natural and perfectly clear.

"Then you say to the kid, Look, we have commitments to each
other that are serious and we both have to do our best to live up to
them.

"One commitment you make to me is that you're not going to use
drugs or alcohol or engage in violence while you're in Covenant
House.

"Another commitment—and it's important to be clear about it—is
that any kind of sexual activity here is just not a good idea.

"And finally, you promise, as much as you can, that you're going
to try really hard to get your life together, and to let us help you, if
we can.

"There are no strings to this," I said. "No limits. No conditions.
Just a couple of people who are trying to care about each other, to
respect each other, to help each other, to be grateful for the good we
can for each other."

"Bruce, can't we at least *call* them regulations?"

I groaned, moaned, whimpered, rolled my eyes—I really put on an
act—and yelled, "No! There are no regulations, no rules that can get
between us and the kids.

"They've lived by rules too long," I said. "The wrong kind of
rules. On the street the rules are very clear: seduce or be seduced;
intimidate or be intimidated; get over on before somebody gets over
on you. Don't believe anybody. Don't trust anybody.

"These rules have killed plenty of kids," I said. "Kids have died
trying to live by these rules," I said.

"If you set up a bunch of rules and regulations for the kids to observe, they won't relate to you at all," I said. "The rules will be the most important thing in their lives. They won't care about their relationship with us. They won't be accountable to us. They won't feel responsibility and commitment to us but to a rule book. And the most important thing will be if they can get over on the rules. And kids always can," I said. "Everybody can!

"Besides," I said, "if a kid breaks a rule you've got to throw him out. You can't negotiate a rule. It just stands there all by itself. It has a life of its own. You can't change it if you're not the boss. You trap a kid's life with a bunch of rules.

"You can negotiate a commitment," I said. "Relationships are infinitely flexible. Commitments and relationships admit to understanding and forgiveness and individual interpretation."

I was getting pretty excited.

"Rules just stand there and spit in your eye," I said. "If you break one you're done, finished, it's over.

"A covenant has a lot of give in it," I said.

"A covenant is a thousand times stronger than a rule," I said.

"Bruce, what do you say to a kid that breaks curfew, and gives the staff a hard time, and maybe comes in a little high one night?" the staff person said. He wasn't about to give up his death grip on the rule book that didn't exist.

"If you believe in rules and regulations you have to throw him out," I said. "You have to discharge him, because you don't have the right to change the rules.

"If you believe in covenants and commitments you negotiate and bend and flex and understand where the kid is coming from. But if you have to, you say to that kid, Look, I'm sorry, but it's over. You didn't keep your commitments, you didn't keep the convenant with me, the promises you made. I don't think you're trying hard enough right now. You shouldn't stay here anymore, for a while.

"Please come back, soon. When you come back, don't go away then. When you come back, I'll be really glad to see you. After I calm down, I'll miss you. We all will. Please come back.

"But you don't throw him out for breaking the rules. There aren't any," I said.

"This is Covenant House," I said. "We don't make contracts with our kids. We don't say, If you do this, I'll do that. We don't say, If you keep the rules, you can stay. We don't want to run their lives.

"We say, Hey, we care about you. We're glad you're here. Don't go away. Please stay. If you stay, we'll love you if we can. If you have to go away, please come back.

"Do you understand?" I asked. "Do you?"

The staff person looked a little doubtful. "I'm beginning to," he said. "I think I am. . . ."

"You've got to work at it," I said. "It doesn't come easy for everybody. Especially if we've been raised to run our life by rules and regulations. A lot of us have," I said.

"We have a Covenant," I said. "With each other and with our kids. There's no difference. It's the same Covenant.

"When we all understand that, and try to live by it," I said, "then this becomes the best place in the world to be."

Kids Like You
Don't Have Funerals

He'll remember the hug. . . .

June 1986

I looked at the boy across my desk, trying to describe him to myself, but it was hard.

Average height, dark blond hair, dusky blue eyes. Bold eyes. Bright eyes. Brave, direct eyes.

"My name is Peter," he said.

Not exactly skinny, but not well muscled. Not exactly effeminate, but not strongly masculine either. Sexually indefinite, I thought. A young-looking sixteen.

"My name is Bruce," I said.

He wore his low-slung jeans and green T-shirt with casually studied nonchalance. The Etonic running shoes looked new. He had big feet.

"That apartment you were in today," I said, "is owned by a guy into sadomasochism, sex with kids your age, and a lot of drugs. He's got a nineteen-year-old lover who makes porn films, with felony warrant for assault out on him."

"I'm sixteen," Peter said. This piece of irrelevance hung in the air between us.

"I know about the guy," Peter said. "The cops told me about him. They wanted me to say that he gave me drugs and had sex with us. I didn't tell them anything."

"My kids tell me you did," I said.

"He treated me good, Bruce. He didn't hurt me. He's real rich. I want some of that, Bruce."

"You want the clothes and the nice apartments and the grass and the trips to the Bahamas, the nice restaurants. . . . He promised you all that," I said. It wasn't a question.

"I can get it, Bruce. I want it. I never want to go home to Georgia. I won't go."

"I called your mother," I said. "She wants you to come home."

"My mother's okay, Bruce, but there's nothing for me in Georgia. I won't go back. I'm going to make it in New York. If the cops send me home I'll just come back to New York."

"This guy will sell you to his friends," I said. "He already has. My kids told me about it. They're worried about you. A kid heading for trouble is how Billy described you."

"I won't let them hurt me, Bruce. If they try I'll blackmail them. I already know a lot about them. I can hurt them."

"They'll kill you," I said. "Real quick. If you try that. You'll fall out of a window. You'll overdose. You'll just disappear. The death certificate—if they find your body, and they don't very often—will just say some dumb kid OD'd or killed himself. There won't be anything to investigate. Kids like you don't have funerals."

The boy didn't turn away. He wasn't embarrassed or ashamed. His dark blue eyes looked at me thoughtfully. "I've thought about all that, Bruce." His voice was soft but definite. "I appreciate your worrying about me. It's nice of you to do that. The cop, too," he said.

"I wasn't trying to scare you," I said. "Just not to scare you. But it's a real bad scene, and most kids never really make it out."

Peter didn't take his eyes off me. He was kind and attentive and listened carefully.

"You're going to be worth too much money to them," I said. "You'll be income-producing property worth tens of thousands of dollars. They won't let you go," I said. "Until it's too late to matter. They'll want you to take your clothes off for a camera and you won't be able to say no."

"I'm going to make it in New York, Bruce. I figure I can make it as a hustler. If I have to."

"What about AIDS?" I said. "Hustlers can't practice safe sex. It's a sure bet you'll get AIDS."

"I hope not, Bruce," he said. "I worry about that. That's the kind of sex I like, Bruce."

"When did you know you were gay?" I said.

"When I was twelve or thirteen I was pretty certain, but I didn't really get into it until I came to New York last week."

"Stay here," I said. "Don't go away. Look, Peter, I can get you a scholarship to this really great prep school. It'll be a good college after that. You're smart," I said. "I can tell. I'll do it, Peter, if you stay. I promise you that, Peter."

"I got straight A's in school, Bruce, but I don't want to go back. I want all the things I never had. I want to be rich, Bruce."

"Don't go, Peter. Don't leave. It's a bad scene. We want you to stay. Think about it, overnight at least."

He smiled at me. A very sad, knowing, direct-in-my-eyes smile. He didn't look away. "Don't feel bad, Bruce. It's okay. I want to do it."

"When it turns sour, Peter, come back. If you ever get in trouble, call me. If you need a place to hide, my number is in the book. Anytime. Until you come back, I'll miss you. . . ." I had to stop. It was getting pretty hard for me to go on.

"Thanks," he said. "I'm glad you care about me."

"I do," I said. "A lot."

"I've got to split, Bruce. I told this guy I'd meet him at six o'clock. I'm staying at his place. Apartment 46B, Bruce. It's on the forty-sixth floor. It's got a great view of the city, Bruce. He's going to buy me some new clothes tomorrow. . . ." His voice trailed off.

"I never knew my father, Bruce," he said suddenly.

He stood up abruptly, and for the first time his composure deserted him.

"Good-bye," he said

"Good-bye," I said.

"Can I hug you?" he said.

"Sure," I said.

We hugged each other hard.

P.S.

Peter will come back. I know he will. He just doesn't understand yet. He wants many things too much and he wants, needs, just one person to care about him.

He's only sixteen—a young sixteen and he's a good kid. You shouldn't think he's not.

It's really important for us to be here when the Peters come back. Older, sadder, wiser. He'll remember the hug.

EPILOGUE

In a certain sense this was an easy book to write.
Most of the newsletters were pressured out of my head by the inexorable deadlines for the monthly newsletter. Only occasionally was the experience itself so vivid, so profoundly moving, so immediate, that I had to write it down immediately to exorcise the hurt and pain.

Once out of my mind and on paper, the letters took on a life of their own. It was a comparatively simple task to pick and choose among fifteen years of letters and compile them into this book.

I am their sole author. Nobody else wrote them. They are true stories about real kids: no embellishments, no hyperboles, no made-up or colored characters or incidents. Names are changed, of course, and occasionally times and geographies are masked to protect the identities of the kids about whom I wrote that month.

I suppose that the letters are inescapably autobiographical in the sense that the only way I knew how to write about the kids was to describe the way they involved themselves in my own life, how they finally came to live in my own heart and mind and to own me. And, in a few cases, let me own them. Quite often, I have skirted that risky edge of self-revelation, and each time just as consciously drawn back from that inviting precipice.

This book is not autobiographical in the usual sense of that term: I have no particular desire to write about my life or to share my inmost thoughts and feelings with the world. I can assure you, therefore, publishers will wait in vain for my autobiography.

In the beginning the letters were written to inform the small band of contributors of what was going on at Covenant House in order to win their financial support that we desperately needed. From that perspective the letters have always had—and always will—a fund-raising purpose.* Without the support of hundreds of thousands of loyal friends over the past almost nineteen years, Covenant House would not have been able to continue to help the thousands of kids who came to us from the streets each year.

Anyone, however, who has read this far will see another purpose clearly evolving: to speak out on behalf of the tens of thousands of good and beautiful and brave kids who have already come to us— and the literally hundreds of thousands of others who still live and die on the streets of our cities.

They need advocates! They need committed, convinced people who will work to change attitudes and laws: attitudes that say it is okay to buy and sell children, and laws and legal structures that permit or even actually encourage it.

Children should not be bought and sold. They should not be ex-ploited. It should not be unspeakably dangerous for a kid to be alone and homeless on the streets of our cities.

The protection of these children has been left in large part, to their peril, to the casual and often unconcerned mercies of the various divisions of our legal systems. The fact is that in most cases we have an abundance of effective and constitutional legislation already on the books that, if properly enforced, could and would protect our children from the kinds of exploitation that annually destroys thousands of them.

The fact is that police do not enforce these laws, prosecutors do not prosecute, and judges are more often than not accustomed to give slap-on-the-wrist sentences that provide no effective deterrent.

The fact is that the learned and facile gobbledygook that emanates from all parts of our legal systems is designed to convince us that the other guy is at fault. The police point fingers at prosecutors, the prosecutors wearily point to the judges, the judges point to over-crowded jails, while legislators assure us that they never have enough money for even more important priorities than the lives and safety of our children.

---

* This is particularly true since C. H. receives very little financial support from gov-ernment agencies—less than 6 percent!

State legislators and our Congress will allocate sufficient resources only if we, their masters, insist on it. We won't do it.

The real truth is that police, prosecutors, and judges will only enforce or pursue vigorously those laws that the citizens think important, and we citizens do not want the laws on our books regarding our sexual misconduct enforced. There are millions of satisfied customers of the porno bookstores and peep shows and theaters, and tens of millions of happy customers of the porno films in our video stores, and hundreds of thousands of us will go looking for some kid hanging out on the street corners of our cities and wait for him to say, "Are you looking for some friendly company?"

A porno film is nothing more than a filmed record of an act of prostitution: sex for money. A peep show, as every customer who has ever been in one knows, is nothing more than a low-class brothel, where young people, imprisoned by fear and need, sell little pieces of their lives for a few dollars at a time. The kid on the street corner? Somebody's son or daughter who smiles because he or she is too afraid to cry.

We live in a sex-for-sale society where it is okay to pay for sex and be paid for it. The merchandise that is bought and sold, the commodities that are exchanged, are young people—more often than not, the kids are down on their luck, the kids who have already learned, in their destroyed and destroying families, that abuse and exploitation are intrinsic to their lives, the kids who have no other option to hundreds of degrading commercial recreational transactions than hunger and homelessness.

It's not going to change until we do. Until we restore to human sexuality the dignity and honor—and privacy—that are intrinsic to its noble purposes.

It's not going to change until we succeed in giving to women a rightful dignity and honor and equality with men that is not based on their equal right to be equally promiscuous and equally concerned with equal salaries. The problem is that men cannot teach men this equality and women by and large are either unwilling or unable or don't know how to—or don't want to. It might mean giving up some privileges and even some measure of control over men.

The churches, by and large, have been singularly unhelpful and ineffective. With a few shining exceptions, the theological hand-wringing engaged in by church leaders over these issues has served only to reveal their powerlessness and lack of leadership.

But that goes back, doesn't it, to their fear of offending the millions of people who sit in their pews every Sunday and who don't want to hear exhortations to change attitudes and behavior. . . .

Our society has been inundated with images of violent and perverse sexuality that alternately fascinate and repel, until, after repeated exposure, we become so desensitized to their impact that we look for even more violent and perverse images to titillate our jaded appetites. The marketers are always there to supply the need. . . .

The American family has been profoundly violated. Its foundations have been seriously eroded. In the United States, in 1987, sex has very little to do with love and marriage and stability and fidelity and responsibility and children. It has everything to do with casual anonymous promiscuity, violence, and sometimes grotesque perversions of human love.

That radically flawed and dangerous view of human sexuality has substantially pervaded our society. We used to bemoan and regret and conceal our vices. Now we celebrate them on dozens of prime-time TV shows and sleazy afternoon soap operas, and in hundreds of first-run Hollywood films.

Our kids are learning what we teach them. The teachers are legion and the message is clear: if it feels good, do it. "Good sex"—meaning as much sex as you can have with about as many partners as you can manage, in as many ways as you can devise—is great, as long as you are protected, of course.

Things will change—and families will be protected—when we do.

Until we do, thousands of murdered children will come walking into Covenant House and look at us with undead eyes.

Thousands more will die unspeakably ugly and lonely deaths on the streets of our cities because nobody reached out to them in time.

This book is dedicated to them. And to the thousands of service providers across the country who, very often working in obscurity and with grossly inadequate resources, try to save them.

1-800-999-9999

If you're a parent, teach this number to your child. This number will connect your child to help from anywhere in the country. It is our "Nineline" number, staffed twenty-four hours a day with trained people who care. People who can and will help your child if a crisis ever arises.

If you'd like more information about how Covenant House is helping America's kids, write to Bruce Ritter at:

460 West 41st Street
New York, N.Y. 10036

Printed in the United States
by Baker & Taylor Publisher Services